LYNCH-LAW

AN INVESTIGATION INTO
THE HISTORY OF LYNCHING
IN THE UNITED STATES

BY

JAMES ELBERT CUTLER, Ph.D.

*Instructor in Economics in Wellesley College; sometime Henry C. Robinson Fellow
and Instructor in Political Economy in Yale University*

NEGRO UNIVERSITIES PRESS
NEW YORK

Originally published in 1905
by the Longmans, Green, and Co.

Reprinted 1969 by
Negro Universities Press
A DIVISION OF GREENWOOD PUBLISHING CORP.
NEW YORK

SBN 8371-1821-2

16748

FOREWORD

FEW people are able to read about lynch-executions, with atrocious forms of torture and cruel death, such as have occurred from time to time within ten years in this country, without a feeling of national shame. It is necessary that facts should be known and that public opinion should be corrected as to the ethics of that mode of dealing with crime. Lynch-law is a very different thing where laws and civil institutions are in full force and activity from what it is where they are wanting. It is not admissible that a self-governing democracy should plead the remissness of its own selected agents as an excuse for mob-violence. It is a disgrace to our civilization that men can be put to death by painful methods, which our laws have discarded as never suitable, and without the proofs of guilt which our laws call for in any case whatsoever. It would be a disgrace to us if amongst us men should burn a rattlesnake or a mad dog. The badness of the victim is not an element in the case at all. Torture and burning are forbidden, not because the victim is not bad enough, but because we are too good. It is on account of what we owe to ourselves that these methods are shameful to us, if we descend to them. It is evident, however, that public opinion is not educated up to this level. The reader of the present book will learn very interesting facts about the causes alleged for lynching, and about the public view of that crime. Many current errors will be corrected, and many notions which are irrelevant, although they are popularly believed to be germane and important, will be set aside.

W. G. SUMNER.

NEW HAVEN, CONN., February, 1905.

PREFACE

In making this investigation into the history of lynching in the United States, my point of view has been that of a student of society and social phenomena. The purpose of the investigation has not been primarily to write the history of lynching, but to determine from the history the causes for the prevalence of the practice, to determine what the social conditions are under which lynch-law operates, and to test the validity of the arguments which have been advanced in justification of lynching.

At the present time many positive opinions are held with reference to lynching, and these are quite at variance one with another. Any one who attempts to investigate a subject under such conditions cannot hope to escape criticism; neither can he hope to have given the subject equal consideration from every standpoint. The most that one can say is that he has pursued the investigation with perfect honesty of purpose and with openness of mind. To this study of the history of lynching I have brought no theories to prove and no conscious prejudices to confirm. My first endeavor has been to obtain all the facts possible; my final endeavor has been to point out the conclusions clearly warranted by such facts.

The material for a study of this nature is found in a wide range of sources and I gratefully record here my obligations to those who have aided me in the task of collecting and sifting this material. For some very valuable notes on the early history of lynch-law I am indebted to Mr. Albert Matthews, of Boston, Massachusetts. Of his notes I have made free use, indicating my obligation to him in each instance, either by the use of the letter (M) or by special mention. Six of the chapters have been read by him in the manuscript, and he has given me much encouragement and kindly criticism during the preparation of these pages for publication.

For many valuable suggestions during the prosecution of this study I am indebted to members of the Faculty of the Social Sciences of Yale University, especially to Professors Sumner, Farnam, Bourne, and Keller. The editors of the *Yale Review* have very courteously permitted me to use in Chapter VIII the material which was published in a condensed form in the *Yale Review* for August, 1904. To many others whom I cannot here mention by name I desire to express my thanks and acknowledge my indebtedness for information given in response to inquiries.

The number of requests which have come to hand for copies of this study, from persons living in various sections of the United States as well as in Europe, and the attention that has been given the subject of lynchings in newspapers and magazines, indicate a desire on the part of the general public to learn the facts concerning lynchings. By many it is believed that in no other respect to-day is American civilization so open to reproach as in its toleration of the practice of lynching, and there is an increasing demand that this summary method of administering justice be suppressed and utterly abolished. That this book may contribute in some measure to a better understanding of this most serious and difficult problem is the hope with which it is placed in the hands of the reader.

J. E. C.

CONTENTS

[xi]

CHARTS

CHARTS

LYNCH-LAW

CHAPTER I

INTRODUCTION

IT has been said that our country's national crime is lynching. We may be reluctant to admit our peculiarity in this respect and it may seem unpatriotic to do so, but the fact remains that lynching is a criminal practice which is peculiar to the United States. The practice whereby mobs capture individuals suspected of crime, or take them from the officers of the law, and execute them without any process at law, or break open jails and hang convicted criminals, with impunity, is to be found in no other country of a high degree of civilization. Riots and mob executions take place in other countries, but there is no such frequent administration of what may be termed popular justice which can properly be compared with lynch-law procedure in the United States. The frequency and impunity of lynchings in the United States is justly regarded as a serious and disquieting symptom of American society.

In general, it may be said that the practice of summarily punishing public offenders and suspected criminals is found in two distinct types of society: first, the frontier type where society is in a formative state and the civil regulations are not sufficiently established to insure the punishment of offenders; and second, the type of society which is found in older communities with well established civil regulations, the people of which are ordinarily law-abiding and conservative citizens. In this second type of society, recourse to lynch-law procedure may be had either in times of popular excitement and social disruption, or when there is a contrast in the population such as is to be seen in the South between the whites and the negroes, or against disreputable characters in the community for whose punishment under the law no tangible evidence can be adduced, or against persons guilty of committing some heinous offense which on account of its atrocity and fiendishness is particularly shocking to the community.

In other countries one or more of these conditions has at times existed, and summary methods of punishment to which lynch-law procedure in the United States bears a close resemblance have been followed. In the course of the settlement and development of this country, however, all of these conditions have existed almost side by side. From colonial times down to the present day there has been a section of the country where the frontier type of society was to be found. At the same time there has been an older, better settled section of the country, forming a different type of society, where, though the judiciary was well established and the apprehension and punishment of public offenders was well provided for in the law, circumstances have arisen of such a nature that the regular and legal administration of justice was deemed inadequate or defective, and was therefore disregarded. As will be made clear in the following pages, lynch-law has been resorted to in the United States in times of popular excitement and social disruption; it has been inflicted upon negroes, Indians, Italians, Mexicans; it has been inflicted upon disreputable characters; it has been inflicted upon persons guilty of heinous offenses.

The practice of lynching does not prevail in Canada[1]; nor is a similar practice to be found in England, France, or Germany. The nearest approach that can be found in Europe to the American practice of lynching exists in the rural districts of little Russia where the peasants sometimes adopt summary measures against horse-thieves. The Russian law provides only a light punishment for horse-stealing, and, since the peasant's horse is almost his only property and is his chief instrument of labor, summary methods seem necessary in order to check the veritable plague of horse-stealing which breaks out every year as soon as the dark nights of autumn begin. When a thief is caught, the common way is for the men of the village to club him to death, each trying to strike in such a way as to inflict no injury more serious than a bruise. Another method is to tie the criminal by the feet to the tail of a young and active colt which is then ridden at a gallop until little is left of the horse-thief. There is also a mode of execution whereby the thief is bound hand and foot to a bench or log, and the women of the village thrust needles and pins into the soles of the victim's feet and other sensitive parts, until death ensues.[2]

Aside from this instance which is found in the loosely organized society of the peasants in the rural districts

[1] Compare statement by William Roberts in *Fortnightly Review*, January, 1892 (57: 92).

[2] The *Times*, Washington, D. C., Dec. 14, 1902.

of Russia, nothing like lynch-law can be said to prevail in Europe. Occasionally mobs put persons to death who have committed some brutal and outrageous crime. A newspaper report states that the burgomaster of Stujhely, Hungary, was lynched in November, 1902, for having set fire to his home in which were his wife, father, mother, and three sisters, all of whom were burned to death. The burgomaster had become angry at the members of his family for some trifling cause, and his method of revenge so enraged his neighbors that they immediately "took summary measures and lynched him."[1] A similar report tells of the lynching of a Bohemian village schoolmaster who suddenly became insane and began shooting his revolver right and left among his pupils, killing three and dangerously wounding three others.[2] People in the lower stages of civilization, such as the Melanesians, Micronesians, and the inhabitants of the Guinea Coast of Africa, often have secret societies which take control of important functions, such as the initiation of young persons arriving at maturity, or the exaction of penalties for the transgression of customs and traditions. In most cases these societies form an essential part of the state, holding quite the place of the chief. Occasionally they degenerate and create a reign of terror by their extortions and exactions. Secret tribunals for thieves and robbers, like the society of the "Old Ox," have existed in China.[3] Such instances, however, merely illustrate the general truth that summary methods of

---

[1] The *Standard Union*, Brooklyn, N. Y., Nov. 14, 1902.

[2] The *New York Evening Telegraph*, Oct. 8, 1902.

[3] See F. Ratzel: "History of Mankind" (trans. by A. J. Butler), I, 125, 281, 282; II, 131; III, 507.

punishing offenders are sometimes resorted to in every country in times of great popular excitement or when some peculiarly atrocious crime has been perpetrated. They in no way invalidate the assertion that the practice of lynching is peculiarly an American institution.

Historically some parallels may be cited showing the execution of summary justice under frontier conditions in other countries. In Brande's Dictionary of Science, Literature, and Art, published in 1842, it was stated that "lynch law may be called a democratic imitation of the old feudal *Vehmgerichte*." Reference was there made to the "irregular and revengeful species of justice administered by the populace in some parts of the United States," evidently meaning the operation of lynch-law on the western frontier at that time. Lynch-law in the United States has never been administered by an organization so perfect and extensive as that of the Vehmic courts.[1] The feudal conditions have been lacking which made that organization possible. It is only in its *raison d'être* that the frontier type of lynch-law may be compared to the Vehmic courts. The early settlers in this country felt themselves compelled to resort to summary proceedings as a means of protection; the civil government was not sufficiently organized and established to insure the punishment of violators of the public peace and security. In the fourteenth and fifteenth centuries utter lawlessness and disregard of authority was prevailing in Germany, and for a time the Vehmic courts afforded some protection against the outrages of the princes and nobles. With the increasing strength of the regular governments, how-

[1] See "Fehmic courts," Encyclopædia Britannica, 9th edition.

ever, the need of special protection diminished and these tribunals gradually disappeared. Like the Vehmic courts, with the establishment of the judiciary and a more effective execution of the laws by the officials, the administration of lynch-law in the western half of the United States has declined.

The tendency, it may be noted, for societies secretly organized for the arbitrary punishment of offenders to pass into the control of the persons against whom they were originally directed, is to be seen not only in the history of the Vehmic courts but also in the history of the Ku-Klux Klan and numerous vigilance societies in the United States. The proceedings of such societies necessarily awaken distrust and fear among the more quiet in the community, while the rogues, whose characters are not yet known, hasten to obtain admittance, both as a shield against enemies and a cloak to cover their own misdeeds. Soon their vindictive actions and their rascalities excite the indignation of the community; a counter-party of "moderators" must be formed to check the "regulators"; then begins a deadly struggle for supremacy. Such, in brief, is the abuse of lynch-law on the frontier. The tyranny of the Vehmic courts becomes the taking of private vengeance, the feud and the *vendetta*, under lynch-law.

The Vehmic courts, however, give no explanation for the presence of lynch-law as an institution in American society. No connection can be traced further than a few similarities in the methods adopted to put down lawlessness at a time when the civil government proved weak and inefficient.

Some writers have stated that lynch-law was anciently known in England by the name of Lydford law and Halifax law, and that the same thing was known in Scotland as Cowper justice and Jeddart or Jedburg justice. Lydford law is defined in a dictionary of the seventeenth century as "a certain Law whereby they first hang a Man and afterwards indite him."[1] One of Grose's Proverbs reads:

> "First hang and draw,
> Then hear the cause by Lidford law."

Westcott, in his "History of Devonshire," has preserved some droll verses about the town of Lydford. The first twelve lines are as follows:

> "I oft have heard of Lydford law,
> How in the morning they hange and draw,
> And sit in judgement after;
> At first I wondered at yt much,
> But since I fynd the reasons such
> As yt deserves no laughter.

> "They have a castle on a hill,
> I tooke it for an old wyndmill,
> The vanes blowen off by weather:
> To lye therein one night, 'tis guest,
> 'Twere better to be ston'd and prest,
> Or hang'd; now chuse you whether."[2]

It has been asserted, therefore, that "Lydford law became a proverbial expression for summary punishment

---

[1] Edward Phillips: "The New World of Words, or a General English Dictionary" (1678, 4th edition).

[2] Grose's "Provincial Glossary" (London, 1811), p. 163.

without trial."[1] This, however, is going further than the facts will allow, and is wholly misleading when thus used to show the connection between Lydford law and lynch-law. It would seem to imply that Lydford law in England was once as well known, as a name for summary punishment, as lynch-law has become in this country. As a proverbial expression Lydford law never came into general use; it was confined to one section of England and never became more than a localism.

In another part of England a certain summary procedure was known by the name of Halifax law. In this case there was a trial followed by immediate punishment. The trial was of a summary nature without adequate opportunity of defense, and the punishment was irrevocable. The name, Halifax law, originated from the so-called *gibbet law* or custom in the forest of Hardwick, coextensive with the parish of Halifax, under which the frith burghers summarily tried any one charged with stealing goods to the value of $13\frac{1}{2}$ d., and could condemn him to be beheaded on the market-day.[2]

Cowper justice is defined by Jamieson to mean "trying a man after execution; the same with Jeddart, or Jedburgh justice," and the latter he defines as "a legal trial after the infliction of punishment." Jeddart justice refers to Jedburgh, a Scotch border town, where many of the border raiders are said to have been hanged without the formality of a trial. It is said that "in mockery of justice, assizes were held upon them after that they had suffered."[3]

[1] See "Lynch Law," International Cyclopædia (1893).
[2] See Century Dictionary under "Law."
[3] John Jamieson: "Etymological Dictionary of the Scottish Language" (1879).

All of these expressions, however, were entirely provincial. They were merely different names used to characterize the methods employed in various parts of England and Scotland for executing popular justice. These practices differ from the administration of lynch-law in not dispensing with all regular proceedings. Further, as will appear later, the death penalty was not at first inflicted under lynch-law; originally, lynching was synonymous with whipping. It is impossible, therefore, to trace lynch-law back to these mediæval practices and find in them any explanation for the existence of the practice of lynching in the United States.

A general idea of the history of lynch-law in the United States is obtained by noting the definitions of the term that have appeared from time to time in the dictionaries. Brande's Dictionary of Science, Literature, and Art (1842)[1] contains the following: "Lynch Law. The irregular and revengeful species of justice administered by the populace in some parts of the United States is said to have been so called from a Virginian farmer of the name of Lynch, who took the law into his hands on some occasion, by chasing a thief, tying him to a tree, and flogging him with his own hands." A "University Edition" of Webster's Dictionary (1845) defines "Lynch-law" as "The practice of punishing men for crime by private, unauthorized persons, without a legal trial"; and gives the verb lynch meaning "to inflict punishment without the forms of law, as by a mob." Worcester's Dictionary (1846) has "Lynch-law. An irregular and revengeful

[1] An American edition, bound under the title, "Brande's Encyclopædia," was published in 1843.

species of justice, administered by the populace or a mob, without any legal authority or trial. Brande." For the verb lynch the meaning is given, "To condemn and execute in obedience to the decree of a multitude or mob, without a legal trial; sometimes practiced in the new settlements in the southwest part of the United States. Qu. Rev." In Webster's Dictionary (1848) "Lynch-law" is defined as "The practice of punishing men for crimes or offenses by private, unauthorized persons, without a legal trial. The term is said to be derived from a Virginia farmer, named Lynch, who thus took the law into his own hands. (U. S.)" [1]

Some important changes are noticeable in the definitions attached to lynch-law forty years later. The Progressive Dictionary of the English Language, edited by Samuel Fallows and published at Chicago in 1885, gives this definition for the verb lynch: "To punish without the forms of law; specifically to hang by mob-law." In a note it is stated that more than one etymology is claimed for the word. John S. Farmer in his "Americanisms," published at London in 1889, says the origin of the term lynch-law "is wrapped in mystery; many explanations

---

[1] The English Dictionary, edited by Rev. John Boag and published at Glasgow in 1848, gives for the verb lynch, "To inflict punishment without the forms of law, as by a mob." The definitions given for the words "lynched" and "lynching" are also very similar to the ones given by Webster. It is fair to presume that Boag consulted Webster and followed his authority, although he did not mark the term as an American word. John Craig's Dictionary of the English Language (London, 1849) gives "lynch, v. a. To punish summarily without judicial investigation, as by a mob. — An American word." The London edition of Nuttall's Dictionary (published about 1863) gives "Lynch, v. a. To inflict pain, or punish without the forms of law, as by an American mob." The dictionaries published in Great Britain previous to 1848 do not contain the verb lynch.

have been put forward; none, however, are conclusive."
In Webster's Dictionary, edition of 1893, the following
definition is found: "Lynch: To inflict punishment upon,
especially death, without the forms of law, as when a mob
captures and hangs a suspected person." Lynch-law is
defined in a general way as "The act or practice by private persons of inflicting punishment for crimes or offenses,
without due process of law," but this note is added: "The
term *Lynch law* is said to be derived from a Virginian
named Lynch, who took the law into his own hands.
But the origin of the term is very doubtful."[1]

There are two differences between the definitions formulated in the forties and those formulated in the eighties
and in recent years. In the later definitions the operation of lynch-law is described as being much more harsh
and severe, and there is an expression of doubt as to the
origin of the term. In the earlier definitions death is not
mentioned as the ordinary penalty administered by
lynch-law and the American origin of the term is accepted
without question. The doubt as to the origin probably
arose because of the number of stories which have appeared, all claiming to account for its origin, and also
because of the lack of any careful investigation to determine the question authentically from historical sources.
The increased harshness expressed in the definitions is,
of course, due to the fact that the punishment inflicted
under the name of lynch-law has become more severe and
inexorable. Lynching is now practically synonymous

[1] The edition of 1901 has the same. The Century Dictionary is the
only recent authoritative work that states unequivocally that lynch-law
was originally the kind of law administered by Charles Lynch of Virginia.

with summary and illegal capital punishment at the hands
of a mob. In the following pages the history of this
change will be traced and the conditions noted which
have led to the continuance of the practice of lynching
and given to it its increased severity.

In the above citations to various definitions that have
been given for lynch-law it was noted that more than one
origin has been claimed for the term. An investigation
into the circumstances surrounding its origin will throw
considerable light on the early history of lynch-law procedure in the United States, and this question will therefore be taken up in some detail.

CHAPTER II

Origin of the Term Lynch-law

MANY and various explanations of the origin of the term Lynch's law, or lynch-law, have been offered. Some of these explanations are evidently nothing more than the offspring of minds fertile in resources; others have the support of tradition and are entitled to consideration. Not infrequently confusion and apparent contradiction have resulted from the failure to distinguish clearly between the practice itself and the name by which it has been known. To follow back through history the successive outbreaks of such practices is not to discover the origin of "lynch-law," the term which has now become so firmly established in the English language. The origin is to be found at that time when these practices first came to be known by the name Lynch's law or lynch-law.

According to one account, given more or less indorsement in the encyclopedias, lynch-law owes its name to James Fitzstephen Lynch, mayor and warden of Galway, Ireland. He was the famous "Warden of Galway" who tried, condemned, and executed his own son in the year 1493. The story is told with varying details. One tradition has it that the mayor sent his son to Spain to purchase a cargo of wine. The young man squandered the money intrusted to him, but succeeded in obtaining a cargo on credit from a Spanish friend of his father. This

gentleman's nephew accompanied him on the return
voyage to Ireland where the money was to be paid.
Young Lynch, to conceal his misuse of the money, caused
the Spaniard to be thrown overboard and returned home
in triumph with his cargo of wine. But a sailor, on his
death-bed, revealed to the mayor of Galway the crime
which his son had committed. The young man was tried
before his father, convicted and sentenced to be hanged.
Another tradition states that the son of the Spanish
friend of his father was visiting him at his home in Ireland.
This son was fast supplanting him in the affections of a
Galway lady to whom he was engaged. One night, in a
fit of jealous passion, he stabbed the Spaniard to the
heart and threw his body into the sea. The crime was
quickly discovered, and on being brought before his
father for trial he was condemned to die as a sacrifice to
public justice. Public sympathy, however, turned in
favor of the young man, and every effort was made to
effect his pardon. The father "undauntedly declared
that the law should take its course." On the way to the
place of execution a mob appeared, led by members of
the mother's family, demanding mercy. The father,
finding that he could not "accomplish the ends of justice
at the accustomed place and by the usual hands," conducted his son up a winding stairway to a window over-
looking the public street. "Here he secured the end of a
rope, which had been previously fixed around the neck of
his son, to an iron staple which projected from the wall,
and, after taking from him a last embrace, he launched
him into eternity." The people, "overawed by the mag-
nanimous act, retired slowly and peaceably to their

several dwellings." In the council books of Galway there is said to be a minute that "James Lynch, mayor of Galway, hanged his own son out of the window for defrauding and killing strangers, without martial or common law, to show a good example to posterity." In commemoration of this "Roman act of justice," a stone sculptured with a skull and crossbones was erected in Lombard Street, Galway, in 1524, and in 1854 was re-erected on the wall of St. Nicholas Churchyard.[1]

This "Galway story" may be dismissed with but little consideration. Howell Colton Featherston of the Lynchburg (Va.) Bar has clearly shown that this act of the mayor of Galway was entirely without any definition ever attached to lynch-law and that there was no reason for bestowing upon it any name, and more particularly his name. Mayor Lynch was the legally constituted authority presiding over the tribunal in which his son had had, presumably, a fair and regular trial. He merely persisted in executing the laws in the face of popular opposition and tumult. Lynch-law has always been considered as operating wholly without, or in opposition to, established laws of government.[2]

Equally fanciful and fictitious but less romantic is the "pirate story" of the origin of the name lynch-law. It is said that about 1687 one Lynch was sent to this country from England under a commission to suppress piracy. He is credited with having faithfully executed, without

---

[1] See Hardiman's History of Galway (Dublin, 1820), p. 70. Also, *Spectator* (London), April 13, 1889 (62: 511). The story can be traced back as far as the year 1674. See Miscellany of the Irish Archæological Society (1846), I, 44–80. (M.)

[2] The *Green Bag*, March, 1900 (12: 150).

the formality of a trial, every pirate that he captured. It is presumed that owing to the difficulty of adhering to the usual forms of law in the colonies, this Judge Lynch was empowered to proceed summarily against pirates and thus gave rise to the term.[1] But whatever the facts may be about the methods employed by this man Lynch to suppress piracy,[2] there is no evidence to show that they were ever known as Lynch's law or had any connection whatever with lynch-law.

On its etymological side the word lynch has been traced to an old Anglo-Saxon verb *linch*, meaning to beat severely with a pliable instrument, to chastise or to maltreat, which is said to have survived in this cognate meaning in America, as have many other words and expressions long obsolete in Great Britain.[3] For this derivation, however, there seems to be no authority. There is no evidence that such a verb "survived" in America; nor is there any evidence that such an Anglo-Saxon verb ever existed.[4] According to Skeat the name Lynch is from

[1] See "lynch law," The American Cyclopædia (edition of 1875). See also, Notes & Queries, 2d Series, Oct. 23, 1858 (6: 338), where reference is made to *London Gazette*, 6–9 February, 1687–8, No. 2319.

[2] That he succeeded in making himself thoroughly unpopular with every one is shown in the Calendars of State Papers, Colonial Series, America & West Indies, 1685–1688, and 1688–1692. (M.)

[3] See "lynch law," Encyclopædia Britannica (9th edition); also, under "to lynch," Bartlett's Dictionary of Americanisms (4th edition, 1877).

C. A. Bristed, in an essay on The English Language in America (Cambridge Essays, 1855, p. 60) says: "*Linch*, in several of the northern-county dialects, means to beat, or maltreat. Lynch Law, then, would be simply equivalent to *club-law;* and the change of a letter may be easily accounted for by the fact that the name of Lynch is as common in some parts of America as in Ireland."

[4] No such verb as *linch* or *linge* is found in Bosworth's Dictionary of the Anglo-Saxon Language, or in Stratmann's Middle-English Dictionary. Murray's Oxford Dictionary (1903) gives the verb *linch* as a variant of *linge*, a word "of obscure origin."

hlinc, an Anlgo-Saxon word meaning a ridge of land.[1]
Furthermore, as was noted in the preceding chapter,
when the word lynch first came into general use, it was
stamped as of American origin.[2] No English lexicographer
recognized the terms lynch or lynch-law until 1848,
and in 1849 Craig gave the verb "lynch" as meaning
"to punish summarily without judicial investigation,
as by a mob.—An American word."[3] The fact that
Wright's English Dialect Dictionary (1902) does not
contain the word lynch, and the further fact that Murray's
Oxford Dictionary (1903) states that the term was originally used in the United States, may be regarded as conclusive evidence that the origin of "lynch-law" is not to
be sought in England.

There is a tradition in the Drake family of South
Carolina which ascribes the origin of the term to the
precipitate hanging, to prevent a rescue, of a Tory named
Major Beard, on Lynch Creek in Franklin County, North
Carolina. The following account of it is given by John
H. Wheeler, to whom it was communicated by Hon. B.
F. Moore, who received it from the Drake family:

"The origin of lynchlaw: During the revolution there was a
noted tory . . . in that portion formerly called Bute County,
now embraced within the counties of Franklin and Nash,
called Major Beard. Major John H. Drake lived near Hil-
liardston; he and his family were decided whigs. He had a

---

[1] See "lynch," Skeat's Etymological Dictionary.

[2] Although Bristed ingeniously traces lynch-law back to the verb *linch*,
he remarks, in passing, that "if there ever was a phrase deemed particularly Trans-atlantic in origin, it is that of Lynch Law for summary and
informal justice."

[3] See p. 10, note 1.

daughter, beautiful and accomplished, by whose charms Beard
was captivated; and the tradition runs, that the handsome
figure and commanding air of Beard had its effect on the young
lady, notwithstanding the difference in politics between him
and her father. On one occasion, Beard encamped for the
night near a mill on Swift Creek. This became known to
Major Drake and other whigs, and they organized a force . . .
and captured him. . . . After some consultation it was resolved to take him as a prisoner to headquarters of Colonel
Seawell, commanding in camp at a ford on Lynch Creek, in
Franklin County, about twenty miles off. He was tied on his
horse and carried under guard. After reaching camp, it was
determined to organize a court-martial, and try him for his
life. But before proceeding to trial, a report came that a
strong body of tories were in pursuit to rescue him; this created
a panic, for they knew his popularity and power, so they hung
him. The reported pursuit proved a false alarm, and it being
suggested that as the sentence had been inflicted before the judgment of the court had been pronounced, therefore it was illegal.
The body was then taken down, the court reorganized, he was
tried, condemned and re-hung by the neck until he was dead.

"The tree on which he was hung stood not far from Rocky
Ford, on Lynch's Creek; and it became a saying in Franklin,
when a person committed any offence of magnitude, that 'he
ought to be taken to Lynch Creek'; and so the word 'Lynch
law' became a fixture in the English language."[1]

In passing, the resemblance of this affair to Lydford
law rather than lynch-law is to be noted, and also the
fact that Wheeler, in his "History of North Carolina,"
published thirty-three years earlier, gives an account
of the hanging of "Captain Beard about 1778," but says

[1] "Reminiscences and Memoirs of North Carolina" (1884), p. 172.

nothing about its being in any way connected with the origin of the term lynch-law. Indeed, according to this earlier account there was nothing irregular in the proceeding; he was hung in accordance with the ordinary rules of war. Beard and one of his band, named Porch, who had been captured with him, "were tried by a court-martial and both were forthwith hung. Such was the end of Captain Beard."[1] The two accounts vary somewhat, but there is no room for doubt as to their having reference to the same occurrence. In short, the "tradition" in the Drake family must have arisen between 1851 and 1884. There is no evidence, further than this statement found in Wheeler's book, that "Lynch law" became a fixture in the English language because of a saying common in Franklin County, North Carolina, that any one who committed a grave offense "ought to be taken to Lynch Creek."

Some evidence has recently been brought forward indicating that lynch-law may have derived its name from Lynch's Creek, South Carolina.[2] Some extracts from Boston newspapers in the year 1768, dated Charlestown, South Carolina, show the existence of "Regulators" at that time, and mention is made of a meeting that they were to have on Lynch's Creek "where it was expected 1,200 would be assembled." It is also evident that one of their methods of inflicting punishment was by whipping. One extract states that "the people called regulators have lately severely chastised one Lum, who is come to town; but we have not yet learnt the real cause

[1] " History of North Carolina " (1851), p. 274.
[2] See article by Albert Matthews in the *Nation*, Dec. 4, 1902 (75: 439).

of this severity to him." The assertion has been made, therefore, that lynch-law derived its name from Lynch's Creek, South Carolina, because at that place the practice of lynching began.

The practice which came to be known as "regulating" had its beginning earlier than 1768, however, and this beginning was not in the neighborhood of Lynch's Creek. As early as 1766 it had begun in North Carolina and had extended from Granville County into Orange and Anson counties. Up to April, 1768, those who had taken part in these proceedings in North Carolina were designated by the appellation of the "Mob," and seem to have adopted it themselves. But on April 4, 1768, at a general meeting, they dropped this name and formally adopted the name of "Regulators."[1] When this practice of "regulating" was started in South Carolina it was instituted by Thomas Woodward, Joseph Kirkland, and Barnaby Pope,[2] who lived in the region between the Catawba and the Saluda Rivers, and not on the Pedee or Lynch's Creek. Thus, a name — that of "Regulation," not "Lynch Law," — had been given this practice before it reached the Pedee section of the Province. If the conduct of the Regulators in South Carolina was to give the name to the practice of illegal punishment, it would have been called, not "Lynch Law," but "Broad River Justice" or "Savannah Law."[3]

[1] Alexander Gregg: "History of the Old Cheraws" (1867), p. 129. F. X. Martin: "History of North Carolina" (1829), II, 228, 233. Hugh Williamson: "History of North Carolina" (1812), II, 128, 131.

[2] J. B. O'Neall: "Annals of Newberry" (1859), p. 76. It is not stated by O'Neall at what time these gentlemen instituted this practice in South Carolina. From the evidence that Gregg gives, it apparently took place in the summer of 1767. See the following chapter, p. 53.

[3] See article by Edward McCrady, in the *Nation*, Jan. 15, 1903 (76: 52). This article as originally written was published in full in the

No evidence has yet been found which shows any connection between "Lynch Law" and "Regulation" at this time.[1] Alexander Gregg, writing of the Regulator movement in the Carolinas, makes the statement: "They called themselves 'Regulators'; and thus 'Lynch law' had its origin at this period."[2] Dr. R. W. Gibbes had written eight years earlier than Gregg: "The Regulation, an association of respectable planters, took the matter in hand, and enforced order by a system of Lynch law."[3] Neither of these writers, however, implies that the Regulation in South Carolina had anything to do with the origin of the term lynch-law. Joseph Johnson, in a book

Sunday News, Charleston, S. C., Jan. 11, 1903. In a letter published in the *Nation*, March 19, 1903 (76: 225), Mr. George S. Wills cites an example of the use of the word lynch in connection with this creek, which is found in a journal kept by the Rev. William H. Wills, a Methodist minister of North Carolina, who traveled in his sulky from Tarboro, North Carolina, to Alabama, in the early summer of 1837. After describing a narrow escape from drowning in an attempt to cross Lynch's Creek while it was swollen, the Rev. Mr. Wills writes in his journal: "Probably I shall never forget Lynches Creek; for it had well nigh Lynch[d] me." — See "Publications of the Southern Historical Association," November, 1902 (6: 479). This example, however, shows no original connection between the term lynch-law and Lynch's Creek, South Carolina. As will appear in the following pages, by the year 1837 the word lynch had come to be widely used to indicate summary punishment. Evidently the writer in this case merely noticed the similarity between the name of the creek and the word which had recently come into use, and so made this play upon words, using the word lynch in a somewhat figurative sense.

[1] See article by Albert Matthews in the *Nation*, Jan. 29, 1903 (76: 91). In a monograph by William A. Schaper, on "Sectionalism and Representation in South Carolina," the statement is made, in reference to the Regulators of 1768, that "the settlers agreed to rely on lynch law, which received its name at this time." — Annual Report of the American Historical Association (1900), I, 337. The author of this statement that lynch-law received its name at this time was, however, unable to cite facts to support it. (M.)

[2] "History of the Old Cheraws" (1867), p. 128.

[3] J. B. O'Neall: "Biographical Sketches of the Bench and Bar of South Carolina" (1859), I, p. x.

published in 1851, gave a brief account of the Regulators and Schofilites. He says, "the most respectable inhabitants united to inflict summary justice on the depredators and called themselves Regulators."[1]   In this connection he does not refer to lynch-law at all. In another connection he writes: "This process, in what is now called 'lynch law,' was then designated 'regulating,' and the associates for this purpose were called 'Regulators.'"[2] No reference to lynch-law is to be found in Ramsay's History of the Revolution in South Carolina which was published in 1785.   Both of the accounts given by Wheeler of the occurrence at Lynch Creek, North Carolina, referred to above, imply that the term lynch-law was not in use any time previous to the Revolutionary War. As will appear later, the terms regulation and lynch-law are not found together until a much later date, and then they are not used in connection with events in the Carolinas.

Still another "Origin of Lynch's law" is given in Niles' Register for August 8, 1835.[3]   An anecdote is related of an occurrence "in Washington County, Pa., many years ago."   A poaching vagabond, long under suspicion, was finally detected and told to leave the neighborhood in twenty-four hours on penalty of prosecution. The poacher refused to comply and a party of five or six of his neighbors went to his home and "proceeded to try him in due form, choosing one of their number, a farmer named Lynch, to be judge."   The judge "decided that the poacher should be tied up and receive three hundred lashes, 'well laid on,' and then be given twenty-four hours

---

[1] " Traditions and Reminiscences," pp. 44–45.
[2] Ibid., p. 544.   [3] Vol. 48, p. 402.

to leave the place under penalty of receiving three hundred more if found after that time. The first part of the sentence was inflicted on the spot, with such *good intent* as to render its repetition unnecessary. The culprit made off as fast as his lacerated limbs would permit him.''

Nothing further is known of this farmer named Lynch, who acted as judge at this impromptu trial, and there is no reason for regarding this incident as in any way connected with the origin of lynch-law. It is merely an instance of recourse to summary procedure against an unpopular individual. It may or may not have been known at the time as punishment by Lynch's law.

We now come to the explanation of the origin of the term which has been most frequently given and which was for years accepted without question. It is to the effect that lynch-law originally had reference to the kind of law administered by Charles Lynch, in Virginia, during the latter part of the Revolutionary War.

It is needless to recount here all the variations in the stories connecting the origin of lynch-law with the Lynch family in Virginia.[1] In certain accounts Charles Lynch has been confused with his older brother, John Lynch, who remained a Quaker all his life and was the founder of Lynchburg, Virginia. Some accounts refer vaguely to a Virginia farmer, or planter, by the name of

[1] One such story will be found in the following chapter on p. 73. For an account of the Lynch family in Virginia, see Mrs. Julia Mayo Cabell: "Sketches and Recollections of Lynchburg" (1858), pp. 9–23. The chief available sources of information for the facts and events pertaining to the life of Charles Lynch are an article by Thomas Walker Page in the *Atlantic Monthly*, December, 1901 (88: 731), and one by Howell Colton Featherston in the *Green Bag*, March, 1900 (12: 150). Both of these articles have been largely drawn upon in the following pages.

Lynch, whose vigorous methods of punishing wrong-doers gave rise to the term lynch-law.[1] Haydn's Dictionary of Dates (1860) apparently is responsible for the fiction that this mode of administering justice began about the end of the seventeenth century and derives its name from John Lynch, a farmer, who exercised it upon the fugitive slaves and criminals dwelling in the Dismal Swamp, North Carolina, when they committed outrages upon persons and property which the law could not promptly repress. This story is repeated in the editions of 1873 and 1885, and is also given in Harpers' Popular Cyclopædia of the History of the United States,[2] and seems to have become generally accepted in France.[3] It is, however, wholly erroneous.

The movement for independence had from the first a great many opponents in the mountainous sections of Virginia, and there was a considerable number of Tories in Bedford County, where Charles Lynch lived.[4] The un-

---

[1] A writer ("Claverhouse") in the *New York Evening Post* for June 2, 1864, says: "In America, the term 'Lynch law' was first used in Piedmont, on the western frontier of Virginia. There was no court within the district, and all controversies were referred to the arbitrament of prominent citizens. Among these was a man by the name of Lynch, whose decisions were so impartial that he was known as Judge Lynch, and the system was called 'Lynch law,' and adopted in our pioneer settlements as an inexpensive and speedy method of obtaining justice."

[2] Edited by Benson J. Lossing, published in 1882.

[3] See article by Arthur Desjardins, *Revue des Deux Mondes*, May, 1891.

[4] Charles Lynch was born in 1736, at Chestnut Hill, his father's estate, upon a part of which the city of Lynchburg now stands. His father was a "redemptioner" who came to Virginia from Ireland about 1725. The young adventurer subsequently married the daughter of the planter to whom the captain of the ship that brought him over had sold him, took up a large tract of land lying between the James and the Staunton rivers, and became a tobacco planter on a large scale. At his death the home on the James fell to his eldest son, John, and Charles took the

settled condition of affairs also led many desperadoes to resort to this section of Virginia. Both Tories and des-

part of the family lands that lay nearer the frontier. The mother, Sarah Lynch, then a widow, had joined the sect of the Quakers at the Cedar Creek meeting on April 16, 1750, and it is in the records of this congregation of Quakers that the following item appears: "14 of Dec., 1754. Charles Lynch and Anne Terrill published for the first Time their Intentions of Marriage." The young couple established their home on the Staunton, in what is now the southwestern part of Campbell County.

For years Charles followed his mother's teachings and was an active member of the Society of Friends; for some time he was "Clerk of the monthly meetings." Later, however, the exigencies of the times caused him to forego some of his scruples and accept public office. In 1767 he became "unsatisfactory" to the peace-loving Quakers and he was "disowned for taking solemn oaths, contrary to the order and discipline of Friends." It was in this year, 1767, that he was elected to the Virginia House of Burgesses, where he held a seat till the colony became an independent State. He was prominent in the earliest organization of Bedford County, formed from Lunenburg County in 1753 (Henry Howe: "Historical Collections of Virginia" (1845), p. 188; Hening's Statutes at Large, VI, 381), and was a member of the Virginia convention of 1776, which, by sending instructions to the delegates from Virginia in the Continental Congress, exercised a decisive influence on the movement for independence. He had been made a justice of the peace under a commission from Governor Dunmore in 1774, and when the county court was reorganized, according to the ordinance of the Convention, passed on the 3d of July, 1776, he retained the position.

At the beginning of the Revolutionary War his Quaker principles seemed still to influence his actions to an extent sufficient to keep him out of active military service. His loyalty was well known, however. Mr. Page says: "He did not enlist in the army, partly because of his Quaker principles, but chiefly because his presence was imperatively necessary at home. He had to rouse the spirit of his constituents to support the action he had advocated in the convention. He had to raise and equip troops for the army. He had, as it were, to mobilize the forces of his country, and attend to all the duties of a commissary department. In addition, he had to make some provision in the event of an attack from hostile Indians." In 1778 the court of Bedford recommended him to the Governor for the office of Colonel of Militia in that county. He accepted the commission and organized a regiment, but the call to the front did not come till two years later when the war was shifted to the south and Lord Cornwallis was sent to co-operate with General Philips and Benedict Arnold in the invasion of Virginia.

The records of the court of Bedford County, the minutes of various Quaker meetings, the journals of the Virginia House of Burgesses and of the first Constitutional Convention, taken together with family documents and traditions, show Charles Lynch to have been a thoroughly capable and highly respected man, a leader among the men in his com-

peradoes harassed the Continentals and plundered their property with impunity.[1] The prices paid by both

munity. Before the close of the war he made a record for himself as an officer in the army. At the battle of Guilford Court House, March 15, 1781, a battalion of riflemen under his command behaved with much gallantry and aided in bringing considerable credit to the Virginia militia. [Henry Howe: "Historical Collections of Virginia" (1845), p. 212. W. G. Simms: "Life of Nathanael Greene" (1859), p. 186. Henry Lee: "Memoirs of the War" (1812), I, 341, 345. William Johnson: "Sketches of Life and Correspondence of Nathanael Greene" (1822), II, 3. Banastre Tarleton: "History of the Campaigns of 1780 and 1781" (1787), p. 272. C. Stedman: "History of the American War" (1794), II, 338.]

He lived for a number of years after peace had been declared with England, and voted for the new constitution. In the family burying-ground on his homestead plantation a tombstone bears the simple inscription:

"In memory of Colonel Charles Lynch, a zealous and active patriot. Died, October 29, 1796; aged 60 years."

Many anecdotes are still in circulation among the old inhabitants of his neighborhood illustrative of his habits and character. The chorus of a once popular patriotic song runs as follows:

"Hurrah for Colonel Lynch,
Captain Bob and Callaway!
They never turned a Tory loose
Until he shouted 'Liberty'!"

Another version of this refrain runs this way:

"Hurrah for Captain Bob,
Colonels Lynch and Callaway!
Who never let a Tory off
Until he cried out ' Liberty!'"

[1] Mr. Page makes no mention of any trouble with desperadoes. Referring to the Tories in Bedford County, he says: "Numerous records of the county courts, taken together with other sources of information, show that here, as in many other western counties, there was a strong and influential party opposed to the struggle for independence. For the most part they were quiet, thrifty men, far different from the ruffians and desperadoes that prejudice has since represented them to be." That there were cliques of depredators and that much lawlessness prevailed in Virginia and the Carolinas at about this time is undoubtedly true, however. William Wirt, in his "Sketches of the Life and Character of Patrick Henry" (p. 217), cites the case of Josiah Philips who, at the head of a band of banditti, spread terror in the counties of Norfolk and Princess Anne, and was made an outlaw by an act of the legislature of Virginia, by which act it became lawful for any person to kill him whenever opportunity offered. Lyman C. Draper presents the record of a great deal of lawlessness and depredation in his "King's Mountain and its Heroes." See pp. 241, 331, 332, 336, 340 note, 343 note, 384, 448–449.

armies for horses made horse-stealing a lucrative practice, and the inefficiency of the judiciary made punishment practically out of the question. The county courts were merely examining courts in all such cases, and the single court for the final trial of felonies sat at Williamsburg, more than two hundred miles away. To take the prisoners thither, and the witnesses necessary to convict them, was next to impossible. Frequently the officers in charge of prisoners would be attacked by outlaws and forced to release their men, or be captured by British troops and themselves made prisoners.

It was under these circumstances that Colonel Lynch conferred with some of his neighbors as to what was best to be done. After deliberation they decided to take matters into their own hands, to punish lawlessness of every kind, and so far as possible restore peace and security to their community. For the purpose of attaining these ends they formed an organization with Mr. Lynch at the head. Under his direction suspected persons were arrested and brought to his house, where they were tried by a court composed of himself, as presiding justice, and his three neighbors, William Preston, Robert Adams, Jr., and James Callaway, sitting as associate justices.

The practice of this court was to have the accused brought face to face with his accusers, permit him to hear the testimony against himself, and to allow him to defend himself by calling witnesses in his behalf and by showing mitigating and extenuating circumstances. If acquitted, he was allowed to go, "often with apologies and reparation." If convicted, he was sentenced to receive thirty-

nine lashes on the bare back, and if he did not then shout
"Liberty Forever," to be hanged up by the thumbs until
he did so. The execution of the sentence took place
immediately upon conviction. The condemned was
tied to a large walnut tree standing in Mr.
Lynch's yard and the stripes inflicted — with such vigor, it is
said, that even the stoutest hearted Tory shouted for
"Liberty" without necessitating a resort to further
punishment.[1]

The news of the invasion of Virginia by Cornwallis
gave the Bedford Tories strong encouragement and a
conspiracy was formed to overthrow the county organization and seize, for the use of Cornwallis on his arrival, the
stores that Lynch had collected for Greene's army in North
Carolina. The conspirator's plans, however, became
known to Colonel Lynch, tradition says through one of
their own number, and he had them all arrested. In the
case of these conspirators, who were guilty of a treasonable
offense, a more serious situation presented itself. Lynch
himself was on the point of setting out with his regiment
for the east to oppose the British under Benedict Arnold.
It was not wise to inflict the usual punishment and then
give the conspirators their freedom again; neither could
he take them as prisoners along with him on the rapid
march that he was forced to make. After careful deliberation, Colonel Lynch, as the presiding justice, sentenced
them to terms of imprisonment varying from one to five
years. Robert Cowan, who had formerly been a fellow
justice on the county bench and who seems to have been

---

[1] It is to be understood that these statements are based on tradition
and not on contemporary evidence.

the ringleader, was sentenced to a year's imprisonment and a fine of £20,000.[1]

This court, even though it be considered as still the regular county court, had clearly transcended its powers; the General Court alone had jurisdiction in cases of treason. After the war, therefore, the Tories who had suffered at his hands threatened to prosecute Colonel Lynch and his friends. To avoid lawsuits and as a means of finally settling the affair, Lynch brought the whole matter before the Virginia legislature. After a lengthy debate, which, according to Mr. Page, "aroused the interest of the whole country," the following act was passed in October, 1782:

"An act to indemnify certain persons in suppressing a conspiracy against this state.

I. WHEREAS divers evil-disposed persons in the year one thousand seven hundred and eighty, formed a conspiracy and did actually attempt to levy war against the commonwealth; and it is represented to the present general assembly, that William Preston, Robert Adams, junior, James Callaway, and Charles Lynch, and other faithful citizens, aided by detachments of volunteers from different parts of the state, did, by timely and effectual measures, suppress such conspiracy: And whereas the measures taken for that purpose may not be strictly warranted by law, although justifiable from the imminence of the danger;

II. BE IT THEREFORE ENACTED, That the said William Preston, Robert Adams, junior, James Callaway and Charles Lynch, and all other persons whatsoever, concerned in

---

[1] Mr. Page remarks that the fine was not so heavy as it seems, for in that year the prices fixed by the court were: rum and brandy per gallon, £40, corn and oats per gallon, £2 8s., dinner at an "ordinary," £4 10s., &c.

suppressing the said conspiracy, or in advising, issuing, or executing any orders, or measures taken for that purpose, stand indemnified and exonerated of and from all pains, penalties, prosecutions, actions, suits, and damages, on account thereof. And that if any indictment, prosecution, action, or suit, shall be laid or brought against them, or any of them, for any act or thing done therein, the defendant, or defendants may plead in bar, or the general issue, and give this act in evidence."[1]

"The proceedings in Bedford, which the legislature thus pronounced to be illegal, but justifiable, were imitated in other parts of the State, and came to be known by the name of Lynch's Law. In justice to Colonel Lynch, it should be remembered that his action was taken at a time when the State was in the throes of a hostile invasion. The General Court, before which the conspirators should have been tried, was temporarily dispersed. Thomas Jefferson, then the governor of the State, was proving himself peculiarly incompetent to fill the position. The whole executive department was in a state of partial paralysis. It was, therefore, no spirit of insubordination or disregard of the law that induced Lynch to act as he did. There were few men living more inclined than this simple Quaker farmer to render due respect in word and deed to the established authorities."[2]

The old walnut tree on which lynch-law is said to have been first administered was still standing, in 1900,[3] on

---

[1] Hening's Statutes at Large, XI, 134–135.

[2] Quoted from the article by Mr. Page. No evidence is cited in support of the statement that the proceedings in Bedford were imitated in other parts of the State and came to be known by the name of Lynch's Law.

[3] See article by Mr. Featherston. A drawing of this tree "from a sketch from nature" may be found in the *Green Bag*, December, 1892 (4: 561).

the lawn of the Lynch homestead, two miles from the village of Lynch Station on the Southern Railway. A part of it was dead but the rest was still vigorous and bore its annual crop of nuts. The death penalty, however, was never inflicted under its shadow. Some say that the Quaker proclivities of "Judge Lynch"[1] prevented him from passing sentence of death; others say that it was due to his native sense of humanity. Mr. Page presents some evidence showing that "both custom and sentiment were violently opposed to visiting capital punishment upon the detected Tory conspirators."[2]

[1] Mr. Featherston states that Charles Lynch was often called "Judge Lynch" by his neighbors. He seems to have been more commonly known as "Colonel Lynch."

[2] "The infliction of capital punishment was extremely rare. There were only three instances of it, and these for most heinous offenses, between the organization of the county (Bedford) and the Revolution. The first case was on May 24, 1756, when the court assembled 'to hear and determine all Treasons, Petit Treasons, Murders, and other Offenses committed or done by Hampton and Sambo belonging to John Payne of Goochland, Gent.' 'The said Hampton and Sambo were set to the Bar under Custody of Charles Talbot (then sheriff) to whose Custody they were before committed on Suspicion of their being Guilty of the felonious Prepairing and Administering Poysonous Medicines to Ann Payne, and being Arraigned of the Premises pleaded Not Guilty and for their Trial put themselves upon the Court. Whereupon divers Witnesses were charged and they heared in their Defence. On Consideration thereof it is the Opinion of the Court that the said Hampton is guilty in the Manner and Form as in the Indictment. Therefore it is considered that the said Hampton be hanged by the Neck till he be dead, and that he be afterwards cut in Quarters, and his Quarters hung up at the Cross Roads. And it is the Opinion of the Court that the said Sambo is guilty of a Misdemeanor. Therefore it is considered that the said Sambo be burnt in the Hand, and that he also receive thirty-one Lashes on his bare Back at the Whipping Post. Memo: That the said Hampton is adjudged at forty-five Pound which is ordered to be certified to the Assembly (that his owner may be remunerated according to law).' That it was a convincing proof of his guilt, and not race prejudice, that led the court to impose this savage punishment is evident from the fact that in the same year a negro was tried for murder, another for poisoning, and a third for arson, and all were cleared." — Quoted from the article by Mr. Page.

In the determination of origins it is frequently impossible to obtain direct evidence bearing on the point in question. In this case there is direct evidence for connecting the name of Charles Lynch with the origin of "lynch-law."[1] In 1817 Judge Spencer Roane wrote in a letter to William Wirt: "In the year 1792 there were many suits on the south side of James River, for inflicting Lynch's law." Mr. Wirt adds, in a note explanatory of the words "Lynch's law," "Thirty-nine lashes, inflicted without trial or law, on mere suspicion of guilt, which could not be regularly proven. This lawless practice, which, sometimes by the order of a magistrate, sometimes without, prevailed extensively in the upper counties on James River, took its name from the gentleman who set the first example of it."[2] Though Wirt does not mention Charles Lynch by name, he does say that the lawless practice "prevailed extensively in the upper counties on James River," and Charles Lynch was for years closely identified with the interests of Campbell[3] and Bedford counties — two of the upper counties on the James River.

[1] This evidence has been presented by the present writer in a communication to the *Nation*. See issue of May 21, 1903 (76: 415).

[2] William Wirt: "Sketches of the Life and Character of Patrick Henry" (1818), p. 372. Mr. Matthews, in his article in the *Nation*, Dec. 4, 1902 (75: 439), remarks that it is uncertain whether the note was written by Roane or Wirt. In William Wirt Henry's "Life of Patrick Henry," Vol. II, p. 482, the "MS. Letter of Judge Roane to Mr. Wirt" is given, but the note is not included. The note was undoubtedly written by Wirt.

[3] An act for dividing the county of Bedford into two distinct counties, the new county to be known by the name of Campbell, was passed by the General Assembly in 1782. — Hening's Statutes at Large, X, 447; Journal of the House of Delegates, Jan. 5, 1782, p. 73. Howe says that Campbell County was formed from Bedford in 1784, and named in honor of General William Campbell, a distinguished officer of the American Revolution. — "Historical Collections of Virginia." p. 210.

Henry Howe, in his "Historical Collections of Virginia," in a section entitled "Lynch Law," says: "At that time (the time of the Revolution), this country (Campbell County and vicinity) was very thinly settled, and infested by a lawless band of tories and desperadoes. The necessity of the case involved desperate measures, and Col. Lynch, then a leading whig, apprehended and had them punished, without any superfluous ceremony. Hence the origin of the term 'Lynch Law.' This practice of Lynching continued years after the war, and was applied to many cases of mere suspicion of guilt, which could not be regularly proven."[1]

In a book written a few years later than the above, Howe has the following to say on the same subject: "The Lynch Law, as it is termed, originated in Virginia at the time of the American Revolution, and was first adopted by Colonel Lynch against a lawless band of tories and desperadoes, who infested the country at the base of the Blue Ridge. This plan was afterwards followed in the west, and its operation was salutary in ridding the country of miscreants whom the law was not strong enough to punish. The tribunal of *Squire Birch*, as the person who personated the judge was called, was established under a tree in the woods; the culprit being usually found guilty was tied to a tree and lashed without mercy, and then expelled from the country. In general, '*the regu-*

---

[1] Published at Charleston, South Carolina, in 1845. See p. 212 for the quotation. See Mrs. Julia Mayo Cabell: "Sketches and Recollections of Lynchburg" (1858), pp. 9–10, for a similar account of the connection of Colonel Charles Lynch with the origin of "the celebrated code called 'Lynch Law.'" This account is taken from the *St. Louis Republican*, but neither the author's name nor the date of its publication is given.

lators' only exercised this law upon the most base and vile characters."[1]

This account given by Howe cannot be considered as wholly independent of the influence of Wirt. In his "Historical Collections of Virginia," Howe quotes from Wirt's book in substantiation of his statement that the "practice of Lynching continued years after the war." On the other hand, however, the fact that he repeated his assertions in regard to the origin of "Lynch Law" in emphatic terms in his later book, and therewith described the operation of "Lynch Law" in the west, is strong evidence that he had other sources of information than Wirt's book on the matter.[2]

An account, entirely independent of any influence from either Wirt or Howe, is found in "Colonel William Martin's Narrative of Frontier Life," prepared about 1842 for Dr. Lyman C. Draper and now in the Draper MS. Collections in the Wisconsin State Historical Society Library. It is as follows:

"In those times there were a great many bad men settled along the frontiers who by their thefts annoyed the country greatly. Insomuch that the people entered into combinations to suppress them and formed companies called regulators. They formed in military style, with officers, etc.

"They also organized a court and appointed some three or four of their aged, discreet men judges to try criminal causes, award punishment, etc. The company would bring up suspected fellows and the court would try them. But they seldom

<hr>

[1] Henry Howe: "The Great West" (Cincinnati, 1852), p. 183.

[2] The writer is indebted to Mr. Matthews for the suggestion that Howe's allusion to "Squire Birch" points to Judge James Hall's "Letters from the West" as one such source. See Chapter III. p. 81.

extended punishment beyond whipping and driving them from the country, sometimes making them pay for property stolen, when they had the means.

"This method of breaking up combinations of rogues was first set on foot by Col. Charles Lynch, of Bedford county, Va., where I was raised. He and my father were acquainted. (The same man for whom Lynchburg was named.) This plan was started some seventy or eighty years ago.[1]

"The measure seemed to be called for from the situation of the country at the time. And it has been practiced more or less in the settling of new countries from that time until within a few years past, since the laws operate with more efficiency. The authorities generally connived at it from the necessity of the case. And perhaps nowhere has it been more common than in Tennessee. Lynch at first punished with thirty-nine stripes, taking, as I suppose, Moses for his model. And this was for a great while called Lynch's law, meaning all unlawful whipping. Any of the old men now in the South and West can tell the meaning of Lynch's law.

"Lynch, however, has been improved upon and more severe punishments sometimes inflicted. I have given this feature of Western history from the presumption that you may not have known it."[2]

Such is the strongest evidence bearing directly on the point under consideration. It is true that Martin's

[1] There are two errors here. Lynchburg was not named for him but for his brother, John Lynch, and the plan was started later than "some seventy or eighty years ago." Mr. Matthews disagrees with the writer in saying that this account is entirely independent of what Wirt had written on the subject. It seems to the writer, however, that these two inaccuracies indicate that Martin was drawing wholly from his own sources of information. He was, apparently, merely writing down what was considered a matter of common knowledge among the older men in that section of the country, many of whom were emigrants from Virginia.

[2] "Publications of the Southern Historical Association," November, 1900, (4: 463).

account, as well as Howe's, was not written until more than forty years after the death of Charles Lynch. It is true, also, that many stories have referred to a man by the name of Lynch in Virginia, sometimes specifically mentioning Charles Lynch or Colonel Lynch, at other times naming some other Lynch.[1] But it is likewise true that it is in this way that tradition has been persistent in attributing the origin of lynch-law to a member of the Lynch family in Virginia. Furthermore, since no evidence whatsoever has been found for tracing the beginning of lynch-law to any other member of that family, it may be said that tradition has thus persistently pointed to Colonel Charles Lynch as the first lyncher. Traditions are in general far from trustworthy, but, on the other hand, they usually have *some* basis in fact. In this case Wirt's statement gives, at the very least, a presumption in favor of the tradition, which facts to the contrary only can remove.[2]

The earliest use of the expression "Lynch's law" that

[1] Charles Augustus Murray, in his "Travels in North America during the years 1834, 1835, and 1836" (2 vol., N. Y., 1839), gives a traditional account of the origin of the term "lynch-law," such a one as might be given around a camp-fire. He also describes the operation of lynch-law at that time in the Mississippi Valley. See Vol II, p. 79. G. W. Featherstonhaugh, in his "Excursion through the Slave States" (N. Y., 1844), gives "An account of the first Judge Lynch, and the state of Legal Practice in his Court," pp. 89–90. He speaks of a certain Judge Lynch in Arkansas and of "a famous Virginia ancestor of his." He says that "this ancestor, the first Judge Lynch, was a miller and a justice of the peace in the back woods," and then gives a traditional account of his methods of inflicting punishment. See also David Schenck: "North Carolina, 1780–81" (1889), pp. 309–310. L. P. Summers: "History of Southwest Virginia and Washington County" (1903), p. 243.

[2] Mr. Matthews holds a somewhat different view. See article, "The Term Lynch Law," *Modern Philology*, Vol. II, No. 2, October, 1904. This article should be consulted by any one desiring to investigate this matter further.

is known at the present time is this one found in Wirt's book which was published in 1818. Judge Roane wrote that there were many suits in the year 1792 for inflicting Lynch's law. From his statement it does not follow that the term Lynch's law was in use in the year 1792. It does follow, however, that the term was at least a localism in Virginia in the year 1817.

Other terms were also in use for summary and illegal punishment in the period 1780–1830. The following appeared in the Salem Gazette of October 2, 1812: "People who clamored violently against Mr. Adams' 'gag law' in '99, see nothing to disapprove in the 'club law' enacted at Baltimore, as a substitute for it. — *Messenger.*"[1]

In the year 1819 two passages entitled "Summary justice" appeared in Niles' Register. They read as follows: "*Summary justice.* — A tin pedlar at Easton, Pa. was discovered to have two negro children in his cart. On examination, one of the little sufferers was found to have been crammed in such a manner, that his ear was rubbed off! The people indignantly rose and cut off the fellow's ear. I am no advocate for the violation of the laws, but from my heart I can't feel sorry for him. — *Village Recorder.*"[2] "*Summary justice.* After a late extensive fire which happened at Charleston, a fellow was found secreting some goods that had been stolen during the calamity. The alternative was offered to him, whether he would be prosecuted at law, or suffer punishment on

[1] In the *Salem Gazette*, July 17, 1812, p. 3, the rise and domination of mobs in a community was characterized as "Mob Law." (M.)

[2] Jan. 9, 1819 (15: 384). (M.)

the spot; he chose the latter, was tied to a tree, received
fifty lashes well laid on, and got off *clear*, having restored
the stolen goods."[1]

In the year 1822 Niles' Register contained the following: "*Riot*. A parcel of Irish laborers employed in the
navy yard at Charlestown, lately attempted to rescue
some property of one of their fellows out of the hands
of the sheriff. The affray was a severe one — but 'club
law' did not prevail. Captain Hull exposed himself considerably to quell the riot."[2]

Writing under the date of November 29, 1819, W.
Faux describes an instance of the use of summary methods
against an unpopular individual in Princeton, Indiana,
and says: "The people of the place deputed four persons
to inform him, that unless he quitted the town and the
state immediately, he should receive Lynch's law, that is,
whipping in the woods."[3] Under the date of December
16, 1819, referring to "the Rowdies of Kentucky," the
same author writes: "These regulators are self-appointed
ministers of justice, to punish or destroy those whom the
law cannot touch."[4]

On July 17, 1824, Niles' Register published the information that several murders had been committed in Kentucky "by persons who called themselves 'regulators.'"[5]

W. N. Blane published in London in 1824 an account
of his travels in America and described "the practice of
Regulating" that then existed in parts of Kentucky,

---

[1] July 24, 1819 (16: 368). (M.)
[2] June 1, 1822 (22: 224). (M.)
[3] "Memorable Days in America" (1823), p. 304.
[4] Ibid., p. 318.   [5] Vol. 26, p. 326.

Indiana, and Illinois. He tells how the bands of Regulators were organized and their methods of inflicting punishment, but does not use the term lynch or lynchlaw.[1]

Judge James Hall, in his "Letters from the West," published in 1828, uses the following words: "No commentator has taken any notice of *Linch's Law*, which was once the *lex loci* of the frontier. The citizens formed themselves into a '*regulating company*.' Sometimes the sufferers resorted to courts of justice for remuneration, and there have been instances of heavy damages being recovered of the regulators."[2]

It thus appears that summary and illegal methods of punishing offenders were known under various names between 1780 and 1830. The term Lynch's law was not exclusively applied to such practices. The evidence obtainable at present, therefore, indicates that at some time between 1780 and 1817 the term Lynch's law became a localism in Virginia in the region of the James River. By the year 1819 it had spread as far west as Indiana, and by 1828 it had become still more widely used but had not superseded all other terms for the popular administration of justice.

To the question why or how Lynch's name came to be attached to this practice, there is at present no conclusive answer. It may be said that Colonel Charles Lynch was a prominent man in his community, and when he adopted extra-legal methods of punishing public offenders during

---

[1] "An Excursion through the United States and Canada," pp. 233–236. (M.) An extended extract is given in the following chapter on p. 79.

[2] pp. 291, 292. A more extended extract is given in the following chapter on p. 81.

the troublous times of the Revolution, he no doubt attracted considerable attention to himself, and thus his name became identified with such practices. It may also be said that the uniqueness of some of his punishments, such as compelling the Tories to shout "Liberty forever," probably brought his name into prominence with the practice. The fact remains, however, that no contemporaneous evidence has yet been discovered which will explain why Lynch's name came to be applied to the practice. We know definitely only that the form of the expression was at first Lynch's law, and that tradition, supported by all the evidence that we have, ascribes its origin to Colonel Lynch. Equally certain it is that Lynch's law originally signified a whipping for reformatory purposes with more or less disregard for its legality, and was so used at a time subsequent to the American Revolution and not before that time. Evidently the term originated in Virginia, and as the tide of emigration moved westward it was carried along the frontier where conditions were such as to encourage the use of extra-legal methods against public offenders.

This becomes more evident when the early history of the popular administration of punishment in the United States is taken into account. A consideration of early lynch-law, or lynch-law down to 1830, constitutes the following chapter.

CHAPTER III

EARLY LYNCH-LAW

IN the preceding chapter we have been concerned with the origin of the term by which the practice has come to be known. In this chapter we are concerned with the practice itself. Something of the nature of lynch-law procedure during the Revolutionary epoch has already become apparent, but a more detailed investigation into the early history of such procedure will reveal other characteristics.

It has been said by some that the first instance of the operation of lynch-law in America was in December, 1763, at Paxtang (now Harrisburg), Pennsylvania. Indian scalping parties had been laying waste the settlements with relentless fury, and the appeals of the settlers to the Quaker government for help had been treated with contempt. Exasperated at the policy pursued by the Quakers toward the Indians, the Scotch-Irish who had settled in Lancaster and Cumberland counties formed several companies of Rangers to patrol the borders and give protection. "About the middle of December, word was brought to the settlers living at Paxtang, that an Indian known to have committed depredations in the vicinity had been traced to Conestoga. Matthew Smith, a man of influence and popularity among his associates, called together a number of the Paxtang Rangers, and

[41]

led them to the Conestoga settlement. One of the men saw an Indian issuing from a house, and thought that he recognized him as the savage who had killed his own mother. Firing his rifle, he brought the Indian down. Then, with a loud shout, the furious mob rushed into the cabins, and killed all the Indians whom they found there, some six in number. Fourteen of the Conestogas managed to escape, and, fleeing to Lancaster, were given a place of refuge in the county jail. While there, word was again carried to the Paxtang men that an Indian, known to have murdered the relatives of one of their number, was among those who had received the protection of the Lancaster magistrates. This again aroused a feeling of rage and resentment amongst the Rangers. On December 27, some fifty of them, under the leadership of Lazarus Stewart, marched to Lancaster, broke open the jail, and with the fury of a mob massacred every Indian contained therein, man, woman, and child."[1]

In connection with this incident it has been suggested that the Scotch-Irish are to blame for the introduction of lynch-law in America; that they brought with them traditions of the administration of summary justice in Mediæval Scotland, and, amidst the perils of the frontier, quickly resorted to the ancient methods of suppressing violence and depredation. The case of the Regulators in the Carolinas is also cited as an instance of the Scotch-Irish backwoodsmen taking the administration of justice into their own hands, when their rulers failed to provide for them a safe government. It is said that this same self-reliant spirit is exhibited in the "family feuds of Ken-

[1] C. A. Hanna: "The Scotch-Irish" (1902), p. 60.

tucky, which for the most part seem peculiar to families bearing Scottish names." [1]

Undoubtedly the Scotch-Irish played an important part in the early history of lynch-law in the United States. But it was rather because they were the vanguard of a new civilization than because they were of Scottish descent that they played this important part. Environmental influences of old had made them pioneers. Before coming to this country they had behind them a century of frontier life. Their experience in Ireland, where the soil was poor and where by reason of the difference in religion they lived apart from, and often in open hostility to, the natives, led them to be self-reliant and self-assertive. Their training had thus made them sturdy frontiersmen, quite the sort to subdue the wilderness and become the founders of a new civilization. Amid the vicissitudes incident to settlement in a virgin territory it was often necessary, as a matter of self-preservation, to use prompt and decisive measures against depredators. That the early settlers did not always observe "due process of law" can scarcely be urged as deserving condemnation. They merely adopted the means which seemed to them the most expedient under the existing circumstances.

The adoption of summary measures by Scotch-Irish Rangers in Pennsylvania in 1763, however, does not furnish an isolated instance, nor indeed the earliest instance, of the use of such measures against Indians. The provincial governments were not infrequently called upon to take note of such occurrences in order to preserve amicable relations with the various Indian tribes, and

[1] C. A. Hanna: "The Scotch-Irish" (1902), p. 60.

considerable difficulty was commonly experienced when the attempt was made to bring to justice white men who had murdered Indians.

In the Province of New Hampshire in June, 1753, two white men killed two Indians who were accused of having carried off two negroes the preceding year. After several months the men were arrested, indicted for the murder, placed in the jail at Portsmouth, and their trial set for March 21, 1754. The night previous to the day appointed for the trial a party of their neighbors appeared in Portsmouth, broke open the jail and set them free. "This outrage produced great excitement in the community — some endeavoring to discover and retake the murderers, and others favoring their escape. Both the murder and the rescue, however, were generally justified in the community. And, although rewards were offered by Governor Wentworth for the apprehension of Bowen and Morrill, yet in a short time they went openly about their business, without fear of molestation, and the men engaged in breaking the jail at Portsmouth, though well known, were never called to account, but, on the contrary, were considered as having performed a most meritorious act. In fact, some of the most substantial men in the country were engaged in the rescue, — by act or advice, — and the Government could not have made an arrest had they made the attempt. Presents were afterwards made to the relatives of these Indians by the Government of New Hampshire, and thus the 'blood was wiped away' to the satisfaction of the Indians."[1]

In May, 1795, in the county of St. Clair in the Illinois

[1] New Hampshire Provincial Papers, VI, 262–266. (M.)

country, two Indians were murdered while they were in the custody of the sheriff who was conveying them to jail upon warrant. An effort was made to bring the murderers to justice, but although "the most positive evidence was adduced to the grand jury against two persons, inhabitants of the county of St. Clair, that the murder was committed by them," no bill of indictment was found against them. Three attempts were made to secure an indictment from the grand jury, all of which were unsuccessful. Referring to another instance where Indians were murdered by whites, which occurred at about the same time but the circumstances of which were "not only not blameable but laudable," Governor St. Clair wrote, in his report to the Secretary of State, "had the affair been ever so criminal in its nature, it would have been, I believe, impossible to have brought the actors to punishment."[1]

In several respects there is a resemblance between the means which were employed by the early settlers for protection against Indian depredators and the methods which have been adopted in more recent years for the punishment of public offenders. In their purpose, in their organization, and in their summary infliction of the death penalty, the Rangers were not unlike the vigilance committees which have been closely identified with the later operation of the frontier type of lynch-law. In breaking open jails, and, as in Lancaster, Pennsylvania, in massacring inmates against whom there was a strong popular resentment, or, as in Portsmouth, New Hampshire, in

[1] W. H. Smith: "The St. Clair Papers" (1882), II, 351, 374, 376, 396-397. (M.)

liberating prisoners whose criminal conduct was generally
justified in the community, there appear some of the distinctive features which have marked the later operation
of lynch-law in well settled communities. It is also
probably true that the antagonistic relations which existed between the whites and the Indians during the early
history of this country directly encouraged a popular
disregard of all legal procedure on the part of the whites
when dealing with Indians. But the use of summary
measures against Indians and the attendant occurrences
can scarcely be said to mark the beginning of the operation of lynch-law in America. The meaning which was
at first attached to the term Lynch's law and the nature
of the practice which first came to be known by that name
preclude such a beginning for the practice. Lynch's law
originally corresponded much more closely to what was
known as "regulating," a practice which was early
adopted not only where the frontier type of society existed,
but also where there was the stable and better organized
form of society characteristic of older communities.

The following appeared in the New York Gazette of
December 18, 1752: "We hear from *Elizabeth-Town*,
that an odd Sect of People have lately appeared there,
who go under the Denomination of *Regulars:* there are
near a Dozen of them, who dress themselves in Women's
Cloaths, and painting their Faces, go in the Evening to
the Houses of such as are reported to have beat their
Wives: where one of them entering in first, seizes the
Delinquent, whilst the rest follow, strip him, turn up his
Posteriors and flog him with Rods most severely, crying
out all the Time, *Wo to the Men that beat their Wives:* —

It seems that several Persons in that Borough, (and 'tis said some very deservedly) have undergone the Discipline, to the no small Terror of others, who are in any Way conscious of deserving the same Punishment. 'Twere to be wish'd, that in order for the more equal Distribution of Justice, there wou'd arise another Sect, under the Title of *Regulatrixes* who should dress themselves in Mens Cloathes, and flagilate the Posteriors of the Scolds, Termagants, &c., &c."[1]

In a letter dated December 7, 1753, "Prudence Goodwife," after relating how her husband beats and maltreats her, writes as follows: "My Case being happily nois'd abroad, induced several generous young Men to discipline him. These young Persons do stile, or are stiled, Regulators: and so they are with Propriety: for they have regulated my dear Husband, and the rest of the bad Ones hereabouts, that they are afraid of using such Barbarity; and I must with Pleasure acknowledge, that since my Husband has felt what whipping was, he has entirely left off whipping me, and promises faithfully he will never begin again. Tho' there are some that are afraid of whipping their Wives, for fear of dancing the same Jigg; yet I understand, they are not afraid of making Application, in order to have those dear Regulators indicted; and if they should it might discourage them for the future, to appear to the Assistance of the Innocent and Helpless; and then poor Wives who have the unhappiness to be lockt in Wedlock with bad Hus-

---

[1] New Jersey Archives (1897), XIX, 225-226. (M.)

bands, take care of your tender Hides; for you may depend upon being bang'd without Mercy."[1]

These may be regarded as sporadic cases of "regulating," as illustrations of the kind of "regulating" which is found in a stable and well organized form of society. They are instances of the infliction of summary corporal punishment upon individuals for whose punishment under the law little tangible evidence can be adduced, and the nature of whose offense is such that legal penalties are popularly believed to be inapplicable.

In North Carolina, from 1765 to 1771, under frontier conditions combined with political dissension, "regulation" assumed a well-organized form and gained considerable strength.[2] The movement was inaugurated in the north-central part of the province to resist what was considered oppressive exactions laid by government officials. Specifically, the grievances were excessive taxes, dishonest sheriffs, and extortionate fees. A meeting "to inquire into the abuse of power and take proper measures for amendment" was held at Maddock's mill on October 10, 1766, and several resolutions were drafted and adopted.[3] Nothing was done by the authorities to alleviate the grievances, however, and a general meeting was held on April 4, 1768, at which the organization into

[1] New Jersey Archives (1897), XIX, 326–327. *New York Gazette*, December 31, 1753. (M.) This is the earliest use of the word regulate in connection with illegal punishment for corrective purposes that has come to the writer's notice.

[2] See monograph on "The Regulators of North Carolina," by Professor John S. Bassett of Trinity College, N. C., for a full and complete account of this organization. It was published in the Annual Report of the American Historical Association for 1894.

[3] F. X. Martin: "History of North Carolina" (1829), II, 218–219. H. Williamson: "History of North Carolina" (1812), II, 130–131, 261.

a body of Regulators was perfected. An agreement was drawn up and the members bound themselves by oath to its observance. This agreement reads as follows:

"We the subscribers do voluntarily agree to form ourselves into an association, to assemble ourselves for conference for regulating public grievances and abuses of power, in the following particulars, with others of the like nature that may occur.

"1. That we will pay no more taxes until we are satisfied they are agreeable to law, and applied to the purposes therein mentioned; unless we cannot help it, or are forced.

"2. That we will pay no officer any more fees than the law allows, unless we are obliged to it; and then to show our dislike, and bear an open testimony against it.

"3. That we will attend our meetings of conference as often as we conveniently can, and is necessary, in order to consult our representatives on the amendment of such laws as may be found grievous or unnecessary; and to choose more suitable men than we have done heretofore for burgesses and vestrymen; and to petition the houses of assembly, governor, council, king and parliament, &c., for redress in such grievances as in the course of the undertaking may occur; and to inform one another, learn, know, and enjoy all the privileges and liberties that are allowed and were settled on us by our worthy ancestors, the founders of our present constitution, in order to preserve it on its ancient foundation, that it may stand firm and unshaken.

"4. That we will contribute to collections for defraying necessary expenses attending the work, according to our abilities.

"5. That in case of difference in judgment, we will submit to the judgment of the majority of our body.

"To all which we solemnly swear, or being a quaker, or otherwise scrupulous in conscience of the common oath, do solemnly affirm, that we will stand true and faithful to this cause, till we bring things to a true regulation, according to the true intent and meaning hereof, in the judgment of the majority of us."[1]

As this agreement indicates, this organization was primarily for the purpose of "regulating public grievances and abuses of power," not for the purpose of bringing to justice public offenders beyond the reach of law, such as horse thieves and desperadoes. Their methods of procedure, however, closely resembled those that have been adopted by other bands of Regulators for the purpose of meting out justice to frontier criminals. Their favorite method seems to have been to administer whippings. In an intercepted letter from Rednap Howell to James Hunter, both leading Regulators, the following passage occurs: "I give out here that the Regulators are determined to whip every one who goes to law, or will not pay his just debts, or will not agree to leave his cause to men, where disputed. That they will choose representatives, but not send them to be put in jail. In short, to stand in defence; and as to thieves, to drive them out of the country."[2] From time to time, however, serious disturbances and riots occurred. In September, 1770, about 150 Regulators attacked the superior court which was in session at Hillsboro, severely whipped several men who had incurred their enmity, and destroyed considerable property. New laws were hurriedly enacted by the legislature and the leaders of the riots were arrested,

[1] H. Williamson: "History of North Carolina" (1812), II, 262–263. J. H. Wheeler: "History of North Carolina" (1851), II, 306.

[2] H. Williamson: "History of North Carolina" (1812), II, 270–271.

but the Regulators were not easily subdued or conciliated. In 1771 Governor Tryon called out the militia, and a battle took place between the Regulators and the militia, in which the Regulators were utterly defeated and their organization broken up. Each side, however, had several men killed and many wounded.

A similar attempt at "regulating" was made in South Carolina at about the same time.[1] The "Back Country," as it was called, had become infested with robbers and brigands. Prior to the year 1769 the only court of criminal and civil jurisdiction in the Province — except the courts of Justices of the Peace, which had jurisdiction in civil causes as high as twenty pounds current money — "was holden in Charles-town." This gave practical immunity from punishment to those who were lawlessly inclined in the distant parts of the Province. As early as the year 1752, the inhabitants along the Pedee River near the mouth of Lynche's Creek petitioned the Upper House of Assembly for the creation of a new county in which twelve or more Justices should be appointed who should have a general jurisdiction over both civil and criminal causes. This and other petitions which were presented in the following years from different parts of the Province received scant attention on the part of the Provincial Government. For several years the Government did not seem to comprehend the real nature of the evils, or the remedies necessary to be applied. Consequently, there

---

[1] See Alexander Gregg: "History of the Old Cheraws" (1867), Ch. VII. This chapter contains quotations from original sources on the Regulation movement in South Carolina, and has, therefore, considerable value.

was a very decided opposition between the Regulators and the Government.

The earliest account we have of the operations of the organization which became known as the Regulators is in thé South Carolina Gazette of May 26, 1767, in an extract from a letter from Pine Tree Hill (Camden), dated May 14, 1767. It is as follows: "On the 6th inst., a number of armed men, being in search of Horse Stealers, robbers, &c., discovered a parcel of them in camp on Broad River, where an engagement soon ensued, and the Thieves were put to flight; and though none of them were taken, it is reasonable to suppose, from the quantity of blood on the ground, that some of them were killed. They left behind them ten horses, thirteen saddles, some guns, &c."[1]

The South Carolina Gazette of July 27 — August 3, in the same year, made this statement: "The gang of Villains from Virginia and North Carolina, who have for some years past, in small parties, under particular leaders, infested the back parts of the Southern Provinces, stealing horses from one, and selling them in the next, notwithstanding the late public examples made of several of them, we hear are more formidable than ever as to numbers, and more audacious and cruel in their thefts and outrages. 'Tis reported that they consist of more than 200, form a chain of communication with each other, and have places of general meeting; where (in imitation of Councils of War) they form plans of operation and defence, and (alluding to their secrecy and fidelity to each other) call their places Free Mason Lodges. In-

[1] See Gregg's "History of The Old Cheraws," p. 134.

stances of their cruelty to the people in the back settlements, where they rob or otherwise abuse, are so numerous and shocking, that a narrative of them would fill
a whole *Gazette*, and every reader with horror. They at
present range in the Forks between Broad, Saludy, and
Savannah Rivers. Two of the gang were hanged last
week at Savannah, viz., Lundy Hart and Obadiah Green-
age. Two others, James Ferguson and Jesse Hamber-
sam, were killed when these were taken."[1]

Apparently, it was for the purpose of breaking up and
bringing to justice this "gang of Villains" that Thomas
Woodward, Joseph Kirkland, and Barnaby Pope "instituted the Regulation."[2] At any rate, an organization
had been formed in the region surrounding the Broad
River, and, as early as 1767, the members of this organization had come to be known as Regulators. In an
address to both Houses of Assembly, November 5, 1767,
the Governor of the Province, referring to the "unhappy
situation in the Back Parts of this Country," made the
following statement: "The means to suppress those
licentious spirits that have so lately appeared in the distant parts of the Province, and, assuming the name of
Regulators, have, in defiance of Government, and to the
subversion of good order, illegally tried, condemned, and
punished many persons, require an attentive deliberation."[3]

The courts that were asked for by the inhabitants were

---

[1] See Gregg's "History of The Old Cheraws," p. 134.

[2] J. B. O'Neall: "The Annals of Newberry" (1859), pp. 75–76.

[3] See Gregg's "History of the Old Cheraws," p. 136. This is the
earliest use of the word Regulator in connection with the disturbances
in the Carolinas known to the present writer.

not established, however, and the "regulation" continued. The following is taken from the South Carolina Gazette of June 13, 1768: "It seems hardly probable that the disturbances in our back settlements will entirely subside, notwithstanding all the prudent steps that have been taken, or can be taken, by the Government to suppress them, until the late Act of the General Assembly of this Province for establishing Circuit Courts,[1] takes effect: for we daily hear of new irregularities committed by the people called Regulators, who, seeming to despair of rooting out those desperate villains that remain among them any other way, still take upon themselves to punish such offenders as they can catch. We hear, that within this month, one Watts and one Distoe, have received 500 lashes each by their direction; and that an infamous woman has also received corporal punishment. We hear, also, that one John Bowles has lately lost his life in attempting to take Mr. Woodward, one of the leaders of the people called Regulators. According to our account, Woodward, refusing to surrender himself, Bowles fired at, and would have killed him, but the ball struck the barrel of a gun which he held across his breast, upon which, some people in company with Woodward, fired, and killed Bowles."[2]

On July 25, the following intelligence was given in the South Carolina Gazette: "The last accounts from the Back Settlements say, that the People called the Regulators were to have a meeting at Lynche's Creek, on last

[1] On April 18, a Circuit Court Act was passed, but afterwards failed to become a law.

[2] See Gregg's "History of The Old Cheraws," p. 138.

Friday, where it was expected 1200 would be assembled. The occasion of this meeting is said to be, a Party of them lately having been roughly used by a Gang of Banditti, consisting of Mulattoes, Free Negroes, &c., notorious Harborers of runaway slaves, at a place called Thompson's Creek, whom they ordered to remove. It is added, they anxiously wait to hear the fate of the Act for establishing Circuit Courts in this Province, sent home for the Royal approbation, which, if it obtains, will restore good order in those parts." [1]

The Governor of the Province, not understanding the situation in the remote settlements, made an attempt to enforce order and compel obedience to law by sending an officer with full discretionary power against the Regulators. The course of events is described by Ramsay in the following words: "The extreme difficulty of bringing criminals from the remote settlements to a legal condemnation had induced a number of men, who called themselves regulators, to take the law into their hands. They, by their own authority, inflicted corporal punishment on sundry persons without any regular condemnation. To remedy abuses of this kind, lord Charles Greville Montague, then governor of the province, advanced to the rank of colonel a man of low character, of the name of Scovil, and employed him to enforce regular law among these self-constituted regulators. In execution of his commission he adopted severe measures, which involved multitudes in great distress." [2] This

[1] See Gregg's " History of The Old Cheraws," p. 139.

[2] David Ramsay: "History of the Revolution in South Carolina" (1785), I, 63–64. According to this author these events took place "about the year 1770." O'Neall says (Annals of Newberry, p. 75):

Colonel Scovil (or Schovel — his name is written in various ways), instead of redressing the grievances on both sides, armed the depredators and paraded them for battle. Before a battle took place, however, between the Regulators and the Schofilites, as they were known from the name of their leader, wiser counsels prevailed and both parties sent delegates to the Governor asking for his intervention.[1] In this way the disastrous results of the conflict in North Carolina between the Regulators and the Government were avoided in South Carolina.

Finally, the necessity for courts in the interior of the Province could no longer be denied. The Royal approval was given, and in the year 1769 seven new courts, with suitable jails and court-houses, were established in different parts of the interior.[2] This marked the end of the

---

"The Regulators and Scofelites, in 1764, met in battle array," &c. Johnson says (Traditions and Reminiscences, p. 92): "In 1769 great commotions arose in the upper parts of the State, between what were called 'Regulators' and 'Schofilites.'" In reality, the crisis in the strife between the Regulators and Schofilites occurred in March, 1769. This is shown by the following extract, dated Charlestown, (South Carolina), April 6, which appeared in the *Boston Chronicle* of May 11-15, 1769 (No. 92, II, 155): "The prudent conduct of government, in ordering Joseph Coffill, who had assumed the title of Colonel, and some extraordinary powers, and with his party had committed divers excesses, to disperse, has had the happy effect of once more restoring peace and good order amongst the inhabitants of the western settlements, who, exasperated by the tyrannical conduct of this man, has assembled in a large body towards the close of last month, in order to compel him to shew what powers he was invested with, and if they had found that he was not cloathed with authority, to have brought him to justice, at all events. Both parties were incamped within musket shot of each other, on Saludy river, when the orders to Coffill arrived, and thus a great deal of bloodshed was prevented. The Colonels Richardson, Thompson, and M'Girt, gentlemen of great reputation, and highly esteemed by the whole body of honest back settlers, we are told, exerted themselves upon this occasion, with great spirit, discretion, and success."

[1] Joseph Johnson: "Traditions and Reminiscences" (1851), p. 45.

[2] Ibid.

Regulation movement in South Carolina. The condition of affairs which had called it into existence had ceased to prevail and the practice of "regulating" was, therefore, discontinued.

A single quotation will conclude all that need here be said in regard to the Regulation in South Carolina. It is an "extract of a letter from a Gentleman at Pedee, to his friend in Town," and appeared in the South Carolina Gazette, September 2, 1768. It reads as follows:

"I wish you would inform me what is generally thought in town of the Regulators, who now reign uncontrolled in all the remote parts of the Province. In June, they held a Congress at the Congarees, where a vast number of people assembled; several of the principal settlers on this River, men of property, among them. When these returned, they requested the most respectable people in these parts to meet on a certain day; they did so, and, upon the report made to them, they unanimously adopted the Plan of Regulation, and are now executing it with indefatigable ardour. Their resolution is, in general, effectually to deny the Jurisdiction of the Courts holden in Charles-town over those parts of the Province that ought to be by right out of it; to purge, by methods of their own, the country of all idle persons, all that have not a visible way of getting an honest living, all that are suspected or known to be guilty of malpractices, and also to prevent the service of any writ or warrant from Charles-town; so that a Deputy Marshal would be handled by them with severity. Against those they breathe high indignation. They are every day, excepting Sundays, employed in this Regulation work, as they term it. They have brought many under the lash, and are scourging and banishing the baser sort of people, such as the above, with universal diligence.

"Such as they think reclaimable, they are a little tender of; and those they task, giving them so many acres to tend in so many days, on pain of flagellation, that they may not be reduced to poverty, and by that be led to steal from their industrious neighbours. This course, they say, they are determined to pursue, with every other effectual measure, that will answer their purpose; and that they will defend themselves in it to the last extremity. They hold correspondence with others in the same plan, and are engaged to abide by and support each other whenever they may be called upon for that purpose. This, it seems, they are to continue till County Courts, as well as Circuit Courts, shall be rightly established, that they may enjoy, by that means, the rights and privileges of British subjects, which they think themselves now deprived of. They imagine that, as the Jurisdiction of the Courts in Charles-town extends all over the Province, Government is not a protection, but an oppression; that they are not tried there by their Peers; and that the accumulated expenses of a law-suit, or prosecution, puts justice out of their power; by which means the honest man is not secure in his property, and villainy becomes rampant with impunity.

"Indeed, the grievances they complain of are many, and the spirit of Regulation rises higher and spreads wider every day. What this is to end in, I know not; but thus matters are situated; an account of which, I imagine, is not unacceptable, though perhaps disagreeable to hear."[1]

This letter may be regarded, upon the whole, as an impartial account of the Regulation movement in South Carolina.[2] It exhibits the character of those who were taking the lead in the matter, and indicates the objects which they proposed to accomplish. It also indicates

[1] See Gregg's "History of the Old Cheraws," pp. 151–152.
[2] This is likewise Gregg's view of the matter.

that their usual procedure was to whip and banish all persons whom they considered inimical to the interests of the community. In this respect the Regulation movement in South Carolina closely resembled the Regulation movement in North Carolina. It may be said, therefore, that lynch-law was in operation at this time in the Carolinas, though not known by that name. The practice of administering corporal punishment for reformatory or corrective purposes, the practice of "regulating" public offenders and public grievances, is the essence of lynch-law procedure.

As events shaped themselves for the outbreak of the Revolution in 1775, conditions became such as to encourage the frequent use of summary methods of redressing grievances in all of the colonies. The increasing dissatisfaction among the colonists with the way they were being governed by the mother country, the obnoxious Stamp Act and other measures which they thought to be unjustly imposed upon them, rendered recourse to summary procedure not only easy but popularly justifiable.[1] It was a time of excitement when neighbor looked upon neighbor with suspicion and the slightest offense was

[1] In the year 1765 and for several succeeding years the "Sons of Liberty" were particularly active in stirring up resistance to the acts of the British government, which were considered oppressive. The "Sons of Liberty," elsewhere as well as in Boston, seem to have been regularly organized and to have held secret meetings at which resolutions were adopted and definite plans of action were determined upon for either driving away or punishing certain "Stamp Masters," "infamous importers," and "informers." Warning notices were frequently posted and published, signed by "P. P., Clerk," "M. Y., Secretary," &c. Hanging and burning in effigy, flagellation, tarring and feathering, and ducking, were the punitive measures generally threatened and not infrequently carried into effect. — These statements are based on a collection of notes on "Sons of Liberty" which were loaned to the writer by Mr. Albert Matthews.

deemed worthy of severe punishment. Social conditions were unsettled; the civil authorities were fast losing the respect and support of the people in the community; threats and taunts, satire and insult, were prevalent.[1] Under such conditions it is not strange that summary procedure came to be in vogue from Maine to Georgia.

Furthermore, during the entire period of the Revolutionary War not only were the usual unsettled conditions incident to a war prevailing, but, in addition, there was disaffection and disagreement among the colonists themselves. Almost every community had its Tories who frequently sought, openly or secretly, to further the Royal cause and injure the American cause. In return, the American sympathizers often adopted retaliatory measures against the Tories. In such cases it was hopeless to appeal to the civil or the judicial powers for they were badly disorganized. Not infrequently conditions were such as to preclude action under martial law, and thus the only recourse possible was the popular administration of justice in the form of summary procedure of one sort or another.

Particularly characteristic of the Revolutionary period was the practice of tarring and feathering.[2] It has been

[1] For an exposition of the condition of society, its state of dissolution and lack of organization, during the Revolutionary period and subsequent to that period, see W. G. Sumner: "Alexander Hamilton" (1890). On page 13 this statement is made: "The Union was from the start at war with the turbulent, anarchistic elements which the Revolution had set loose."

[2] A correspondent of the *New England Gazette* in 1776 asked "whether it would be featherable for a man to be detected with one of them (pardons from the king) in his pocket." — Frank Moore: "Diary of the Revolution (1875), p. 226. Paul Leicester Ford, when writing his historical novel "Janice Meredith," treated tarring and feathering as an ordinary incident of Revolutionary times. See Chapters XVII, XXXVIII.

said that "this singular punishment" was begun in
America by British troops who tarred and feathered an
inhabitant of the town of Billerica, Massachusetts, on
March 9, 1775.[1] But a number of instances may be cited
showing that this punishment had been administered in
more than one of the colonies several years earlier. It
is probable that many of the early immigrants knew of
this manner of punishment before they left their native
shores[2]; at any rate, they did not wait until 1775 for the
British troops to set them an example.[3]

On September 7, 1768, at Salem, Massachusetts, a
"Custom-House Waiter" informed an officer of the customs that some measures had been taken on board a
vessel, in the harbor to elude the payment of certain

[1] John Drayton: "Memoirs of the American Revolution" (1821), I,
273. Frank Moore: "Diary of the Revolution" (1875), p. 44. Joseph
Johnson: "Traditions and Reminiscences" (1851), p. 70. Edward
McCrady: "South Carolina in the Revolution 1775–1780" (1901), p. 24.
The date on which the tarring and feathering of Thomas Ditson of the
town of Billerica took place was March 9, not March 8, as given by the
above writers. For an explanation of the discrepancy in the date and
for a description of the occurrence, see *Boston Gazette*, March 13, 1775
(No. 1039, p. 3); March 20, 1775 (No. 1040, p. 3).

[2] Joseph Johnson: "Traditions and Reminiscences" (1851), p. 71.
"The punishment of banishment, preceded by the more dreadful opera-
tion of tarring and feathering," was put in execution by a "judicial Association" in the early days of a settlement on the Bay of Islands, New
Zealand. See R. G. Jameson: "New Zealand, South Australia, and
New South Wales" (London, 1842), pp. 190–191.
The *Yankee*, June 4, 1813, p. 4, cited one of the laws of the naval code
established during the reign of Richard I as the "Origin of Tarring and
Feathering." By this law any one lawfully convicted of stealing should
have his head shorn, and boiling pitch poured upon his head, and feathers
or down strewed upon the same, whereby he might be known until the
next landing place was reached, where he was to be left. — See Hakluyt's
"Voyages," II, 21.

[3] The writer is indebted to Mr. Albert Matthews for the facts which
are here presented in regard to the practice of tarring and feathering
previous to the year 1775.

duties. This "engaged the Attention of a Number of the Inhabitants. Between the Hours of Ten and Eleven, A.M. he was taken from one of the Wharves, and conducted to the common, where his Head, Body and Limbs were covered with warm Tar, and then a large Quantity of Feathers were applied to all Parts. The poor Waiter was then exalted to a Seat on the Front of a Cart, and in this Manner led into the Main Street, where a Paper, with the Word *Informer* thereon, in large Letters, was affixed to his Breast, and another Paper, with the same Word, to his Back. This Scene drew together, within a few Minutes, several Hundred People, who proceeded, with Huzzas and loud Acclamations, through the Town." [1]

On Saturday, September 10, 1768, "two Informers, an Englishman and a Frenchman, were taken up by the Populace at Newbury-Port, (Mass.) who tarred them & feathered them; but being late they were hand-cuffed and put into custody until the Sabbath was over: — Accordingly on Monday Morning, they were again tarred and rolled in Feathers, then fixed in a Cart with Halters, and carried thro' the principal Streets of the Town." [2] Upon his release the Englishman, Joshua Vickery by name, went before a justice of the peace and took oath "that he never did directly or indirectly make or give any Information to any Officer of the Customs nor to any other Person either against Capt. John Emmery, or any other Man whatever; that he was no ways concerned with Francis Magno in his Information, nor ever wrote one

---

[1] *Salem Gazette*, Sept. 6–13, 1768 (No. 7, p. 27). *Boston Evening Post*, Sept. 12, 1768 (No. 1720, p. 3). "Diaries of B. Lynde & B. Lynde, Jr." (1880), p. 192.

[2] *Boston Evening Post*, Sept. 19, 1768 (No. 1721, p. 3).

Line for the said Francis, on that Account."[1] These statements were corroborated by the Frenchman and it was shown that the only ground for suspicion against Vickery was the fact that he had been in the company of the Frenchman on the day that the "Information" was given.

On the evening of May 18, 1769, at Providence, Rhode Island, Jesse Saville, "a Tidesman belonging to the Custom-House" who was accused of "Informing," was seized by a number of people, stripped naked, covered from head to foot with turpentine and feathers and severely beaten. "For the better bringing to Justice and condign Punishment the Authors of this daring & atrocious Outrage, the Commissioners of His Majesty's Customs" offered a reward of fifty pounds sterling for their discovery and conviction.[2]

A similar case of tarring and feathering, the offender being "a Person who had informed against a Merchant, respecting a Vessel then in the West-Indies," occurred in New Haven, Connecticut, in September, 1769.[3]

In New York, in October, 1769, "one Kelly, an Oyster-man, Mitchner, a Tavern-keeper, and one or two more, having, it is said, made an Information to the Custom-House Officers, which occasioned the Seizure of a few Casks of Wine belonging to the Mate of a Vessel, and was, it is said, the whole Saving he had made of three Years Wages: The Populace being greatly incensed against the Informers, after several Days Search, found and seized

---

[1] *Essex Gazette*, Sept. 20–27, 1768 (No. 9, p. 37).

[2] *Boston Evening-Post*, June 19, 1769 (No. 1760, p. 3).

[3] *Boston Gazette*, Sept. 25, 1769 (No. 755, p. 3).

them, placed and tied them in Carts, and carried them thro' great Part of the City, attended with many Thousand People, who huzza'd, insulted and treated them with the utmost Indignity, often besmearing their Faces and Clothes with Tar, and sprinkling them with Feathers. . . . The Magistrates interposed, but were for some Time unable to stop the Cavalcade, till the Populace had in some Measure satiated their Resentment."[1]

The Boston Chronicle for October 26-30, 1769,[2] contained the following under the heading of "Boston": "Last Saturday evening, a person suspected to be an informer, was stripped naked, put in a Cart, where he was first tarred, then feathered, and in this condition, carried through the principal streets of the town, followed by a great concourse of people."

During the year 1770 there was much popular feeling against merchants who imported goods contrary to the non-importation agreement. Such importers were threatened with many dire punishments including tar and feathers, and in several instances the threatened punishments were administered.[3]

At Philadelphia, in October, 1773, a certain Ebenezer Richardson, accused of "seeking an opportunity to distress the Trade of Philadelphia," was publicly notified,

[1] *Boston Gazette*, Oct. 16, 1769 (No. 758, p. 2).

[2] No. 140, II, 351.

[3] *Boston Gazette*, Jan. 1, 1770 (No. 769, p. 1); June 11, 1770 (No. 792, p. 2); July 2, 1770 (No. 795, p. 2); August 20, 1770 (No. 802, p. 1); *Boston-Gazette* Supplement July 30, 1770 (No. 799, p. 2); Aug. 6, 1770 (No. 800, p. 2); *Boston News-Letter*, June 21, 1770 (No. 3480, p. 3); *Essex Gazette*, June 19–26, 1770, II, p. 191; June 26 — July 3, 1770, II, p. 195; Aug. 7–14, 1770, III, p. 11; *London Gazetteer*, Nov. 17, 1770 (No. 13016, p. 2); "The Letters of James Murray, Loyalist," edited by Nina Moore Tiffany (1901), pp. 165, 175–178.

by "Tar *and* Feathers," of the punishment which was in store for him, a punishment which he narrowly escaped by leaving the city "closely pursued by many well-wishers to peace and good order."[1]

On November 1, 1773, John Malcolm who had rendered himself obnoxious "by being an Informer" was "genteely *Tarr'd* and *Feather'd*" by "about 30 Sailors" at Pownalborough (Mass.).[2] On January 25, 1774, Malcolm was in Boston, and when some taunting remarks were made to him to the effect that he had been tarred and feathered but not in the proper manner, he dared any one to do it better and assaulted one man, slightly injuring him. In the evening a number of people took Malcolm out, stripped him, tarred his head and his body, feathered him, set him in a chair in a cart, and thus carried him through the streets, finally whipping and beating him before they let him go.[3] On the morning of January 30 the following handbill[4] was found pasted up in the most public places:

BRETHREN, AND FELLOW-CITIZENS!

THIS is to Certify, That the modern Punishment lately inflicted on the ignoble JOHN MALCOM, was not done by

[1] *Boston Gazette*, Nov. 1, 1773 (No. 969, pp. 1, 3). See also *Boston News-Letter*, Jan. 27, 1774 (No. 3669, p. 2).

[2] *Boston Gazette*, Nov. 15, 1773 (No. 971, p. 3).

[3] *Boston News-Letter*, Jan. 27, 1774 (No. 3669, p. 2); Feb. 3, 1774 (No. 3670, p. 2); *Massachusetts Spy*, Jan. 27, 1774 (No. 156, p. 3).

[4] *Boston Gazette*, Jan, 31. 1774 (No. 982, p. 3); *Massachusetts Spy*, Feb. 3, 1774 (No. 157, p. 2).

On January 17 a handbill signed in the same way had been distributed, giving notice that any "TEA CONSIGNEES" who should come to reside again in Boston would be given "such a Reception as such vile Ingrates deserve." — *Boston Gazette*, Jan. 17, 1774 (No. 980, p. 3); *Boston Evening Transcript*, Feb. 27, 1903, p. 14.

our Order — We reserve that Method for bringing Villains of greater Consequence to a Sense of Guilt and Infamy.

JOYCE, jun[r].

(Chairman of the Committee for Taring *and* Feathering.

☞ If any Person should be so hardy as to tear this down, they may expect my severest Resentment.   J. jun.

During the years 1773 and 1774 tea commissioners and tea consignees, in addition to customs informers and importers of British goods, fell into popular disfavor, and thus became subjects for tarring and feathering. "Tiewaghnodago" in the Boston Gazette, December 20, 1773,[1] said that he had been informed that "some *little* Shopkeepers in this Town," finding that tea was not likely to be used, had raised the price of coffee a few coppers per pound, and he asked "whether *Tar* and *Feathers* would not be a constitutional encouragement for such eminent Patriotism."

In the period 1765–1775 there were likewise cases of mob violence where houses were attacked and damaged by having missiles thrown at them and where property was destroyed.[2] In one instance at least the owner of goods which were destroyed by a mob recovered damages in the courts. Early in the year 1772, according to S. G. Arnold,[3] there occurred "a memorable instance of the triumph of law over popular prejudice." One David Hill was detected in selling goods included in the non-importation agreement, and the goods were seized and destroyed by a mob. Hill brought action in the Rhode

[1] No. 976, p. 3.
[2] *Boston News-Letter*, Nov. 18, 1773 (No. 3659, p. 2).
[3] "History of Rhode Island" (1878), II, 308–309.

Island courts, and the superior court confirmed the judgment of the inferior court and gave the plaintiff two hundred and eighty-two pounds damages and costs.

Tarring and feathering was not reserved for certain
informers and importers or for tea consignees alone,
however. This punishment was administered in at least
two instances for offenses other than those growing out
of the political controversies of the time.

The Boston Gazette for November 6, 1769,[1] contained
the following item: "Last Thursday Afternoon a young
Woman from the Country was decoyed into one of the
Barracks in Town, and most shamefully abused by some
of the Soldiers there: — the Person that enticed her
thither with promises of disposing of all her marketing
there (who also belonged to the Country) was afterwards
taken by the Populace and several times duck'd in the
Water at one of the Docks in Town; but luckily for him
he made his escape from them sooner than was intended;
— however, we hear, that after he had crossed the Ferry
to Charlestown, on his return home, the People there
being informed of the base part he had been acting, took
him and placed him in a Cart, and after tarring and
feathering him (the present popular Punishment for
modern delinquents) they carted him about that Town
for two or three Hours, as a Spectacle of Contempt and a
Warning to others from practising such vile Artifices for
the Delusion and Ruin of the virtuous and innocent:
He was then dismissed, and permitted to proceed to the
Town where he belonged, for them to act with as they
should see fit."

[1] No. 761, p. 3.

In January, 1774, smallpox became prevalent in Marblehead, Massachusetts, and an inoculating hospital was erected on Cat Island as a private enterprise. This hospital, however, was popularly regarded with suspicion and disfavor, for it was thought to be a source of contagion. When four men were detected in the act of stealing clothing from the hospital, they were promptly tarred and feathered, and, after being placed in a cart and exhibited through the principal streets of the town, were carried to Salem, accompanied by a procession of men and boys, marching to the music of a fife and several drums. A number of new cases of smallpox developed soon after this affair, and popular indignation ran so high against the proprietors of the hospital that they were openly threatened with personal violence and were finally compelled to close its doors. Subsequently a rumor that the hospital was to be opened again awakened fresh opposition, and on January 26 a party of disguised men visited the island, and as a result of their visit the building was completely destroyed by fire. Two men were arrested as being implicated in the incendiarism and were confined in the Salem jail, but a large number of men from Marblehead marched to Salem, surrounded the jail, broke open the doors, overpowered the jailer and his assistants, released the two prisoners and conducted them home in triumph. A force of citizens was later organized by the sheriff for the purpose of going to Marblehead to recapture the men, but when it became known that an equally large force was organizing and arming in Marblehead to protect them, the sheriff abandoned his purpose and no further effort was made to prosecute the incen-

diaries. Before the trouble connected with the hospital
was finally ended, however, one of the four men who had
been tarred and feathered was again the subject of popular
indignation because of his bringing away clothing from
Cat Island. He was taken from his bed one night by a
mob and carried to the public whipping-post where he
was severely whipped and beaten.[1]

During the year 1775, when the spirit of rebellion rose
to the height of armed resistance and open warfare, there
was increased occasion for recourse to summary procedure.
In that year mobs gathered in many places,[2] riots were
numerous and cases of tarring and feathering occurred
in several of the colonies.

In June, 1775, Laughlin Martin and James Dealy were
stripped of their clothes, tarred and feathered, and carted
through the Streets of Charleston, South Carolina, by
order of the "Secret Committee," one of the committees
which had been formed to carry on an independent
government in that Province.[3] In August of the same
year, this committee had another man, "a Mr. Walker,
Gunner of Fort Johnston," treated in the same way.[4]

---

[1] *Boston News-Letter*, Jan. 27, 1774 (No. 3669, p. 2); *Massachusetts Spy*, Jan. 27, 1774 (No. 156, p. 2); *Essex Gazette*, Jan. 25—Feb. 1, 1774 (No. 288, VI, p. 107); March 1–8, 1774 (No. 293, VI, p. 127); *Boston Gazette*, Feb. 28, 1774 (No. 986, p. 2); March 14, 1774 (No. 988, p. 1). For a brief account of the whole affair see S. Roads, Jr.: "History and Traditions of Marblehead" (1880), pp. 91–94.

[2] For an account of the doings of mobs in Massachusetts see Frank Moore: "Diary of the American Revolution "(1875), pp. 37–42.

[3] John Drayton: "Memoirs of the American Revolution" (1821), I, 273–274. Frank Moore: "Diary of the Revolution" (1875), pp. 90–91. Edward McCrady: "South Carolina in the Revolution, 1775–1780" (1901), p. 24.

[4] John Drayton: "Memoirs of the American Revolution" (1821), II, 17.

In September, 1775, James Smith, a judge of the Court of Common Pleas for Duchess County, New York, together with Coen Smith of the same place, were "handsomely tarred and feathered" for acting in open contempt of the resolves of the County Committee. "The judge undertook to sue for, and recover the arms taken from the Tories by order of said committee, and actually committed one of the committee, who assisted at disarming the Tories, which enraged the people so much, that they rose and rescued the prisoner, and poured out their resentment on this villanous retailer of the law."[1]

In December, 1775, "at Quibbletown, New Jersey, Thomas Randolph, cooper, who had publicly proved himself an enemy to his country, by reviling and using his utmost endeavors to oppose the proceedings of the continental and provincial conventions, in defence of their rights and liberties; and being judged a person not of consequence enough for a severer punishment, was ordered to be stripped naked, well coated with tar and feathers, and carried in a wagon publicly around the town — which punishment was accordingly inflicted. As soon as he became duly sensible of his offence, for which he earnestly begged pardon, and promised to atone, as far as he was able, by a contrary behavior for the future, he was released and suffered to return to his home, in less than half an hour. The whole was conducted with that regularity and decorum that ought to be observed in all public punishments."[2]

In the later years of the Revolution, also, there were

[1] Frank Moore: "Diary of the Revolution" (1875), p. 138.
[2] Ibid., p. 178.

cases of tarring and feathering. At Charleston, South
Carolina, in 1776, "John Roberts, a dissenting minister,
was seized on suspicion of being an enemy to the rights
of America, when he was tarred and feathered; after
which, the populace, whose fury could not be appeased,
erected a gibbet on which they hanged him, and afterwards made a bonfire, in which Roberts, together with
the gibbet, was consumed to ashes."[1]

During the campaign of April to December, 1776, for
the possession of the Hudson River, Tryon, who when
governor of North Carolina had led the militia against
the Regulators, was "fomenting plots of a most dastardly
character against the persons and property of patriots.
One of these was the seizure of Washington himself.
The plotters were sometimes discovered, and, when they
were, such was the exasperation of the New York patriots
that they did not hesitate to cruelly maltreat them, a coat
of tar and feathers being among the lightest penalties."[2]

In Virginia the manner of punishing by tarring and
feathering was likewise sometimes followed. According
to Wirt, "The name of 'British tory' was of itself enough,
at that period (the close of the Revolution), to throw
almost any company in Virginia into flames, and was
pretty generally a signal for a coat of tar and feathers;
a signal which was not very often disobeyed."[3]

The practice of tarring and feathering was thus mainly
confined to cases in which popular indignation was aroused

[1] Frank Moore: "Diary of the Revolution" (1875), p. 359.
[2] W. M. Sloane: "The French War and the Revolution" (1893),
p. 239.
[3] "Sketches of the Life and Character of Patrick Henry" (1818),
pp. 232-233.

against Tories, or against persons expressing Tory sentiments and conspiring to injure the American cause. It is this fact that makes tarring and feathering particularly characteristic of Revolutionary times. It is to be remembered, however, that summary punishment was also administered in other ways. Various other forms of corporal punishment, as well as the occasional infliction of capital punishment, were very frequently adopted during the period of the Revolution.

In the preceding chapter, in the discussion of the origin of the term lynch-law, the legislative act was cited which indemnified Charles Lynch and some others for the part which they had taken in suppressing a conspiracy. A similar act of indemnification was passed by the legislature of Virginia in the year 1779. This act reads as follows:

"WHEREAS divers evil disposed persons on the frontiers of this commonwealth had broke out into an open insurrection and conspiracy, and actually levied war against the commonwealth, and it is represented to the present general assembly, that William Campbell, Walter Crockett, and other liege subjects of the commonwealth, aided by detachments of the militia and volunteers from the county of Washington, and other parts of the frontiers did by timely and effectual exertion, suppress and defeat such conspiracy: And whereas the necessary measures taken for that purpose may not be strictly warranted by law, although justifiable from the immediate urgency and imminence of the danger: *Be it therefore declared and enacted*, That the said William Campbell, Walter Crockett, and all other persons whatsoever concerned in suppressing the said conspiracy and insurrection, or in advising, issuing or executing any orders or measures taken for that purpose, stand indemnified and clearly exonerated of, and from all pains, penalties, prosecutions, actions, suits, and damages on account thereof: And that if any indictment, prosecution, action, or suit, shall be laid or brought against them, or any of them, for any act or thing done therein, the defendant or defendants may plead in bar, or the general issue, and give this act in evidence."[1]

In the year 1836 the editor of the Southern Literary Messenger said that frequent inquiry had been made in the preceding year as to the origin of Lynch's law. After an allusion to the historical interest of the subject, he answered the inquiry in the following words:

"It will be perceived from the annexed paper, that the law, so called, originated in 1780, in Pittsylvania, Virginia. Colonel William Lynch, of that county, was its author; and we are informed by a resident, who was a member of a body formed for the purpose of carrying it into effect, that the efforts of the association were wholly successful. A trained band of villains, whose operations extended from North to South, whose well concerted schemes had bidden defiance to the ordinary laws of the land, and whose success encouraged them to persevere in depredations upon an unoffending community, was dispersed and laid prostrate under the infliction of Lynch's law. Of how many terrible, and deeply to be lamented consequences — of how great an amount of permanent evil — has the partial and temporary good been productive!

" ' Whereas, many of the inhabitants of the county of Pittsylvania, as well as elsewhere, have sustained great and intolerable

---

[1] Hening's " Statutes at Large," X, 195.

For an account of the measures taken which were not strictly warranted by law, see L. C. Draper : " King's Mountain and its Heroes" (1881), pp. 384–387.

" An act to indemnify Thomas Nelson, Junior, esquire, late governor of this commonwealth, and to legalize certain acts of his administration," was passed in 1781. — Hening's "Statutes at Large," X, 478.

losses by a set of lawless men who have banded themselves together to deprive honest men of their just rights and property, by stealing their horses, counterfeiting, and passing paper currency, and committing many other species of villainy, too tedious to mention, and that those vile miscreants do still persist in their diabolical practices, and have hitherto escaped the civil power with impunity, it being almost useless and unnecessary to have recourse to our laws to suppress and punish those freebooters, they having it in their power to extricate themselves when brought to justice by suborning witnesess who do swear them clear — we, the subscribers, being determined to put a stop to the iniquitous practices of those unlawful and abandoned wretches, do enter into the following association, to wit: that next to our consciences, soul and body, we hold our rights and property, sacred and inviolable. We solemnly protest before God and the world, that (for the future) upon hearing or having sufficient reason to believe, that any villainy or species of villainy having been committed within our neighborhood, we will forthwith embody ourselves, and repair immediately to the person or persons suspected, or those under suspicious characters, harboring, aiding, or assisting those villains, and if they will not desist from their evil practices, we will inflict such corporeal punishment on him or them, as to us shall seem adequate to the crime committed or the damage sustained; that we will protect and defend each and every one of us, the subscribers, as well jointly as severally, from the insults and assaults offered by any other person in their behalf: and further, we do bind ourselves jointly and severally, our joint and several heirs &c. to pay or cause to be paid, all damages that shall or may accrue in consequence of this our laudable undertaking, and will pay an equal proportion according to our several abilities; and we, after having a sufficient number of subscribers to this association, will convene ourselves to some convenient place, and will make choice of our body five of the best and most discreet men belonging to our body, to direct and govern the whole, and we will strictly adhere to their determinations in all cases whatsoever relative to the above undertaking; and if any of our body summoned to attend the execution of this our plan, and fail so to do without a reasonable excuse, they shall forfeit and pay the sum of one hundred pounds current money of Virginia, to be appropriated toward defraying the contingent expenses of this our undertaking. In witness whereof we have hereunto set our hands, this 22d day September 1780.' "[1]

The only indication of the source from which the editor obtained this agreement is found in the reference to "a resident, who was a member of a body formed for the purpose of carrying it into effect." It is upon this reference that its authenticity depends. The agreement sounds genuine and is not out of harmony with the condition of affairs at that time in Virginia. Nothing is known, however, of any Colonel William Lynch in the county of Pittsylvania, Virginia.[2] It is possible that

---

[1] *Southern Literary Messenger*, II, 389 (May, 1836).
This reference comes to the present writer through Mr. J. P. Lamberton of Philadelphia, Mr. Edward Ingle, the author of "Southern Sidelights" (See pp. 191–193), and Mr. Albert Matthews.

[2] The name of one of the younger sons of John Lynch, the founder of Lynchburg, was William, and Mrs. Cabell says that he was a "Colonel in the late war." This William Lynch, however, married in early life and made his home in the city of Lynchburg. See Mrs. Julia Mayo Cabell: "Sketches and Recollections of Lynchburg" (1858), p. 20.
A writer in *Harper's Magazine* for May, 1859 (p. 794) refers to a "Mr. Lynch" who "was for many years the senior and presiding Justice of the County Court of Pittsylvania." This writer also says that Lynchburg was named for this Mr. Lynch, and that his advanced age prevented him from taking the field during the War of Independence. This, however, is an account from memory of a story heard when a mere boy from an old man, and, as there are inaccuracies in several particulars, it cannot be regarded as reliable.

the man referred to was Colonel Charles Lynch of Bedford County.

An instance of summary corporal punishment occurred in Virginia on October 10, 1783, as is shown by the following act entitled "*An act of indemnity to certain persons*": "*Be it enacted by the General Assembly*, That all and every person or persons who either directly or indirectly committed any insult or injury against the person of a certain Joseph Williamson, on the tenth day of October, in the year one thousand seven hundred and eighty three, or breach of the peace on that occasion, and which was previous to the ratification of the definitive treaty between Great Britain and America, shall be, and they are hereby respectively indemnified for the same, and shall be exonerated and discharged of and from any fines, penalties, or forfeitures, which they might have incurred thereby."[1]

Judge Roane's statement that there were many suits in 1792 for inflicting Lynch's law indicates that there were many cases of its infliction in the years preceding that date. It seems probable, therefore, that the practice of administering corporal punishment in a summary manner was very prevalent in Virginia from 1780 to 1792.

During the period 1792–1819 accounts of lynch-law procedure are very rare. There are but few sources of information on the subject during that period. Indeed, it is true that the chief source of information on the subject from 1792 to 1830 is the writings of travelers who have chanced to witness or hear of instances of such procedure.

Under the date of November 29, 1819, W. Faux

---

[1] Hening's "Statutes at Large," XI, 373.

describes the treatment given a young Yankee, of the name of Williams, near Princeton, Indiana, two years earlier. He was suspected of having robbed a store, but only circumstantial evidence could be adduced against him and he was acquitted. "The people of the place, however, prejudiced against him, as a Yankee, deputed four persons to inform him, that unless he quitted the town and state immediately, he should receive Lynch's law, that is, a whipping in the woods. He departed, with his wife and child, next day, on foot; but in the woods, four miles from Princeton, they were overtaken by two men, armed with guns, dogs, and a whip, who said they came to whip him, unless he would confess and discover to them the stolen money, so that they might have it. He vainly expostulated with them; but, in consideration of his wife's entreaties and cries, they remitted his sentence to thirteen lashes. One man then bound him to a tree and lashed him with a cow-hide whip, while the other held and gagged him; the alarmed wife, all the time, shrieking murder. He was then untied, and told to depart from the state immediately, or he should receive another whipping on the morrow, as a warning and terror to all future coming Yankees.

"This poor fellow was of respectable parents at Berlin, in the state of New York, and possessed a well-informed mind. He quitted the state, and returning, soon after, to prosecute his executioners, died at Evansville, before he had effected so desirable an object."[1]

In "Letters from Illinois," the second edition of which was published in London in 1818, Morris Birkbeck writes:

[1] "Memorable Days in America" (London, 1823), pp. 304, 305.

"There is nothing that I anticipate with so much satisfaction and security as the rapid development of society in our new country. Its elements are rude certainly, and heterogeneous. The first settlers, unprotected, and unassisted amid dangers and difficulties, have been accustomed from early youth to rely on their own powers; and they surrender with reluctance, and only by halves, their right of defence against every aggression, even to the laws which themselves have constituted.

"They have been anxiously studious of mildness in the forming of these laws, and when, in practice, they seem inefficient, they too frequently proceed with Indian perseverance to acts of vengeance, inconsistent with the duty of forbearance essential to social man. Hence deeds of savage and even ferocious violence are too common to be viewed with the abhorrence due to them.

"This disposition is evinced continually, and acted on without any feeling of private or personal animosity.

"If a man, whom the public voice has proclaimed a thief or a swindler, escapes from justice for want of a legal proof of his guilt, though the law and a jury of his fellow citizens have acquitted him, ten to one but he is met with before he can quit the neighborhood, and, tied up to a sapling, receives a scourging that marks him for the rest of his life.

"In Kentucky, whose institutions have acquired greater maturity, such events *have* taken place some years ago; but now they would scarcely be tolerated, and they will soon be matter of history only, in Indiana and Illinois.

"No crime but murder 'of the first degree' is punished with death, in any of the western states, nor, I believe, in the Union. In Kentucky there is a general penitentiary, for the punishment of other offences by imprisonment and labour."[1]

William Newnham Blane, who traveled through the United States and Canada in the years 1822 and 1823,

[1] See pp. 96–98 for this extract. (M.)

described the lynch-law procedure of that time as
follows:

"After leaving Carlyle, I took the Shawnee town road, that
branches off to the S. E., and passed the Walnut Hills, and
Moore's Prairie. These two places had a year or two before
been infested by a notorious gang of robbers and forgers, who
had fixed themselves in these wild parts, in order to avoid
justice. As the country became more settled, these desperadoes became more and more troublesome. The inhabitants
therefore took that method of getting rid of them, that had
been adopted not many years ago in Hopkinson and Henderson
counties Kentucky, and which is absolutely necessary in new
and thinly settled districts, where it is almost impossible to
punish a criminal according to legal forms.

"On such occasions therefore, all the quiet and industrious
men of a district form themselves into companies, under the
name of 'Regulators.' They appoint officers, put themselves
under their orders, and bind themselves to assist and stand by
each other. The first step they then take, is to send notice to
any notorious vagabonds, desiring them to quit the State in a
certain number of days, under the penalty of receiving a domi-
ciliary visit. Should the person who receives the notice refuse
to comply, they suddenly assemble, and when unexpected, go,
in the night time, to the rogue's house, take him out, tie him to
a tree, and give him a severe whipping, every one of the party
striking him a certain number of times.

"This discipline is generally sufficient to drive off the culprit;
but should he continue obstinate, and refuse to avail himself of
another warning, the Regulators pay him a second visit, inflict
a still severer whipping, with the addition probably of cutting
off both his ears. No culprit has ever been known to remain
after a second visit. For instance, an old man, the father of a
family, all of whom he educated as robbers, fixed himself at

Moore's Prairie, and committed numerous thefts, &c. &c. He was hardy enough to remain after the first visit, when both he and his sons received a whipping. At the second visit the Regulators punished him very severely, and cut off his ears. This drove him off, together with his whole gang; and travellers can now pass in perfect safety, where it was once dangerous to travel alone.

"There is also a company of Regulators near Vincennes, who have broken up a notorious gang of coiners and thieves who had fixed themselves near that place. These rascals, before they were driven off, had parties settled at different distances in the woods, and thus held communication and passed horses and stolen goods from one to another, from the Ohio to Lake Erie, and from thence into Canada or the New England States. Thus it was next to impossible to detect the robbers, or to recover the stolen property.

"While I was staying at the house of a Mr. Mulligan in Illinois, thirty miles from St. Louis, one of the men, who had belonged to the gang near Vincennes, was taken up on the charge of passing counterfeit money. . . .

"This practice of *Regulating* seems very strange to an European. I have talked with some of the chief men of the Regulators, who all lamented the necessity of such a system. They very sensibly remarked, that when the country became more thickly settled, there would no longer be any necessity for such proceedings, and that they should all be delighted at being able to obtain justice in a more formal manner. I forgot to mention, that the rascals punished, have sometimes prosecuted the Regulators, for an assault. The juries however, knowing the bad characters of the prosecutors, would give but trifling damages, which divided among so many, amounted to next to nothing for each individual."[1]

[1] W. N. Blane: "An Excursion through the United States and Canada, 1822–1823" (London, 1824), pp. 233–236.

In a book entitled "Letters from the West," which was published in London in 1828, Judge James Hall wrote on the subject of lynch-law as follows:

"Among the early settlers there was a way of trying causes, which may perhaps be new to you. No commentator has taken any notice of *Linch's Law*, which was once the *lex loci* of the frontiers. Its operation was as follows: When a horse thief, a counterfeiter, or any other desperate vagabond, infested a neighborhood, evading justice by cunning, or by a strong arm, or by the number of his confederates, the citizens formed themselves into a '*regulating company*,' a kind of holy brotherhood, whose duty was to purge the community of its unruly members. Mounted, armed, and commanded by a leader, they proceeded to arrest such notorious offenders as were deemed fit subjects of exemplary justice; their operations were generally carried on in the night. Squire Birch, who was personated by one of the party, established his tribunal under a tree in the woods, and the culprit was brought before him, tried, and generally convicted; he was then tied to a tree, lashed without mercy, and ordered to leave the country within a given time, under pain of a second visitation. It seldom happened, that more than one or two were thus punished; their confederates took the hint and fled, or were admonished to quit the neighborhood. Neither the justice nor the policy of this practice can be defended; but it was often resorted to from necessity, and its operation was salutary, in ridding the country of miscreants whom the law was not strong enough to punish. It was liable to abuse, and was sometimes abused; but in general, it was conducted with moderation, and only exerted upon the basest and most lawless men. Sometimes the sufferers resorted to courts of justice for remuneration, and there have been instances of heavy damages being recovered of the *regulators*. Whenever a county became strong enough to enforce the laws, these high-handed doings ceased to be tolerated."[1]

In the above extracts we have a fair description of the operation of lynch-law as it was carried westward by the emigrants from Virginia and the neighboring States. The weakness and inadequacy of the civil regulations, and the presence of such criminals as the horse-thief, the counter-feiter, the robber, and the desperado, who find the frontier both a retreat from the consequences of past crime and a new theater for the perpetration of crime, gave a constant justification for recourse to lynch-law.

The usual manner of proceeding was for the settlers to consult together and in a more or less formal way to establish "the institution of Regulators." Sometimes the Regulators were small bodies of men chosen by the people to look after the interests of the community — in effect, they were committees of safety. At other times, the Regulators were bodies of men who voluntarily assumed the duty of policing a district. The duties of such companies, whether known as Regulators or as Rangers or by some other name, were to ferret out and punish criminals, to drive out "suspicious characters," and to exercise a general supervision over the interests of the settlements in which they lived. Their statute-book was the "code of his honor, Judge Lynch"[2]; their

---

[1] See pp. 291–292 for this extract. The letters which compose Judge Hall's book were mostly printed in *The Port Folio* between 1821 and 1825, but the letter in which he speaks of lynch-law first appeared in the printed volume of 1828. (M.)

[2] This expression is used in the Illinois agreement of 1820 (see below), and that document, if genuine, furnishes the earliest instance of its use known to the present writer.

order of trial was similar to that of a "drum-head court-martial"; the principles of their punishment were certainty, rapidity, and inexorability. They were in themselves judges, juries, witnesses, and executioners.

These bodies of men bound themselves by a regular compact, to the people and to each other, to rid the community of all thieves, robbers, plunderers, and villains of every description. Such compacts were usually verbal but they were sometimes in writing.[1] The compact entered into by the Regulators of North Carolina has already been cited. If the agreement of 1780 in Virginia, to which the editor of the Southern Literary Messenger gave his indorsement, be accepted as genuine, we have a record of another such compact. There is recorded, also, a compact entered into by a company of Regulators in Illinois in 1820. It reads as follows:

"*Know all men by these presents:*
"That we (*here follow twelve names*), citizens of ———— settlement, in the state of Illinois, have this day, *jointly and severally*, bound themselves together as a company of Rangers and Regulators, to protect this settlement against the crimes and misdemeanors of, all and singular, every person or persons whomsoever, and especially against *all horse-thieves, and renegades, and robbers*. And we do by these presents, hereby bind ourselves, jointly and severally as aforesaid, unto each other, and to the fellow-citizens of this settlement, to punish, according to the code of his honor, Judge Lynch, all violations of the law, *against the peace and dignity of the said people of* ———— settlement; and to discover and bring to speedy punishment,

---

[1] This statement is made on the authority of McConnel (see below), but compare C. J. Latrobe: "Ramble in America," (N. Y., 1836, 2d ed.), Let. VII,I, 96.

all illegal combinations — to rid the country of such as are
dangerous to the welfare of this settlement — to preserve the
peace, and *generally to vindicate the law*, within the settlement
aforesaid. All of which purposes we are to accomplish as
peaceably as possible: *but we are to accomplish them one way
or another.*

"In testimony whereof, we have hereunto set our hands and
affixed our seals, this twelfth day of October, *Anno Domini*,
eighteen hundred and twenty.

(Signed by twelve men.)
"Acknowledged and subscribed in the presence of
"C—— T. H——n,
"J—— P. D——n,"

and five others, who seem to have been a portion of
"the fellow-citizens of this settlement," referred to in the
document.[1]

The companies of Regulators were generally organized
only temporarily to meet some emergency in particular
communities. The one striking exception is the Regulation movement in the Carolinas. The circumstances
surrounding that movement, however, were not paralleled
elsewhere. The duration and strength of the organiza-

[1] J. L. McConnel: "Western Characters or Types of Border Life in
the Western States" (1853), pp. 244–245. (M.) This extract is copied
verbatim, the names of the twelve men being omitted by McConnel.
Of the genuineness of the document McConnel says: "I am not sure that
I can vouch for its authenticity, but all who are familiar with the history
of those times, will recognise, in its peculiarities, the characteristics of
the people who then inhabited this country. The affectation of legal
form in such a document as this would be rather amusing, were it not
quite too significant; at all events, it is entirely 'in keeping' with the constitution of a race who had some regard for law and its vindication, even
in their most high-handed acts. The technical phraseology, used so
strangely, is easily traceable to the little 'Justice's Form Book,' which
was then almost the only law document in the country; and though the
words are rather awkwardly combined, they no doubt gave solemnity to
the act in the eyes of its sturdy signers."

tion there, was undoubtedly due to the prominence of the political factor in its existence. Leaving out of consideration the Carolina Regulation and the summary practices which were incident to the Revolutionary War, there existed almost exclusively down to 1830 what may be called the frontier type of lynch-law pure and simple. This form of lynch-law procedure has always been justified on the ground of necessity, and has been condemned only because of its liability to abuse. As one writer has said, referring to the Regulators: "Their acts may sometimes have been high-handed and unjustifiable, but on the whole — and it is only in such a view that social institutions are to be estimated — they were the preservers of the communities for whom they acted. In time, it is true, they degenerated, and sometimes the corps fell into the hands of the very men they were organized to punish.

"Every social organization is liable to misdirection, and this, among others, has been perverted to the furtherance of selfish and unprincipled purposes; for, like prejudices and habits of thought, organized institutions frequently survive the necessities which call them into existence. Abuses grow up under all systems; and, perhaps, the worst abuse of all, is a measure or expedient, good though temporary, retained after the passing away of the time for which it was adopted."[1]

If it be said that "all law emanates from the people, and is, in fact, whether written or not, nothing more or less than certain rules of action by which a people agree to be governed," then the frontier type of lynch-law is

[1] J. L. McConnel: "Western Characters," &c., p. 176.

scarcely more than one step removed from genuine law. For instance, in the year 1834, a large number of persons, citizens of the United States, but of no particular state or territory, and beyond the pale of the regular operations of the law, were collected at a place called *Dubuque's mines*, west of the Mississippi, and north of the State of Missouri. On May 29 of that year, Patrick O'Conner, who had the reputation of being a desperate character, shot and killed George O'Keefe. O'Conner "was arrested by mutual consent of all parties, and, on the next day, was duly tried, by a jury of twelve citizens, taken from the multitude. Privilege was given to the prisoner to object to all such as he chose not to be tried by, and he made no objections to the mode of trial. He was allowed the privilege of choosing a friend to counsel with him, and assist in conducting the trial."

After hearing the testimony of the witnesses that were called, the jury retired, and "after a session of about two hours," returned the following verdict: "We, the jury selected to try Patrick O'Conner, for the murder of George O'Keefe, on the 29th inst. after examining the witnesses on oath, and attentively hearing and considering the testimony against the prisoner, do unanimously agree that the said O'Conner is guilty of murder in the highest degree, and are of opinion that the said O'Conner has done an act which, in a land of laws, would forfeit his life. And inasmuch as the security of the lives of the good citizens of this country requires that an example should be made, to preserve order and convince evil disposed persons that this is not a place where the lives of men may be taken with impunity — we are of opinion that the said O'Conner should be carefully secured until the 20th day of June, and that, at the hour of 12 o'clock, of said day, the said Patrick O'Conner be conducted to the place of execution, and there be hung by the neck until he is dead." This verdict was signed by the twelve members of the jury.

Pursuant to a public notice, a meeting of the citizens was held on June 17 to make arrangements for the execution of O'Conner on June 20. L. Wheeler was requested to take command of a company of volunteers to act as a guard. A committee of three was appointed to make the necessary arrangements for the execution and burial of O'Conner. Henry Adams was requested to act as sheriff on the day of the execution. A committee of three was appointed to collect sums to defray the necessary expense "for the keeping, executing, burial, &c., of said O'Conner." It was voted that the sheriff be allowed the sum of twenty-five dollars for the keeping and execution of said O'Conner; and that if there were anything over and above that amount, after all necessary expenses were paid, the same should go to the executioner.

"At 12 o'clock, on the day of the execution, the prisoner was taken from his place of confinement, under a guard of a company of volunteers, commanded by L. Wheeler, to the place of execution, where had assembled about 1,500 citizens. He was placed on a cart, the rope was made fast to the gallows, when the cart was driven away, leaving the prisoner suspended between the heavens and the earth.

"The whole proceedings were carried on with the utmost regularity and good order. By mutual consent of all, every coffee house was kept closed, and not a drop of spirits was sold until after the execution."[1]

At the time of this affair no judicial or civil regulations were yet established in that region. Under these circumstances, then, was Patrick O'Conner legally executed or was he executed by lynch-law? Doubtless most men will agree that he was, to all intents and purposes, legally executed, and yet many instances of the operation of lynch-law on the frontier were scarcely less justifiable, though the trial and infliction of punishment may have been far more summary.

In general, the punishments administered under lynch-law previous to 1830 were not severe, usually consisting of a whipping, or some other form of corporal punishment, and banishment after a specified time. Niles' Register for July 17, 1824 (26: 326) contains the following: "Kentucky. — Several murders have lately been committed in this state by persons who call themselves 'regulators' — but effectual measures have been taken to arrest and punish them." This case was evidently an abuse of lynch-law; a band of desperadoes, presumably, adopted the name of "regulators" as a cloak for their misdeeds, and thus sought immunity from punishment. Capital punishment was very rarely inflicted by the substantial and respectable settlers who sometimes found it necessary to use lynch-law methods at this early period.

It thus appears that the summary and extra-legal methods of punishment adopted during colonial times, and the summary practices of the time of the Revolution, were carried by the emigrants from the original colonies

[1] *Niles' Register*, July 19, 1834 (46: 352).

as they pushed the line of the frontier further and further to the westward. Frequent occasion was found on the frontier for the use of such methods and practices to curb the activity of the lawless and the vicious. When the legislature of Virginia authoritatively declared that circumstances may arise under which measures, though not strictly warranted by law, are justifiable from the imminence of the danger, it gave expression to a principle which found ready acceptance among the early settlers exposed to the dangers and vicissitudes of frontier life. Though the statement of the principle by the legislature of Virginia may not have been known, and probably was not known, to very many of those who took an active part in the subsequent history of lynch-law, nevertheless the principle itself was a matter of common knowledge, for it was in the air, as it were, and it was repeatedly embodied in action. In reality, the subsequent history of lynch-law is but the working out of this principle under varying conditions.

CHAPTER IV

Lynch-law 1830–1860

With the exception of the summary practices characteristic of Revolutionary times, the lynch-law procedure that prevailed prior to 1830 was largely of the frontier type. Even in Revolutionary times, however, when war and political controversies had brought about a state of social disruption leading to the adoption of lynch-law procedure in well settled communities, many of the instances of such procedure might properly be classified under the frontier type. In remote parts of many of the colonies the civil regulations had never been sufficiently established to insure the punishment of public offenders, and recourse was had to summary and extra-legal methods on the ground that there was a lack of courts and other requisites for legal procedure. The Regulation movement in the Carolinas, though stimulated by political dissension, had its basis and origin in frontier conditions; and it is obvious that lynch-law operated under frontier conditions in the rough-and-ready methods of administering justice which were adopted by the pioneers who moved westward over the Alleghanies into the valley of the Mississippi. Before about the year 1830, then, lynch-law was confined almost entirely to the border settlements, and was generally excused and justified on the ground of necessity. It was not regarded as a serious menace to law and order. It was adopted merely as a temporary expedient which was expected to fall into disuse when the civil government and the judiciary became firmly established.

Soon after 1830 a change took place. The anti-slavery agitation was accompanied by a revival of lynch-law, and the practice spread throughout the country. Not only did lynch-law continue to be exercised occasionally in the border settlements, but it was revived in well-established communities for the purpose of putting down abolitionism. The early thirties witnessed many acts of violence. The following appeared in the Massachusetts Journal in the year 1831: "Progress of Violence. — It ought to be observed that there never was a time of peace in which violence was so common in this country as at this period. . . . Citizens who feel offended take the law into their own hands without ceremony." Then follows a recital of thirteen cases of violence which occurred within two or three months, including riots, duels, insurrections of negroes, persecutions of abolitionists, &c.[1]

The following instances, selected with reference to the localities in which they occurred, indicate the extent of territory over which lynch-law practices prevailed at this time:

"Wilmington, N. C., Sept. 28. — Three ringleaders of the late diabolical conspiracy were executed at Onslow Court House, on Friday evening last, 23d inst.

---

[1] The *Liberator*, Nov. 5, 1831 (1: 180).

The publication of this paper was begun in Boston in 1831, by William Lloyd Garrison, the enthusiastic agitator of the anti-slavery cause. His efforts to make his lists of "Southern Atrocities" as large as possible render his paper a valuable source of information on the subject of lynch-law, particularly lynch-law as applied to negroes prior to the Civil War.

by the people. There was a fourth, who escaped during the tumult."[1] The editor of the Liberator adds: "'Executed by the people' doubtless means executed by a mob, on suspicion of guilt, without investigation or trial."

A Mr. Robinson was lashed on the bare back at Petersburg, Virginia, for saying ";that black men have, in the abstract, a right to their freedom." After the scourging he was told to leave Petersburg and never return or he would be treated "worser."[2]

In Georgia, a man, named John Lamb, was severely treated because he had subscribed to the Liberator. "A mob of unprincipled vagabonds assembled around his house and violently took him out and tarred and feathered him. They then poured oil on his head and set fire to it. They next carried him on a rail to the river and ducked him. And then they returned with him to a post near Darraugh and Simms' Tavern, and whipped him."[3]

The slave insurrection in Virginia under the leadership of Nat Turner took place in August of the year 1831. The nature and extent of this insurrection has been frequently misunderstood. On the one hand, it has been represented as having been confined to a magisterial district; on the other hand, its leader is said to have recruited his forces through all Eastern Virginia and through North Carolina. Both of these views are in a measure true.[4]

---

[1] *Liberator*, Oct. 29, 1831 (1: 174).

[2] Ibid., Oct. 1, 1831 (1: 157).

[3] Ibid., Dec. 3, 1831 (1: 194).

[4] For the fullest and, on the whole, most trustworthy account of this insurrection, see W. S. Drewry: "Slave Insurrections in Virginia"

Nat was a negro endowed with a mind capable of high attainments. He was a careful student of the Bible and a Baptist preacher. He read the newspapers and every book within his reach, and he was an attentive listener at discussions of the political and social questions of the day. But his mind grappled with things beyond its reach. The example of Toussaint L'Ouverture in the island of Hayti, and that of Gabriel Prosser in Richmond in 1800, together with the speeches and writings of abolitionists, inspired him to make an attempt to "call the attention of the civilized world to the condition of his race." He became a complete fanatic and believed that the Lord had destined him to free his race. The red tint of the autumn leaves was a sign of the blood which was to be shed. The eclipse of the sun in February and its peculiar appearance in August, 1831, were to him omens indicating that the time had come for him to put his plans into operation.

For several years plans for insurrection had been maturing in Nat's mind, and by Februray, 1831, he had so far determined upon his scheme that he related it to four of the most influential negroes of his section. From that time every effort was made to enlist the co-operation of other slaves, but with the greatest patience and prudence. He deemed it possible to conquer the county of Southampton, march to the Dismal Swamp, collecting the slaves

(1900). This book has been very largely drawn upon for what is here said on the subject.
   See also, *Liberator*, Oct. 1, 1831 (1: 159); Dec. 10, 1831 (1: 198); Dec. 17, 1831 (1: 202); Dec. 24, 1831 (1: 206).
   See also, *Niles' Register*, Aug. 27, 1831 (40: 455); Sept. 3, 1831 (41: 4); Sept. 10, 1831 (41: 19); Sept. 17, 1831 (41: 35); Jan. 7, 1832 (41: 350).

as he went, and so gradually overcome the State, as the Americans had the British in the Revolutionary War.

On the night of Sunday, August 21, Nat opened the insurrection. A misunderstanding in regard to the date deprived him of a few of his followers, but, at the head of a small party which increased in numbers as it proceeded, he went from house to house murdering every white person that could be found. It is characterized as a massacre "barbarous beyond degree." Depredations, murders, and the most revolting crimes were committed in cold blood. Before the insurrection was put down about sixty whites, — men, women and children, — were slaughtered. The condition of affairs in Southampton for about ten days after the massacre is best described by a committee of citizens in a letter to President Jackson, on the 29th of August, of which the following is an extract: "Most of the havoc has been confined to a limited section of our county, but so inhuman has been the butchery, so indiscriminate the carnage, that the tomahawk and scalping knife have now no horrors. Along the road traveled by our rebellious blacks, comprising a distance of something like twenty-seven miles, no white soul now lives to tell how fiendlike was their purpose. In the bosom of almost every family this enemy still exists. Our homes, those near the scenes of havoc, as well as others more remote, have all been deserted and our families gathered together and guarded at public places in the county; and, still further, the excitement is so great that were the justices to pronounce a slave innocent, we fear a mob would be the consequence."[1]

[1] See p. 84 in Drewry's book.

Many of the rebellious slaves were shot on sight and some innocent negroes suffered. Some prisoners taken near Cross Keys were shot by the Murfreesboro troops and their heads were left for weeks stuck up on poles as a warning to all who should undertake a similar plot. The captain of the marines, as they marched through Vicksville on their way home, bore upon his sword the head of a rebel. A negress who attempted to kill a Mrs. Francis was dragged out, after she had been taken prisoner, tied to an oak tree, and her body riddled with bullets. It is said that some of the slaves suffered fearful torture, being burnt with red-hot irons and their bodies being horribly mutilated, before death came to their relief. Nat was persecuted with pin-pricks and soundly whipped before he was put in jail to await his trial.

According to Drewry, however, although "much excitement and rashness had prevailed in the pursuit and capture of the rebels, the cases of mercy and humanity overshadow those of barbarity and leave the decision in favor of the former." Fifty-three of the sixty or seventy negroes connected with the massacre were brought before the county court. Of these seventeen were executed and twelve transported. The rest were discharged, except the four free negroes who were sent on to the Superior Court, three of whom were executed. Nat and his three associate-leaders, Hark, Nelson, and Sam, were hung according to the sentence of the court. "The bodies of those executed, with one exception, were buried in a decent and becoming manner. That of Nat Turner was delivered to the doctors, who skinned it and made grease of the flesh."

The execution of the plot was thus confined to a magisterial district of three thousand inhabitants. Yet every effort had been made to rouse the negroes of neighboring counties in Virginia and North Carolina. The influence of the insurrection was wide-spread, extending to the North as well as the South. The immediate result in many parts of the South was the greatest excitement, alarm, and confusion. "Men went about in groups, the militia drills were renewed, and the arms called in a few months before, reissued." Thomas Gray, who lived in Southampton, said: "It is the first instance in our history of an open rebellion of the slaves, and attended with such atrocious circumstances of cruelty and destruction as could not fail to leave a deep impression, not only on the minds of the community where the fearful tragedy was wrought, but throughout every portion of our country in which this population is found." In the North the immediate effect was a more pronounced conviction of the evils of slavery. In general, the effect of the Southampton insurrection was to center public consideration on the slave question.[1] Its influence was indirect, rather than direct, in stimulating recourse to lynch-law in the country.

[1] The slavery question was the subject of prolonged debate at the next session of the Virginia House of Delegates. See *Niles' Register*, Jan. 28, 1832 (41: 393).

In a speech made during the course of this debate, William H. Broadnax said: "I have certainly heard, if incorrectly, the gentleman from Southampton will put me right, that of the large cargo of emigrants lately transported from that county to Liberia, all of whom *professed* to be *willing* to go, were rendered so by some such severe ministrations as these I have described. A lynch club — a committee of vigilance — could easily exercise a kind of inquisitorial *surveillance* over any neighborhood, and convert any desired number, I have no doubt, at any time, into a willingness to be removed." See W. L. Garrison: "Thoughts on African Colonization" (1832), p. 74. This reference comes to the present writer through Mr. W. P. Garrison and Mr. Albert Matthews.

During the spring and summer of 1834 there was a great deal of rioting in which Irishmen were principally concerned. Several riots occurred in New York City and in Philadelphia between whites and blacks, which were said to be due to the abolitionists having stirred up the blacks.[1] The following appeared in the Boston Whig in October, 1834: "The history of the proceedings of the past year furnishes examples of outrage and violence altogether unprecedented in the annals of our country. It would seem that the supremacy of the laws is to be no farther regarded than it coincides with the caprices and prejudices of an infuriated and misguided and ignorant populace. . . . Mobs, which now seem to be the order of the day, are of recent origin among us. . . . Our newspapers now, with a few honorable exceptions, encourage these outrages and barbarous proceedings, and by the inflammatory articles in their columns, incite to the commission of the most heinous crimes."[2]

The expression "Lynch's law" first appears in the Liberator in the issue of September 27, 1834 (4: 153), in an extract from the Lancaster (Pennsylvania) Journal. The passage quoted is as follows: "In our quiet village of New Holland, we understand *Lynch's law* was carried into execution last week, against a stranger who had given some offence to the inhabitants. The man was taken from his domicile, tarred and feathered in the true Yankee style, marched out of town and let run. We have not heard the cause of this summary proceeding."

[1] See *Niles' Register* for the year 1834.

[2] *Liberator*, Oct. 18, 1834 (4: 168).

The *New England Magazine*, November, 1834 (7: 409), gives some comments on the times under the heading "The March of Anarchy."

Another extract from the Lancaster Journal reads as follows: "We have heard of another case of an appeal to Lynch's code. A celebrated Philadelphia doctor, a disciple of the Tappan school, who could not find room for the overflowings of his milk of human kindness in the city of brotherly love, paid a visit to Columbia, in this county, a few days since, prepared, it is said, to deliver a course of amalgamation lectures. A barrel of tar was purchased, and a pillow well stuffed with feathers procured for the occasion. A hint of these proceedings was given to the learned Doctor's friends, who did not keep the secret, and the Doctor not wishing to be exhibited in the costume of a goose, took wing in an eastern direction, and has not been heard of since."[1]

The expression "Lynch's law" first appears in Niles' Register under the date of October 5, 1833 (45: 87), in an extract from the St. Louis Republican. The quotation is as follows: "'Lynch's Law.' We have heard, that capt. *Slick* summoned his corps the other night, and obtained possession of a man with whose misdeeds they had become familiar, carried him to the prairie near town, and administered 'Lynch's Law' upon him in fine style. He received about fifty lashes — and was ordered to decamp. The offence consisted in cheating at the gaming table — whereof he was over-fond. . . . Several very effective demonstrations have been made upon the gamblers in and about town, and they have been obliged to make themselves scarce. This is as it should be."

Lynch-law proceedings were inaugurated against gamblers in Virginia about a year later. Niles' Register for

---

[1] *Liberator*, Sept. 27, 1834 (4: 153).

October 4, 1834 (47:66) says: "Large nests of gamblers in Richmond and Norfolk were completely routed, a short time ago, by summary processes — numerous bodies of young men having taken the matter in charge. They broke into the gambling houses, and destroyed all the apparatus and furniture — but farther than this, committed no acts of violence. Some curious disclosures of the great profits made by the knaves have been brought to light by these proceedings."

The most notorious case of an appeal to summary procedure against gamblers occurred in July, 1835, at Vicksburg, Mississippi. Professional gamblers had for years made Vicksburg their rendezvous and certain sections of the city were almost wholly given over to them. Frequently, in armed bodies, they disturbed the good order of public assemblages, insulted citizens on the streets, and openly defied the civil authorities. The laws were found ineffectual for their punishment; their numbers and their crimes continually increased.[1] At a barbecue on the Fourth of July one of these gamblers, named Cakler, became insolent and created a disturbance. Later a meeting was held and an anti-gambling society was organized. "It was determined to take him (Cakler) into the woods and *Lynch* him — which is a mode of punishment provided for such as become obnoxious in a manner which the law cannot reach. He was immediately carried out under a guard, attended by a crowd of respectable citizens — tied to a tree, punished with stripes —

---

[1] Conditions were apparently much like those which existed recently in Memphis, Tennessee, when a Committee of Public Safety was organized and a crusade started against gambling. See *New York Times*, July 14, 1904; July 17, 1904.

tarred and feathered; and ordered to leave town in forty-
eight hours." The following morning public notice was
given that all gamblers must leave the town in twenty-
four hours. That night another was "Lynched." The
next morning the citizens understood that a noted gambler,
named North, had defied them, barricaded his house, and
together with some of his fellows had made preparations
to stay in the town. The volunteers were immediately
assembled and, followed by a crowd of citizens, marched
to North's residence and demanded an unconditional
surrender. This was refused. The house was then surrounded and an attempt made to force an entrance. Just
as the door was burst open, Dr. H. S. Bodley, a highly
respected citizen, was shot and instantly killed by the
gamblers. Greatly incensed at this, the crowd rushed
into the building and dragged out the inmates, one of
whom had been seriously wounded, hurried them without
ceremony to the common gallows and hanged them. Five
gamblers were thus executed at this time and their bodies
left suspended for twenty-four hours.[1]

About the time of the Vicksburg affair suspicion was
aroused in Madison County, Mississippi, that the Murrell
gang had organized the blacks for an insurrection.[2]
"Two individuals, by name Cotton and Saunders, both
of them steam doctors by profession," were thought to
be prominently connected with the scheme. A "committee of investigation" was appointed by a mass-meet-

[1] See *Niles' Register*, July 25, 1835 (48: 363); Aug. 1, 1835 (48: 381).
Also *Liberator*, Aug. 8, 1835 (5: 126–7).

[2] For a brief account of the conspiracy led by Murrell, see *Niles' Register*,
Aug. 8, 1835 (48· 403–4). A complete account may be found in the *American Whig Review*, November, 1850 (12: 494); March, 1851 (13: 213).

ing of the citizens and as a result of the investigation the
two "steam doctors" and three other white men were
hanged, and also several negroes, "some ten or fifteen,"
without any process at law.[1]

J. H. Ingraham, writing of conditions in Mississippi
at about this time, after describing a "chain gang" of
negroes, uses the following language: "In Natchez, negro
criminals only are thus honored — a 'coat of tar and
feathers' being applied to those white men who may require some kind of discipline not provided by the courts
of justice. This last summary process of popular justice,
or more properly excitement, termed 'Lynch's law', I
believe, from its originator, is too much in vogue in this
state. In the resentment of public as well as private
wrongs, individuals have long been in the habit of fore-
stalling and improving upon the decisions of the courts,
by taking the execution of the laws into their own hands.
. . . The want of a penitentiary has had a tendency to
keep this custom alive in this state longer than it would
otherwise have existed. When an individual is guilty
of any offence, which renders him amenable to the
laws, he must either be acquitted altogether or suffer
death."[2]

Lynch-law was also known in the eastern states at this
time. Not only were there mobs which dealt summarily
with offenders, as in the year 1831, but their proceedings
were known by a different name. It was now no longer
simply "mobs" and "mobocracy," but "Lynch's law,"

[1] See *Liberator*, Aug. 8, 1835 (5: 126–7).

[2] The "South-West," II, p. 185–7. In Mississippi, at this time,
eleven crimes were punishable by death.

and "Judge Lynch's court" as well. The Boston Daily
Advertiser in July, 1835, gave expression to the following,
under the heading "Lynch's Law": "We have had occasion of late to advert to the use of this term in our paper,
as indicating punishments, wantonly and in disregard of
law, applied in certain portions of our country to individuals suspected or guilty of crime."[1] On the night of
September 10, 1835, a gallows was erected in Brighton
Street, Boston, in front of Mr. Garrison's house, with
two ropes suspended therefrom. On the crossbar was the
inscription "Judge Lynch's law."[2]

The following appeared in Niles' Register, October 3,
1835 (49:76–7): "Our village (Kanawha Salines, W. Va.)
was thrown into considerable commotion on Friday
morning last in consequence of the arrival of judge Lynch
among us. His business was soon ascertained, and by
his authority four white men from Ohio were soon arrested and tried before 12 intelligent persons of our county,
for endeavoring to persuade several slaves to leave their
masters, for some free state. . . . These congenial spirits
of Garrison, Tappan & Co. were arrested in the neighborhood of our village, tried, condemned, and received
the sentence pronounced on them by the jury. That is
to say, Joe Gill and the elder Drake to receive nine and
thirty lashes each, and leave the county in 24 hours; the
younger Drake, with Ross, to be discharged for want of
evidence, but with a promise from them that they would
also quit the county in 24 hours. The evidence . . . produced an unanimous verdict on the part of the jury, that

---

[1] See *Liberator*, Aug. 1, 1835 (5: 123).
[2] *Boston Advertiser*, Sept. 12, p. 2.

two should be *lynched* and the other two excused, provided they would leave this part of the country."

The following appeared in Niles' Register, December 5, 1835 (49:228): "Lynch law in Colerain. The sect known as perfectionists have recently been making some converts in Colerain (Franklin County, Mass.), and holding meetings there considerably to the annoyance of the majority of the inhabitants. We learn that one of the leaders . . . who was suspected of taking with his female disciples some liberties inconsistent with the holiness of his profession, was taken out a few days since, ridden nearly three miles upon a rail, tarred and feathered, and dismissed, with an admonition to quit the town — a piece of advice with which he has since complied."[1]

Some idea of the prevalence of mob violence and lynch-law procedure in 1835 is obtained from the following editorials in Niles' Register:

"Meetings have been held at Danville, Kentucky; at Richmond and Petersburg and many other towns in Virginia; at Charleston, South Carolina; at many places in Mississippi; and, indeed, it may be generally said in all the south and southwest in consequence of the flood of incendiary publications let loose by a few 'anti-slavery' men of the north, inciting the negroes to insurrection, and murder, and desolation; and, at as many places, perhaps, a like spirit has been shown against *gamblers.* Anti-gaming societies have been introduced in a number of cities and towns. *Executions* by 'Lynch law,' have been numerous. Acts of personal violence, on other accounts,

---

[1] Similar punishments have been inflicted upon Mormons. Joseph Smith, Jr., and Sidney Rigdon were tarred and feathered on the night of March 25, 1832. — See W. A. Linn: "The Story of the Mormons" (1902), pp. 133–137.

some of which are terrific, also abound. Society is in an awful state. What is the cause of it?"[1]

"During the last and the present week we have cut out and laid aside more than 500 articles, relating to the various *excitements* now acting on the people of the United States, public and private! *Society seems everywhere unhinged,* and the demon of 'blood and slaughter' has been let loose upon us! We have the *slave* question in many different forms, including the proceedings of *kidnappers* and *manstealers* — and others belonging to the *free negroes:* the proscription and prosecution of *gamblers;* with mobs growing out of *local matters* — and a great collection of acts of violence of a *private,* or *personal* nature, ending in death; and regret to believe, also, that an awful *political* outcry is about to be raised to rally the 'poor against the rich'! We have executions, and murders, and riots to the utmost limits of the union. The character of our countrymen seems suddenly changed, and thousands interpret the law in their own way — sometimes in one case, and then in another, guided apparently only by their own will! . . . We lately gave, by way of a specimen, a few articles of a nature similar to those now in our possession. We cannot consent to hold up our country to the contempt and scorn of the old world, and shall, therefore, generally suppress them, though some cases of peculiar atrocity must be inserted. Let the laws rule. And let no one do anything that may have a tendency to bring them into popular disrespect!"[2]

Even though some allowance for exaggeration in the above statements may be necessary, there yet remains unquestionable evidence of a very unsettled state of affairs.[3] An editorial written in a less sensational style

[1] Issue of Aug. 22, 1835 (48: 439).
[2] Issue of Sept. 5, 1835 (49: 1).
[3] See also Harriet Martineau "Society in America" (1837), I, 120, 121, 122.

appeared in the Register in October. The first sentences are as follows: "Meetings of the people have been held in nearly all the chief cities and towns in the northern states — at which the proceedings of the abolitionists were rejected and disavowed, with great unanimity and much zeal. And in the south we almost daily hear of 'judge Lynch,' and of persons who are flogged and driven away, or 'executed,' under sentences rendered by him."[1]

Judge Jay in a charge to a Grand Jury at White Plains, New York, in November, 1835, referred to the "spirit of lawless violence" that was abroad in the land, and spoke of the danger to civil and religious liberty if it were not arrested. About the same time, Judge Cranch, in a similar charge to a Grand Jury in the District of Columbia, spoke of the "state of excitement" which existed in some parts of the country.[2]

Some attributed the cause of all this excitement to the abolitionists.[3] A correspondent of the Medina (Ohio) Free Press early in the year 1836 wrote as follows: "When a body of men with such feelings and principles, begin to distract the nation with their mad schemes, it is high time for a community to notice them. I am no advocate of Lynch law, but I must say that if Lynch law must be practised, I know of no fitter subjects for its operation than such fanatics."[4] The following appears in an

---

[1] *Niles' Register*, Oct. 3, 1835 (49: 65).
  For a caustic satire on the "proceedings of Judge Lynch," see "The Enemies of the Constitution Discovered," &c., by Defensor (N. Y., 1835), pp. 48–52.

[2] *Liberator*, Nov. 21, 1835 (5: 188).

[3] See *Liberator*, June 8, 1838 (8: 89), for an editorial from the *Philadelphia Daily Focus*.

[4] *Liberator*, April 16, 1836 (6: 63).

article on Lynch Law in America published in England
in 1877: "Among the institutions specially American,
few have had worse odour in England than what is commonly known as 'Lynch law.' In the time of the anti-
slavery agitation the recourse to Lynch law by the
supporters of 'the domestic institution,' or 'involuntary
servitude,' as it was euphoniously called, caused just indignation. It was by Lynch law that men who dared to
speak against slavery were silenced in the Slave States."[1]
Thus, the defenders of slavery in the Southern States were
highly incensed at the interference of abolitionists whom
they felt knew but little about the actual conditions, and
laid upon the shoulders of these "fanatics" the blame
for the necessity of resorting to lynch-law; the abolitionists, on the other hand, said that lawless violence was the
direct result of slavery[2] and the attempt of the South to
put down free discussion by means of force.

The years of Jackson's presidency, 1829–1837, have
been distinguished by political writers as the Jacksonian
period, — a period in which there was an unusual amount
of turbulence and violence. It has been repeatedly suggested that Jackson's own arbitrary temperament and example did something to set this fashion. "It is, however,
more just to see, both in the President himself and in the
mobs of his time of power, symptoms of one and the same
thing; namely, a great democratic upheaval, the wilful
self-assertion of a masterful people, and of a man who
was their true representative. . . . During Jackson's eight

---

[1] *Leisure Hour*, Nov. 24, 1877, p. 750.

[2] This was Garrison's view of the matter. See *Liberator*, Aug. 10,
1838 (8: 127).

years everything is changing; both society and politics are undergoing revolution; deep organic processes are in progress; significant atmospheric changes are setting in."[1] "It is not possible that a growing nation should spread over new territory, and feel the thrill of its own young energies contending successfully with nature in all her rude force, without social commotions and a certain recklessness and uproar. The contagion of these forms of disorder produces other and less excusable forms."[2]

The cause for all the turbulence and violence lay deeper than abolitionism, slavery, or the character of political leaders. These were merely the manifestations of the disruption of underlying social forces which were warring against each other while seeking to come to a stable equilibrium under new and changed conditions. Society was in process of reorganization. It was a time of social readjustment. This was the condition of society which existed, and it was a condition conducive to the spread of lynch-law.

It was due to this fact that the term lynch-law gained a permanent place in the English language. Early in the forties, as mentioned in the introduction, the dictionaries admitted the term to their list and thus gave to it the seal of their approval. A writer in Harper's Magazine for May, 1859 (p. 794) says: "I think I had never heard of lynch-law until about the year 1834, when the citizens of Vicksburg organized themselves into a Court of Uncommon Pleas, with special reference to certain

[1] Woodrow Wilson: "Division and Reunion" (Edition of 1898), pp. 115, 117.
[2] W. G. Sumner: "Andrew Jackson" (1882), pp. 364–365; pp. 428–429, in edition of 1899 in American Statesmen series.

men in their midst who were, or were said to be, 'living on the borders of the law.' And I well remember, boy as I was, the sensation with which the news of the hanging of the Vicksburg gamblers was received in the old States, and how soon the terms 'Lynch law' and 'lynching' became familiar as household words." It was the application of lynch-law, then, to the gamblers infesting the towns along the Mississippi River that familiarized the public with the term, and it was the constant exercise of summary methods of punishment against abolitionists and other unpopular individuals in various parts of the country that furnished the occasion for its continued use.

In the month of May, 1835, two negroes were burned to death near Mobile, Alabama, for "most barbarously murdering" two children. The murderers had their trial, the result of which is given in the following paragraph taken from a Mobile paper: "As the Court pronounced the only sentence known to the law — the smothered flame broke forth. The laws of the country had never conceived that crimes could be perpetrated with such peculiar circumstances of barbarity, and had therefore provided no adequate punishment. Their lives were justly forfeited to the laws of the country, but the peculiar circumstances demanded that the ordinary punishment should be departed from — they were seized, taken to the place where they had perpetrated the act, and burned to death."[1]

A case of burning alive, which on account of the subsequent events gained great notoriety, occurred at St. Louis, Missouri, April 28, 1836. One writer designated it as

[1] *Liberator*, July 4, 1835 (5: 108).

"the execution of 'Lynch Law' upon a yellow fellow, by means of a slow fire." A colored man was arrested on board a boat by a deputy sheriff and a constable. Another colored man, a free mulatto, assisted him to escape, and the officers immediately arrested the mulatto. He, however, turned upon the officers, drew a knife and stabbed Deputy Sheriff Hammond, killing him instantly, and also seriously wounded Mr. Mull, the constable. He was finally captured, however, and locked up in the jail. Later the people assembled and, after threatening to tear down the jail if he was not delivered to them, secured the prisoner, conducted him to the outskirts of the city, placed a chain round his neck and a rope round his body, and thus fastened him to a tree a few feet from the ground. A fire was then placed round the tree and he was roasted alive.[1]

When this case came up for consideration before the Grand Jury of St. Louis County, Judge Lawless — according to subsequent comments rightly named — made the following charge:

"I have reflected much on this matter, and after weighing all the considerations that present themselves as bearing upon it, I feel it my duty to state my opinion to be, that whether the Grand Jury shall act at all, depends upon the solution of this preliminary question, namely, whether the destruction of McIntosh was the act of the 'few' or the act of the 'many.'

"If on a calm view of the circumstances attending this

---

[1] See *Niles' Register*, June 4, 1836 (50: 234).
Also *Liberator*, May 14, 1836 (6: 79), and May 21, 1836 (6: 83).
A negro slave was burned to death in a similar way in Arkansas in November, 1836, for murdering his master and several negroes. See extract from the *Arkansas Gazette* in *Niles' Register*, Dec. 31, 1836 (51: 275).

dreadful transaction, you shall be of opinion that it was perpetrated by a definite, and, compared to the population of St.
Louis, a *small* number of individuals, separate from the mass,
and evidently taking upon themselves, as contradistinguished
from the multitude, the responsibility of the act, my opinion is
that you ought to indict them all, without a single exception.

"If on the other hand, the destruction of the murderer of
Hammond was the act as I have said, of the many — of the
multitude, in the ordinary sense of those words — not the act
of numerable and ascertainable malefactors, but of congre-
gated thousands, seized upon and impelled by that mysterious,
metaphysical, and almost electric phrenzy, which, in all nations
and ages, has hurried on the infuriated multitude to deeds of
death and destruction — then, I say, act not at all in the matter
— the case then transcends your jurisdiction — it is beyond
the reach of human law."[1]

It was for denouncing the burning of this colored man
and violently attacking Judge Lawless in his Observer
that the Rev. E. P. Lovejoy had his printing-office destroyed by a mob in St. Louis, and was forced to remove
his paper to Alton, Illinois. He did not cease to express
his convictions, however, and neither did his persecutions
cease. Three times his press was destroyed by mobs.
On November 7, 1837, while endeavoring to protect his
property, he met his death at the hands of an Alton
mob.

In an address on "The Perpetuation of our Political
Institutions," delivered before the Young Men's Lyceum
of Springfield, Illinois, on January 27, 1837, Abraham
Lincoln characterized the spirit of the times in the following way:

[1] *Liberator,* June 25, 1836 (6: 102).

"Accounts of outrages committed by mobs form the every-day news of the times. They have pervaded the country from New England to Louisiana; they are neither peculiar to the eternal snows of the former nor the burning suns of the latter; they are not the creature of climate, neither are they confined to the slaveholding or the non-slaveholding States. Alike they spring up among the pleasure-hunting masters of Southern slaves, and the order-loving citizens of the land of steady habits. Whatever then their cause may be, it is common to the whole country.

"It would be tedious as well as useless to recount the horrors of all of them. Those happening in the State of Mississippi and at St. Louis are perhaps the most dangerous in example and revolting to humanity. In the Mississippi case they first commenced by hanging the regular gamblers — a set of men certainly not following for a livelihood a very useful or very honest occupation, but one which, so far from being forbidden by the laws, was actually licensed by an act of the legislature passed but a single year before. Next, negroes suspected of conspiring to rise an insurrection were caught up and hanged in all parts of the State; then, white men supposed to be leagued with the negroes; and finally, strangers from neighboring States, going thither on business, were in many instances sub-jected to the same fate. Thus went on this process of hanging, from gamblers to negroes, from negroes to white citizens, and from these to strangers, till dead men were literally dangling from the boughs of trees by every roadside, and in numbers almost sufficient to rival the native Spanish moss of the country as a drapery of the forest.

"Turn then to that horror-striking scene at St. Louis. A single victim only was sacrificed there. This story is very short, and is perhaps the most highly tragic of anything of its length that has ever been witnessed in real life. A mulatto

man by the name of McIntosh was seized in the street, dragged
to the suburbs of the city, chained to a tree, and actually burned
to death; and all within a single hour from the time he had
been a freeman attending to his own business and at peace
with the world.

"Such are the effects of mob law, and such are the scenes
becoming more and more frequent in this land so lately famed
for love of law and order, and the stories of which have even
now grown too familiar to attract anything more than an idle
remark." [1]

The following paragraph appeared in the Southern
Literary Messenger in the year 1839 (5: 218): "Forty
years ago, the practice of wreaking private vengeance,
or of inflicting summary and illegal punishment for crimes,
actual or pretended, which has been glossed over by the
name of *Lynch's Law*, was hardly known except in sparse,
frontier settlements, beyond the reach of courts and legal
proceedings."

The above quotations set forth clearly the condition
of affairs in the United States at this time. It was the
spirit of the times, rather than any particular cause,
which brought about recourse to lynch-law practices.
Lynch-law was invoked for no particular offense to the
exclusion of all other offenses; neither was it peculiar to
any one section of the country. From having been practised only in the border settlements as a temporary means
of suppressing lawlessness until the civil regulations
could be established, lynch-law methods had come to
prevail even in well settled communities. Those writers
who expressed the opinion about 1830 that lynch-law was

[1] "Abraham Lincoln, Works," I, pp. 9–10.

dying out did not foresee the great popular excitement which existed during Jackson's administration. The anti-slavery agitation acted as a spark in a tinder-box and seemed to beget a spirit of lawlessness in every part of the country. To the inflamed imagination of the popular mind the slightest provocation seemed a serious offense. The law did not reach such offenses, or they were deemed to be inadequately punished by the law, and this seemed to the people a justification for summary punishment.

In the slave States such punishment was generally a whipping or flogging, often followed by tarring and feathering, inflicted upon abolitionists or any persons suspected of "tampering with the slaves," or distributing "incendiary tracts." In cases of a suspected conspiracy for an insurrection among the slaves the supposed leaders were often summarily punished, sometimes by the infliction of the death penalty.

Along the Mississippi River, the gamblers had aroused the resentment of the peace-loving portion of the community by their vices and excesses of various kinds. In many places they were able to bid defiance to the civil authorities and laugh at threats of enforcing the law against them. Here again the exigencies of the situation seemed to the people to justify the adoption of lynch-law. This case of the summary treatment of the gamblers may be regarded as a transition from the frontier type of lynch-law to the sporadic and epidemical type which later prevailed in the well settled States.

The author of a book published in London in 1837 wrote: "The Lynch-law, is not, properly speaking, an opposition to the established laws of the country, or, is at least, not contemplated as such by its adherents; but rather as a supplement to them, — a species of *common* law, which is as old as the country, and which, whatever may be the notion of 'the *learned* in the law,' has nevertheless been productive of some of the happiest results."[1]

In 1839, F. Marryat wrote: "The Lynch law of the present day, as practiced in the States of the West and South, may be divided into two different heads: the first is, the administration of it in cases in which the laws of the States are considered by the majority as not having awarded a punishment adequate, in their opinion, to the offence committed; and the other, when from excitement the majority will not wait for the law to act, but inflict the punishment with their own hands."[2]

Occasionally innocent persons suffered the violence of lynching mobs,[3] and sometimes damages were secured through the courts for having suffered lynch-law. Cases of this nature were not uncommon in the early history of the operation of lynch-law in Virginia,[4] and in the later thirties similar suits were instituted in the courts. On September 4, 1835, certain inhabitants of Brownsville, Tennessee, constituted themselves a lynch court for the trial of Anson Moody, suspected of being a kidnapper, or slave stealer. They seized him in the dead of night, tried him, convicted him, and then proceeded to punishment by inflicting one hundred lashes with a "cowskin,"

[1] F. J. Grund: "The Americans in their moral, social, and political relations" (London, 1837), I, 323. (M.)

[2] "Diary in America" (1839), III, 232–233.

[3] Harriet Martineau: "Retrospect of Western Travel" (1838), I, 236–237. Marryat: "Diary in America" (1839), II, 201. *Liberator*, Aug. 24, 1838 (8: 135), &c.

[4] See Chapter II.

branding him on the cheek with the letter R and commanding him to leave the country. A jury in the Circuit
Court of the United States for the District of West Tennessee gave him a verdict of $2,000 and costs against
five of the members of the Lynch court.[1]

In Yazoo, Mississippi, a Mr. Harris, for some real or
supposed offense, was "severely lynched" by H. W.
Dunn, C. W. Bain, and others. He prosecuted those
two individuals for the outrage, and the case was tried in
the circuit court of Yazoo County. The jury returned a
verdict for the plaintiff of $20,000.[2]

Two young men in Fayette County, Tennessee, were
sentenced to three months' imprisonment and to pay a
fine of $50 each for assisting to ride John T. Foster on a
rail. The said Foster died in consequence of the injuries
he received during the outrage.[3]

Sherman Thompson and Samuel Thompson, of Meriden,
Connecticut, were sentenced to pay a fine of $20 each and
to suffer imprisonment in the common jail for the term of
six months for having participated in an outrage upon
the Rev. Mr. Ludlow in October, 1837.[4]

The Grand Jury of Alton, Illinois, found bills of indictment against a number of individuals concerned in
the affair of November 7, 1837, when Lovejoy was killed,
but the suits were evidently not pushed against them.
In the trial of Rock, one of the assailants, which came up
before the municipal court, the jury returned a special

[1] *Liberator*, Oct. 27, 1837 (7: 174).
[2] *Niles' Register*, June 15, 1839 (56: 256).
[3] *Liberator*, Sept. 14, 1838 (8: 146).
[4] *Liberator*, March 16, 1838 (8: 44).

verdict that the defendant, in their opinion, was guilty
of the various charges in the indictment, but that they
return him not guilty on a question of jurisdiction.[1]

Previous to 1840 the verb lynch was occasionally used
to include capital punishment, but the common and general
use was to indicate a personal castigation of some sort.
"To lynch" had not then undergone a change in meaning and acquired the sense of "to put to death."[2] Webster's
Dictionary, edition of 1848, gives: "Lynch, v. t. To inflict pain, or punish, without the forms of law, as by a
mob, or by unauthorized persons," and "Lynched, pp.
Punished or abused without the forms of law." These
same definitions still stand in the edition of 1876. It was
not until a time subsequent to the Civil War that the verb
lynch came to carry the idea of putting to death. Men
were punished with death "by Lynch-law" and "by order
of Judge Lynch," but it is so stated in every such case
that death was inflicted.

A few typical instances of the use of the word will
illustrate the point. The St. Louis Bulletin, November
21, 1835, contained the following item: "Fuller and
Bridges, the men suspected of having kidnapped Major
Dougherty's slaves : . . were soundly flogged, or in
other words — Lynched, and set on the opposite side of
the river, with the positive assurance that, if they were
again found within the limits of the State of Missouri,
their fate should be death by hanging."[3]

---

[1] *Liberator*, Feb. 9, 1838 (8: 24).

[2] This is not wholly in accord with the opinion expressed by Mr. Albert Matthews in the *Nation*, Dec. 4, 1902 (75: 441), but in a private
letter to the writer Mr. Matthews has accepted this modification.

[3] See *Liberator*, Dec. 19, 1835 (5: 204).

Niles' Register for December 5, 1835 (49:228) heads
a paragraph taken from the Louisiana Advertiser "More
Lynching." The paragraph tells of the murder of John
W. Brock by John Joseph Short, who was "tried in a
summary manner, and executed, by hanging."

Under the title "Lynchers Lynched" the following
language was used in the Liberator for September 24,
1836 (6:155): "A party of from 6 to 12 persons proceeded
to the house of Judge Bermudez last night . . . their object being, as it is supposed, to assault or Lynch the Judge."

The following passage is from the Liberator, August 17,
1838 (8:131): "Lynching. A man named John Miles,
who hails from Cincinnati, received 100 lashes in Adams
county, Mississippi, for endeavoring to entice negroes
away."

Under the heading "Horrible Lynching" the following item, taken from the Southern Mississippi Sun of the
19th ult., appears in Niles' Register for December 14, 1839
(57:256): "Crook and Carter who were confined in the
jail of Scott county for murder, have been taken by force
from prison by some of the citizens of that county and
hung! It will be recollected that they once made their
escape from the jail and were retaken. — They were
brought to Rankin county two or three weeks since for
trial, but were remanded for want of some testimony.
The people have taken the law into their own hands, and
executed them without a trial."

The ordinary use of the term at this time was very well
stated by Philip Hone when he wrote in his diary on
August 2, 1835: "A terrible system prevails in some of the
Southern and Western States, which consists in . . . beat-

ing, tarring and feathering, and in some cases hanging the unhappy object of their vengeance, and this is generally called 'Lynch's Law.'" [1]

Instances may be cited showing that the term continued to be used in this way down to 1860. Niles' Register for August 24, 1844 (66: 428) has this paragraph: "Judge Lynch. Four men, Rea, Mitchell, White and Jones, were tried and condemned before his honor, Chief Justice Lynch, on the 16th inst. at South Sulphur, Texas, for killing two men and one boy of the Delaware tribe of friendly Indians. They were executed under said sentence, the next day, in the presence of a large number of persons."

In the year 1845 there were some lawless proceedings in Scott County, Missouri. Niles' Register for July 26, 1845 (68: 325) describes the occurrence in the following way: "A party of men . . . were charged with burning the houses, stocks, etc. and doing other injuries to a man named Lane. Some of his neighbors collected and caught several of the persons charged, lynched them, and ordered them to leave the county, which they did. A few days ago, they returned with a considerable party and avowed their determination to drive out or be avenged on Lane and those who had assisted to lynch and drive them away."

The following item is taken from the St. Louis Reveille for October 2, 1845: "It is reported that the two men named Redman, brothers, with five others, were recently arrested in the vicinity of Davenport, charged with the murder of Colonel Davenport. Suspicion was strong as

[1] Philip Hone: "Diary 1828–1851" (1889), I, 150. (M.)

to their guilt. We have heard rumors that Lynch law had been inflicted upon both the Redmans since their arrest — that they both were hung."[1]

Niles' Register for January 17, 1846 (69: 320) gives the following: "Lynching in Florida. A man by the name of Yeoman, accused of being a noted slave stealer — having been discharged by Judge Warren, of Baker County, Georgia, on a writ of *habeas corpus* . . . on his arrival at Jefferson County, Florida, ninety citizens assembled and took a formal vote, which stood 67 for and 23 against hanging him. He was executed accordingly at 12 o'clock, on the 2d inst."[2]

In 1855 several negroes were summarily executed by mobs in Tennessee. The Liberator gives an account of these occurrences under the heading, "Hanging Negroes in Tennessee by Judge Lynch's Code."[3]

In the Liberator, January 18, 1856 (p. 12), it is stated that "Judge Thomas Clingman, of Carroll county, Missouri, was murdered, about the middle of October, by one of his field slaves. The murderer was instantly hung by Lynch law."

The Liberator, May 2, 1856 (p. 72), contains this paragraph, taken from the Western Herald: "Lynch Law in Virginia. — A man named William Hornbeck, living in Lewis County, Virginia, for the alleged ill-treatment of his family, was lynched by the young men in the neighborhood, one night last week. — Stripped of his clothing,

---

[1] See *Niles' Register*, Oct. 25, 1845 (69: 115).

[2] Sir Charles Lyell, who was in Macon, Georgia, a short time after this occurred, gives an account of it in his book, "A Second Visit to the United States of America" (1850), II, 31-32.

[3] *Liberator*, Oct. 19, 1855 (25: 168).

rode on a rail, made to run through a briar patch, a stout paddle used to keep him going, and a coat of tar and feathers applied."

The Liberator, December 4, 1857 (p. 196) copies the following account of the manner in which an abolitionist was lynched in Mississippi: ". . . A crowd took him to the woods, told him to strip, carried to a hollow and tied around a tree. He was then told what was their intention: to lynch him until he told something. The lashing was commenced by two who used straps fastened to sticks about 10 in. long. . . ."

The same issue of the Liberator contains the following: "Lynch Law Proceedings. — In Barton County, Southwestern Missouri, great excitement has recently existed on account of the doings of a set of lawless wretches called 'Slickers,' who pretended to be after a horse-thief, but who 'slicked'[1] or barbarously beat several men until their lives were dispaired of, and when women interfered, some were badly beaten and others violated. . . ."

The following paragraph appeared in the Liberator, December 31, 1860 (p. 211): "Lynch Law Again. — Two white men named Waters and a mulatto named Wilson, at Mosely Hall, a village in North Carolina, were arrested a few days ago for hurraing for Lincoln and the Abolitionists and severely beating a citizen who remonstrated with them. They were immediately tried by a jury, who ordered them to be whipped, and to have their heads shaved. The verdict was carried out on the spot."

---

[1] During the period 1830–1860 the word "slick" was occasionally used at places in the Mississippi Valley, in the same sense as "lynch." See *Liberator*, Oct. 3, 1835 (5: 157), and compare *Niles' Register*, Oct. 5, 1833 (45: 87).

The use of the word lynch in a story entitled "Jack Long; or lynch-law and vengeance," which appeared in the American Whig Review for February, 1845, purporting to be a true story of frontier life in Shelby County, Texas, fully bears out the assertion that "to lynch" was generally understood at that time to mean to whip or to maltreat. According to the story a band of men calling themselves "Regulators," led by a ruffian, terrorized the county. Once they lynched, that is, lashed to a tree, whipped and beat, Jack Long, leaving him for dead. He recovered and left the county in obedience to their orders, but later came back and shot all but two of the "Regulators."

It should be said, however, that the instances of the application of lynch-law which are given in Niles' Register and the Liberator from 1830 to 1860 show an increase in the severity of the punishment administered. As the slavery controversy went on and the breach widened between the North and the South, it was but natural that such should be the case. Many people in the South felt that no punishment was quite severe enough for an abolitionist. Crimes committed by negroes were also treated with greater severity. The following extract from a private letter, dated Houston, Texas, August 23, 1860, to a friend in Hartford, Connecticut, expresses a sentiment felt at that time in many sections of the South: "Tell your abolition friends to go on and soon they will have the pleasure of seeing the negro reduced to such a state of hopeless bondage that they may well pity them. I solemnly declare that to-day the negro is not as free as he was two or five years ago; and why? Simply because his master has been goaded on to desperation by incendiary acts and speeches. Now he fears the negro, and binds him down as you would a savage animal. One year ago, all was peace and quietness here. The negro was allowed to go out, to have dances and frolics; to-day one dare not show his head after nine o'clock in the evening. Seven companies of patrols are organized and guard the city each night, sixteen horse-patrol scour the country around. Forty-eight vigilance men say live, banish or die, as the proof may go to show. And so it is all over the country. Men are hung every day by the decision of planters, lawyers, judges and ministers. It is no hot impetuous act, but cool, stern justice. It is the saving of wife and daughter, mother and sister from the hand of desecration. It is the stopping of scenes that would make the Druses and Turks blush for shame."[1]

At the time this letter was written, and during the three years preceding, there was a great deal of excitement in Texas. Vigilance societies were in active operation against desperadoes and abolitionists. In 1857 a vigilance committee in the "upper country," as it was then called, was "raking the country fore and aft and swinging every horsethief and murderer," that could be found. A traveler saw twelve bodies suspended from one tree and on another tree five.[2] In the summer of 1860 there was an insurrection and conspiracy in Dallas, Ellis, Tarrant and Denton counties, in northern Texas. The three ringleaders, Sam, Cato, and Patrick, were hung by a vigilance committee on July 24. Twenty-two insur-

---

[1] *Liberator*, Sept. 14, 1860 (30: 146).
[2] See *Liberator*, Oct. 2, 1857 (27: 160).

rectionists in all were said to have been hanged.[1] This condition of affairs must be taken into consideration in connection with the statements made in the above letter and the fears and prejudice therein expressed.

When drawing any conclusions from the instances recorded in the newspapers as to the history of lynch-law during this period, there is another fact to be kept in mind. During the later years the facilities for obtaining news were greatly increased; the means of communication between different parts of the country were very much improved and the number of newspapers published had rapidly increased. There were no doubt many cases of the administration of summary justice in the remote districts during the thirties and the early forties which never came to the notice of either the Liberator or Niles' Register. There is, however, abundant evidence to make the conclusion a safe one that lynch-law was more and more resorted to during this period and that the punishments administered under that name by vigilance committees and mobs came to be more and more severe, death being frequently inflicted during the later years.

The Parkville (Mo.) Democrat made the following statement in the year 1856: "Deeds of daring and outrages perpetrated by negroes, are constantly becoming more frequent. We hope that the proper authorities will see to it that all such cases are punished to the extent of the law."[2] The Liberator for May 2, 1856 (p. 72) contains an item which reads in this way: "In Hancock County, La., Samuel L. Watson, a negro overseer, whipped

---

[1] See *Liberator*, Aug. 24, 1860 (30: 160).
[2] See *Liberator*, Jan. 18, 1856 (26: 12).

one of the negroes under him, and a few days after, the negro caught him in a field and beat him with a club till he died. The tragedy closed in the usual way, by the summary hanging of the negro by the populace." There are indications, therefore, that crime was on the increase among the negroes at this time and that the whites had cause for inflicting more rigorous punishment.

The following editorial appeared in the Liberator, December 19, 1856 (p. 204): "A record of the cases of 'Lynch Law' in the Southern States reveals the startling fact, that within twenty years, over three hundred white persons have been murdered upon the accusation — in most cases unsupported by legal proof — of carrying among slave-holders arguments addressed expressly to their own intellects and consciences, as to the morality and expediency of slavery." If this figure may be accepted as reliable for the whites, it is within the truth to say that a considerably larger number of negroes met with summary capital punishment during the various insurrection excitements which occurred.

The summary execution of negroes did not, however, become a serious evil previous to the Civil War. So long as the negroes were valuable as slaves, it was a direct economic loss to the slaveholder if an able-bodied slave were put to death. In general, it was only in cases of real or supposed conspiracy against the whites, or in cases of insurrection, that the negroes were killed in a summary manner. Such was the case in Virginia at the time of the Nat Turner insurrection; such was the case in Mississippi in 1835 when it was discovered that the Murrell gang had laid plans for a general uprising among the slaves. A similar condition of affairs existed in northern Texas in 1860, when it was thought that strychnine had been distributed among the negroes and they had been instructed to put it in the wells and in the food of their masters.

Damages were sometimes claimed by owners for the loss of their slaves through illegal procedure. A suit was instituted in the year 1857 in the Jefferson Circuit Court of Kentucky against the city of Louisville for the value of the slaves George, Bill, and Jack, the murderers of the Joyce family. George and Bill had been hung by an infuriated mob, and Jack had cut his own throat in jail, in order to escape the fate which befell his companions. $1,500 each was claimed as damages by the owners of the negroes. The Louisville Courier in commenting upon the case said the suit would be of interest and importance, involving some delicate principles of law.[1] In 1858 a vigilance committee was established in Shelby County, Kentucky, whose method of procedure was described as follows: "They order white men and free negroes who have been concerned in evil deeds, to leave the county within three days. Any property belonging to a white man is to be appraised by three disinterested persons, and the price paid, after such person has been directed to leave the county. Slaves who are vicious must be removed, also, from Shelby county, by their masters."[2] The property right in the slaves was generally recognized in cases where they committed offenses against a neighbor or a neighbor's slaves. A common way of

[1] *Liberator*, Oct. 16, 1857 (27: 167).
[2] *Liberator*, Sept. 24, 1858 (28: 155).

settling such matters was for a number of the planters to meet together and decide upon the amount of damages to be paid and what should constitute an equitable settlement, without going through any formal legal procedure. In Louisiana a tribunal formed in this way tried and gave sentence of death upon two negroes for violating the person of a young white girl on Christmas eve, 1856.[1]

An examination of the files of the Liberator shows that, during the ten years 1830–1840, in cases where masters, overseers, or mistresses were murdered by slaves, the law was allowed to take its course almost without exception. The same is true in the case of rape committed upon white women by negroes. The record stands, three slaves and one free negro legally executed for rape and two slaves legally executed for attempted rape. There are some instances reported of summary punishment, not death, being administered to negroes for inducing white girls to run away with them, or for living with white women.

There were also three instances of burning negroes at the stake during this period. These cases have been described above: one was the burning of two slaves near Mobile, Alabama, for murdering two children; another was the burning of the free mulatto at St. Louis for killing an officer; and the other was the burning of a slave in Arkansas for the murder of his master.

For the ten years 1850–1860, the record is somewhat different. Out of forty-six negroes put to death for the murder of owners or overseers, twenty were legally executed and twenty-six were summarily executed. Of the

---

[1] *Liberator*, April 3, 1857 (27 : 56).

latter, one was a female slave who was taken from the constable and hanged upon a tree for the crime of beating her mistress to death, and another was a negro woman who was burned to death for poisoning her master. Eight of the remaining twenty-four negroes were summarily executed by being burned at the stake. For the crime of rape upon white women, three negroes were legally executed, and for attempted rape two were legally executed; while twelve negroes were more or less brutually put to death by mobs for having committed the crime. Of the latter, four were burned at the stake, three of whom had committed the double crime of rape and murder. Some other instances of rape and of attempted rape are reported, but no statement is made as to the manner or the nature of the punishment inflicted.

It cannot be said, however, that these cases of the infliction of capital punishment upon negroes without process of law were anything more than sporadic and isolated cases. They were scarcely more than local in their influence. The most important thing brought to light by the above comparison of the two ten-year periods is the tendency, in the later period, toward less reliance on legal procedure and toward greater readiness on the part of the people to take matters into their own hands. The newspapers in the fifties not only frequently excused summary procedure but often openly advocated it. One instance only will be cited and it is from a southern newspaper. In 1856, a Mr. Pearce, residing in Morgan County, Georgia, attempted to give one of his negroes a flogging for some misdemeanor. The negro picked up an ax and at one blow split his master's head open. He then fled. While he was still at large the Madison Messenger printed the following: "Beyond doubt he will be captured before many hours. If he is, although we admire submission to the course pointed out by the law of the land, in this case so much of the brute has been manifested, we should be glad to see our citizens rise *en masse*, and avail themselves of Lynch law, and hang the rascal without court or jury."[1]

The preceding paragraphs have made it clear that negroes occasionally suffered death under lynch-law previous to the Civil War. It was not common, however, to characterize the summary hanging of negroes as lynching. Such occurrences were neither common nor general enough to give to the verb lynch its modern meaning, even though they had been always designated as lynchings.

It was with reference to the lawless proceedings which took place in the western and southwestern portions of the United States in the fifties that the term lynch was first used in its modern sense. The vigilance committees which were then common in that section of the country often hung desperadoes and horse-thieves, and frequently when such persons were thus executed they were said to have been lynched. A paragraph in the Liberator, November 9, 1860 (p. 179), has the heading: "Four men Lynched in Texas." The paragraph contains a clipping from a Texas paper describing the circumstances under which four men were found one morning hung in the

[1] See *Liberator*, Dec. 19, 1856 (26: 204). It is possibly to this case that F. L. Olmsted refers in "A Journey in the Back Country" (N. Y., 1860), pp. 442–443. He says a negro killed his master "a few months since in Georgia or Alabama"; and "was roasted, at a slow fire, on the spot of the murder, in the presence of many thousand slaves, driven to the ground from all the adjoining counties."

public square of a town in Navarro County, and refers to the "many accounts of lynchings in Texas."

Howitt's Journal for February 12, 1848 (3: 109), contains an article entitled "American Lynching — The Desperadoes of the South-West." The article is really a review of a book published under the title "The Desperadoes of the South-West," which, according to the reviewer, gives a picture of the state of society in that section of the United States. Quotations from the book are given in which the author outlines the way the West was settled up and the difficulty of keeping prisoners until a regular trial could be had, and the exasperating delays and postponements brought about by pettifogging lawyers. The author describes the operation of lynch-law at that time in the following words:

"Then, after all other means of redress have been exhausted, the honest, hard-working portion of the community organize themselves into a community of lynchers, elect a captain, appoint a committee, and, as they say, 'take justice into their own hands.' . . . The company of lynchers once formed, they proceed to the execution of summary justice. It is easy to see what sad work they must make of it, rendered furious, as they have been, by multitudinous wrongs. And accordingly, they whip, bang, torture, burn, flay alive; and however they may begin, end at last by acting like a band of savages. What else could be expected of such men, however honest, however merciful, stung to ungovernable rage by so many injuries, and now placed as judges in their own case, in a position beyond responsibility? By and by, the more cunning rogues take shelter under their protection, and bawl out the loudest for justice. Then the fruit of ruin is ripe. Men accuse their enemies of the most appalling crimes, in order to glut feelings

of private revenge. A hypocritical zeal for honesty becomes
the cloak for rapine and murder. Vengeance supplants law,
and brute force and fury trample down all show of order. . . .
But the force is never wholly on one side only. The lynchers,
or 'regulators,' as they are often called, soon find that their
foes organize also; arm themselves, and prepare for systematic
resistance, under the denomination of 'moderators.' Then
commences a guerilla warfare as dark and deadly in its hate, as
the old English contest between the Red and the White Roses.
It is a war of utter extermination."

Chambers' Journal for February 17, 1855 (23: 101) contains an article entitled "American Jottings. Eccentrici-
ties in criminal jurisprudence — Lynch Law." The following quotations are both illustrative and instructive:

"A respect for law and order is as conspicuous in general
circumstances in the greater part of the United States as it is
in England. This much may be said without prejudice to the
fact, that very strange things occasionally come to pass, particularly in the south and west, in violation of the regular
course of justice. . . . It is doubtless the perfunctoriness in the
administration of justice which at times arouses the indignation of the public and causes them to have recourse to what is
called Lynch Law, in which respect American society, in the
more newly settled parts of the country, may be said to be at
the stage of the rough populace of Edinburgh when they
interrupted the ordinary course of justice, and laid violent
hands on Captain Porteous. It is thus interesting to note how
long it is before a people acquire the habit of implicit submission to the maxims of law — the time, of course, being propor-
tioned according as the administrators of that law are in themselves unworthy of respect. The ancient venality of judges
and juries in Scotland, now the theme of romance, would

appear to be still matched on the banks of the Mississippi, and sometimes, as popular feeling inclines, it leads to similar results. . . . Objectionable and dangerous as lynching may be considered in the abstract there can be little doubt of its propriety practically in certain conditions of American society. When judges and courts are leagued with desperadoes, or when peculiar difficulties stand in the way of a prompt administration of justice, the public, in self-defense, feel impelled to interfere. At the settlement of California, and before society had time to establish regular tribunals, or to give due efficacy to the law, life and property would not have been safe for a moment, unless a Vigilance Committee had charged itself with the duty of lynching. Even when, in such newly opened territories, judges are appointed, only a small advance is made towards a vigorous legal administration. Of American judges it needs to be recollected that their position is often not such as to command respect. A judge of the supreme courts in England is a being aloof in every respect from the people, and he scrupulously abstains from interference personally in matters which might by possibility come before him in his judicial capacity. An American judge, on the other hand, is not dissevered from the ordinary action of society; and if he looks forward to a governorship, or some other high function, he requires to cultivate a certain popularity."

In these extracts there is presented very clearly the character of the illegal and summary proceedings to which the term lynch-law was generally and commonly applied in the fifties. The quoted passages likewise indicate the attitude of public sentiment at that time toward such proceedings and the frequency of their occurrence. The tendency for vigilance societies organized in the interests of law and order to pass quickly into the control of the lawless and the vicious, or for counter-organizations to be formed by the lawless element in the population, is also given due prominence.

The Vigilance Committee movement in the West attained its highest state of organization and effectiveness under the San Francisco Committees of Vigilance of 1851 and of 1856. The discovery of gold in 1848 had brought to California in a few years men from all parts of the world. National characteristics came into conflict. Mexicans, Frenchmen, Irishmen, and Americans were suddenly thrown together in a virgin territory. The establishment of civil government and judicial tribunals could not keep pace with the rapid increase in population. When such civil government was begun, the control which the vicious and corrupt element in the population was able to exercise over it rendered it ineffectual. It was a time of social irresponsibility, and serious crimes were of common occurrence. Out of five hundred and thirty-five homicides which occurred in California during the year 1855, there were but seven legal executions.[1] It was under these conditions and on the ground that some such organization was necessary to bring about order and security, that the two San Francisco Vigilance Committees were organized. "Each hanged four men and banished about thirty. Each rescued two prisoners from

[1] See H. H Bancroft: "Popular Tribunals" (1887), I, 749. In his two volumes on "Popular Tribunals" this author presents very forcibly the arguments and the conditions urged in justification of the acts of these "Tribunals." He also exhibits the methods and inner workings of these organizations. In "Literary Industries" (1890), pp. 655–663, he tells how he obtained his knowledge of what went on behind the scenes.

For a somewhat different view of the Vigilance Committee movement in California, see Josiah Royce: "California" (1886), Chapters IV and V.

See also, John S. Hittell: "History of the City of San Francisco."

the county jail by means of surprise parties. . . . The crimes committed by the victims of the first tribunal were against property and life, while those of the second were strongly tinctured with political immorality. . . . The reformation of 1851 was superficial and temporary; that of 1856 radical and permanent." [1]   On the whole, though the measures taken seem extreme, these committees accomplished their end remarkably well, and it is to their credit that they promptly disbanded when their time of usefulness had passed.

Committees of Vigilance were formed elsewhere than in the city of San Francisco, however. Many places in California during the early history of the State had similar committees, though outside of San Francisco they were usually organized only temporarily to deal with particular cases. Similar "Popular Tribunals" existed in Utah, Nevada, Oregon, Washington, Idaho, Montana, Arizona, New Mexico, and Colorado during the early period of their settlement. Bancroft says at the close of his first volume on Popular Tribunals: "I have given in this volume many examples of Popular Tribunals, but the half has not been told. It is safe to say that thus far in the history of these Pacific States far more has been done toward righting wrongs and administering justice outside the pale of law than within it."

Further evidence of the prevalence of lynch-law during the colonization of the territory west of the Mississippi River is furnished by an editorial in the New York Times of March 19, 1864, written under the title " Judge Lynch." The opening sentences are as follows: " Our fellow-citizens

---

[1] Quoted from Bancroft: "Popular Tribunals" (1887), II, 666.

in the far West, in the mineral territories bordering upon the Rocky Mountains, and in those on the other side of the mountains, are holding Lynch courts in extraordinary number, and carrying out the decrees of that ferocious judge with unprecedented energy. Our latest files from the distant regions of Idaho, Nevada, Utah, &c., contain accounts of executions in numbers that we think were never equalled even in the early days of California settlement, nor in any part of the West." Then follows a recital of various instances, twenty or more robbers and murderers hung in Idaho Territory, four murderers hung by a "Citizens Association" in the Territory of Nevada, &c. It is stated that on Thursday of that week bills were passed in Congress enabling Nevada and two other Territories to form constitutions preparatory to their admission to the Union as States. As a condition to their admission an irrevocable ordinance was provided prohibiting slavery, and the writer of the editorial remarks, "we think lynching might have been added."

Lynch-law prevailed to a large extent, also, during the border troubles attending the outbreak of the Civil War. Particularly was this the case in Kansas where, along with the guerrilla warfare that went on for a number of years, many instances of summary procedure occurred that may be properly classified under lynch-law. A correspondent of the New York Tribune in Lawrence, K. T., wrote on May 30, 1858: "There is a very general disposition to pass over the helplessly useless forms of Territorial law and corrupt Federal courts, and try these parties (*i.e.*, horse-thieves) by Lynch law."[1]

[1] *New York Tribune*, June 7, 1858, p. 3.

The lynch-law procedure of the fifties that was most commonly mentioned and described in the newspapers and periodicals was that that prevailed in the western part of the United States. Bodies of citizens, organized secretly or openly under the names of "vigilance committees," "vigilance societies," "vigilantes," "regulators," "law-and-order men," "Citizens' Associations," &c., punished with summary severity horse-thieves, cattle-thieves, highway robbers, counterfeiters, burglars, and swindlers, as well as murderers. Certain rude forms of trial were generally observed, acquittals were rare but not entirely unknown, and the punishment was usually death by hanging. The frequency with which lynch-law was resorted to at this time is to be referred, both to the lack of a well established civil government, and to a doubt on the part of the people as to the adequacy of the ordinary legal machinery.

It was the use of the word lynching in connection with these summary proceedings against white men of desperate character, the criminals of the frontier region west of the Mississippi, during the period of settlement, that first gave to it its modern meaning of putting to death. After the Civil War, when the Southern States were being reconstructed and the whites were threatened with negro domination, summary practices were adopted against the negroes. The negro had ceased to be valuable as property and was looked upon as a dangerous political factor in the community; to take his life was thought to be the easiest and quickest way to dispose of him. The adoption of this plan in many parts of the South gave for the word lynching a new application. Since the Reconstruction Period, then, to lynch has generally meant to put to death. The infliction of any minor punishment without legal trial still constitutes lynch-law, but the simple term "lynching" usually implies capital punishment. It is in this sense that the term will be used throughout the remainder of this investigation.

CHAPTER V

The Reconstruction Period

A CIVIL war is worse in many respects than a foreign war. When the members of a society are forced to settle any differences that they may have and come together in order to resist the aggressions of a foreign foe, the internal organization of the society is strengthened. A civil war, on the contrary, shakes the very foundations of the social structure. The antagonism of interests which brings on and attends a civil war weakens every social bond and tends to disorganize the society. Hence, a longer period of time is required for the effects of internal dissension to be obliterated. The feelings engendered by such a war are not easily overcome either by the victors or by the vanquished. For men who have fought against each other on the battle-field, quietly to lay aside their arms and at once enter into business and social relations, requires an amount of magnanimity and forbearance that human nature in general does not possess.

At the close of the Civil War in the United States, the South was in a much weaker condition than the North. An attempt had been made to set up a new and separate government, but the attempt had failed utterly. The Union armies had overrun whole sections of the South and left the country desolate. The Emancipation Proclamation had put an end to the institution of negro slavery

on which the whole organization of Southern society had
rested. Out of the ruins of the old must arise a new society
organized on an entirely different basis. It was inevitable that there should be social disturbances and acts of
violence while so great a change was in progress.[1]

Before the passions of war had subsided, however, and
an opportunity had been given the Southerners to accom-
modate themselves to the new order of things, new causes
for irritation and animosity appeared. Politically, the
reconstruction policy adopted by the Federal Congress,
by its lack of wisdom and of efficient leadership, brought
continued humiliation and annoyance. Socially, there
were two causes of vexation and exasperation which the
people were in no mood to bear. The class of individuals
known as "carpet-baggers," by reason of their mercenary
and malicious conduct, aggravated the people beyond
endurance. The second disturbing element was the
negroes.[2]

The history of the reconstruction period — the mistakes, the misunderstandings, the hostility as between
the whites of the North and of the South; the criminal

[1] In a message written by Governor Clarke of Mississippi in 1865, this
passage occurs: "The terrible contest through which the country has just
passed has aroused in every section the fiercest passions of the human
heart. Lawlessness seems to have culminated in the assassination of
Mr. Lincoln." — Quoted in J. W. Garner's "Reconstruction in Mississippi" (1901), p. 59. The message is printed in the *New York Times*
of June 11, 1865.

[2] See "Report on the Condition of the South," No. 261 of Reports of
Committees of House of Representatives for 2d Sess., 43d Cong., 1874–
75.

See, also, article on "The Southern Question" by Charles Gayarré
in *North American Review*, November and December, 1877 (125: 472).

For a comprehensive view, briefly stated, of the great social changes
begun in the South during the reconstruction period, see editorial "The
Way Out," in *Outlook*, Dec. 26, 1903 (75: 984).

dishonesty and knavery of the "carpet-bag governments";
the ignorance and lawlessness prevailing among the
negroes — all this may be read elsewhere. Without attempting to fix the blame for the anomalous condition of
affairs, it is sufficient here to point out that the administration of civil law was only partially and imperfectly
re-established, and that for that reason, and for other
reasons, there was an unusual amount of disorder and
violence prevailing over the country. The proof of this
is to be found not only in the daily newspapers, but also
in the records of the proceedings and debates in Congress
during the twelve years from 1865 to 1877, and especially
in the thirteen volumes embodying the report of the joint
select committee appointed by Congress to investigate
affairs in the insurrectionary States with reference to the
Ku-Klux conspiracy.[1] It is to this so-called Ku-Klux
conspiracy that attention is here to be directed. The
mystery connected with the organization known as the
Ku-Klux Klan and the peculiar history and subsequent
influence of the organization makes it necessary to speak
of it here in some detail.[2]

In May, 1866, a number of young men in the town of
Pulaski, in Giles County, Tennessee, formed a secret

[1] See Reports of Committees of House of Representatives for 2d
Sess., 42d Cong., 1871–72.

[2] The best apparently reliable source for information as to the character and purpose of this organization is a little book entitled "The Ku-
Klux Klan," written by J. C. Lester and D. L. Wilson, and published
at Nashville, Tennessee, in 1884. See also, article "The Ku-Klux Klan,"
signed D. L. Wilson, published in the *Century Magazine*, July, 1884
(6: 398).

A less valuable but an interesting book is "K. K. K. Sketches," by
J. M. Beard, published at Philadelphia in 1877.

Many writers make incidental reference to the Ku-Klux Klan; for
example, Charles Stearns: "The Black Man of the South and the Rebels"

society for the purpose of diversion and amusement to which they gave the name "Ku-Klux Klan."[1] The mystery connected with the name — mysterious because it was meaningless and alliterative — gave it a peculiar potency. This was manifest not only in the impression made by it on the general public, but likewise in the weird influence that it had on the members of the Klan themselves. They had adopted a mysterious name; thereupon the original plan was modified so as to make everything connected with the order harmonize with the name. Amusement was kept as the end in view, but the methods by which they were to obtain it were those of secrecy and mystery. When the report of the committee on rules and ritual came up for consideration, the recommendations were modified to adapt them to the new idea. The report as finally adopted provided for the following officers: a Grand Cyclops or President, a Grand Magi or Vice-President, a Grand Turk or Marshal, a Grand Exchequer or Treasurer, and two Lictors who were the outer and inner guards of the "Den," as the place of meeting was designated.

(1872), Chap. 39; James Bryce: "The American Commonwealth," II, 479.

An account of "The Ku-Klux Movement" is given in W. G. Brown's "Lower South in American History" (1902).

Some of the characteristic, possibly exaggerated, features of the "Ku-Klux Movement" have been presented in fiction. See, for example, A. Conan Doyle: "Adventures of Sherlock Holmes, The Five Orange Pips" (1902), p. 104; Thomas Nelson Page: "Red Rock, a chronicle of Reconstruction" (1898).

[1] The committee appointed to select a name reported among others the name "Kukloi," from the Greek word *kuklos*, meaning a band or circle. At mention of this some one cried out: "Call it 'Ku Klux.'" The word "Klan" at once suggested itself, and was added to complete the alliteration. It has been said that the society was named in imitation of the click heard in cocking the rifle, but this seems to be without foundation in fact.

The members bound themselves by oath to maintain profound and absolute secrecy with reference to the order and everything pertaining to it. This obligation prohibited those who assumed it from disclosing that they were Ku Klux, or the name of any other member, and from soliciting any one to become a member. Each member was required to provide himself with the following outfit: A white mask, a tall cardboard hat so constructed as to increase the wearer's apparent height, a gown or robe of sufficient length to cover the entire person. The matter of color and material was left to the individual's taste and fancy, and each selected what in his judgment would be the most hideous and fantastic. Each member carried also a small whistle with which, by means of a code of signals agreed upon, they held communications with one another.

The "den" was at first in the law office of a member of the Pulaski bar, where the suggestion for the formation of the Klan had been made. But the room was small, and it was too near the business portion of the town to be a suitable place for meeting. On the brow of a ridge that runs along the western outskirts of the town there stood at that time the ruins of an old residence that had been partially demolished by a cyclone. Underneath the portion that remained standing was a large cellar. No other houses stood near, and around these ruins were the storm-torn, limbless trunks of trees which had once formed a magnificent grove. This dreary, desolate and uncanny place was in every way most suitable for a "den," and the Klan appropriated it. When a meeting was held one Lictor was stationed near the house and the other fifty yards from it on the road leading into the town. These were dressed in the fantastic regalia of the order and bore tremendous spears as the badge of their office.

At the close of the war, when the young men of the South who had escaped death on the battle-field returned to their homes, they passed through a period of enforced inactivity. They could not engage at once in business or professional pursuits. In the case of many, business habits were broken up. Few had capital to enter mercantile or agricultural enterprises. There was also a total lack of the amusements and social diversions which prevail wherever society is in a normal condition. The reaction, therefore, which followed the excitement of army scenes and service was intense.

It is not strange, then, that this secret society with its mysterious name and grotesque disguises should awaken profound curiosity in the town of Pulaski. By means of subterfuges members were easily secured without direct solicitation and the order rapidly increased in size. By the time the eligible material in the town had been used up, the young men from the country, whose curiosity had been inflamed by the newspaper notices, began to come in and apply for admission to the Klan. Then "dens" were established at various points in the country. Sometimes a stranger from other parts of Tennessee, or from Mississippi, Alabama, or Texas, visiting in a neighborhood where the order prevailed, would be initiated and on his departure carry with him permission to establish a "den" at home. In fact this was often done without such permission, and thus the connecting link between these "dens" was very fragile. It was only by a sort of tacit agreement that the Pulaski Klan was regarded as the source of power and authority. This was the condition of affairs in April, 1867. During the fall and winter of 1866, the growth of the Klan had been rapid, and it had spread over a wide extent of territory. So far there had appeared no need for a compact organization, rigid rules, and close supervision. The leading members of the Klan were contemplating nothing more serious than amusement. They enjoyed the baffled curiosity and wild speculations of a mystified public even more than the rude sport afforded by the ludicrous initiations.

About this time the combined operation of several causes led to the transformation of the Ku-Klux Klan into a band of "regulators." These causes may be grouped under three heads: (1) The impressions made by the order upon the minds of those who united with it; (2) The impressions upon the public by its weird and mysterious methods; (3) The anomalous and peculiar condition of affairs in the South at this time.

The prevalent idea seems to have been that the Klan contemplated some great and important mission. When admitted to membership this conclusion, in the case of many, was deepened rather than removed by what they saw and heard. There was nothing in the ritual or the obligation or in any part of the ceremony to favor such a conclusion; but the impression still remained that this mysteriousness and secrecy, the high-sounding titles of the officers, the grotesque dress of the members, and the formidable obligation, all meant more than mere sport. Each had his own speculations as to what was to be the character of the serious work which the Klan had to do, but many were satisfied that there was such work.

When the meetings first began to be held in the dilapidated house on the hill passers-by were frequent. Most of them passed the grim and ghostly sentinel by the roadside in silence, but always with a quickened step. Occasionally one would stop and ask: "Who are you?" In awfully sepulchral tones the invariable answer was: "A spirit from the other world. I was killed at Chickamauga." Such an answer, especially when given to a superstitious negro, was extremely terrifying and if, in addition, he heard the uproarious noises issuing from the "den" at the moment of a candidate's investiture with the "regal crown," he had the foundation for a most awe-inspiring story. There came from the country similar stories. The belated laborer, passing after nightfall some lonely and secluded spot, heard horrible noises and saw fearful sights. These stories were repeated with such embellishments as the imagination of the narrator suggested until the feeling of the negroes and of many of the white people, at mention of the Ku-Klux, was one of awe and terror.

In the country it was noticed that the nocturnal perambulations of the colored population diminished or entirely ceased wherever the Ku-Klux appeared. In many ways there was a noticeable improvement in the habits of a large class which had hitherto been causing great annoyance. In this way the Klan gradually realized that the most powerful devices ever invented for controlling the ignorant and superstitious were in their hands. Even the most highly cultured were unable wholly to resist the weird and peculiar feeling which pervaded every community where the Ku-Klux appeared. Circumstances made it evident that the measures and methods employed for sport might be effectually used to subserve the public welfare — to suppress lawlessness and protect property. The very force of circumstances carried the Klan away from its original purpose, so that in the summer of 1867 it was virtually a band of regulators, honestly, but in an injudicious and dangerous way, trying to protect property and preserve peace and order.

It was this conception of the mission of the Klan which led to its reorganization on a plan corresponding to its increased size and new purpose. Some abuses of what was by common consent the law of the Klan and some other evils had already made their appearance. It was hoped also that this danger could be effectually guarded against by reorganization. With these objects in view the Grand Cyclops of the Pulaski "den" sent out a request to all the "dens" of which he had knowledge, to appoint delegates to meet in convention at Nashville, Tennessee, early in the summer of 1867. At the time appointed this convention was held and delegates were present from a number of States.

A plan of reorganization, previously prepared, was submitted to this convention and adopted. The territory covered by the Klan was designated as the "Invisible Empire." This was subdivided into "realms" coterminous with the boundaries of the States. The "realms" were divided into "dominions," corresponding to congressional districts, the "dominions" into "provinces" coterminous with counties, and the "provinces" into "dens." The officers were the Grand Wizard of the Invisible Empire and his ten Genii, the Grand Dragon of the Realm and his eight Hydras, the Grand Titan of the Dominion and his six Furies, the Grand Cyclops of the Den and his two Night Hawks, and other minor officers. The declaration of principles and objects prescribed loyalty to the United States government and opposition to lawlessness and violence of every kind. No material change was made in the methods of the Klan's operations. The essential features of mystery, secrecy, and grotesqueness were retained, but steps were taken with a view to deepening and intensifying the impressions already made upon the public mind. Henceforth the Ku-Klux courted publicity as assiduously as they had formerly seemed to shun it. They appeared at different points at the same time and always when and where they were least expected. Devices were multiplied to deceive people in regard to their numbers and to play upon the fears of the superstitious. On the night of July 4, 1867, public parades were made in many towns in Tennessee.

For several years there existed in the South a spurious and perverted form of the "Union League." Against this organization the Ku-Klux directed their efforts, and this has given color to the assertion that the Ku-Klux Klan was a political organization having only political ends in view. The "Union Leagues" in the South, or the "Loyal Leagues" as they were sometimes called, were generally composed of the disorderly element of the negro population and led by white men who were then considered the basest and meanest of men, the "carpet-baggers" and "scalawags." The depredations committed

by members of these organizations and the general lawlessness then prevailing constitutes the justification for
the Ku-Klux Klan taking upon itself the duty of a vigilance society. In justification of the devices which were
used to terrorize the negroes, it was held that it was not
only better to deter the negroes from theft and other lawlessness in this way than to put them in the penitentiary,
but it was the only way at this time by which they could
be controlled. The jails would not contain them; the
courts could not or would not try them.

At first the Klan seemed to exercise a wholesome influence, but the good effect was short-lived. The order
contained within itself sources of weakness. The devices and disguises by which the Klan deceived outsiders
enabled all who were so disposed, even its own members,
to practice deception on the Klan itself. It placed in the
hands of its own members the facility to do deeds of violence for the gratification of personal feeling and have
them credited to the Klan. Many deeds of violence were
thus done by men who were Ku-Klux, but who, while
acting under cover of their connection with the Klan, were
not under its orders. In addition to this the very class
which the Klan proposed to hold in check and awe into
good behavior soon became wholly unmanageable. Those
who had formerly committed depredations to be laid to
the charge of the negroes, after a brief interval of good
behavior, assumed the guise of Ku-Klux and returned
to their old ways. Outrages were committed by masked
men in regions far remote from any Ku-Klux organizations. Secrecy was the strength of the Ku-Klux Klan so
long as it was conjoined with mystery, but when the masks

and disguises ceased to be mysterious, secrecy was its greatest weakness.

Causes were at work also which led the Klan to adopt measures of greater severity. It had come to pass that all the disorder done in the country was charged upon the Ku-Klux because done under disguises which they had invented and used. They felt that the charge of wrong was unfairly brought against them, and, as is frequently the case, they were carried beyond the limits of prudence and right by a hot zeal for self-vindication against unjust aspersions. The mystery and secrecy that had been courted by the Klan led to the Klan and its objects being wholly misunderstood and misinterpreted. Many people were sure that the Klan meant treason and revolution. A feeling of intense hostility succeeded the first impressions of awe and terror which the Klan had inspired. The negroes formed organizations of a military character the avowed purpose of which was "to make war upon and exterminate the Ku-Klux." On several occasions the Klan was fired into. The effect of such attacks was to provoke counter hostility from the Klan, and so there was irritation and counter irritation till in some places the state of things was little short of open warfare.

Matters continued to grow worse until it was imperatively necessary that there should be interference on the part of the government. In September, 1868, the legislature of Tennessee, in obedience to the call of Governor Brownlow, assembled in extra session and passed a most stringent anti-Ku-Klux statute. In some sections of the State a reign of terror followed and the governor was compelled to send troops and proclaim martial law in certain counties. In March, 1869, the Grand Wizard of the Invisible Empire issued a proclamation to his subjects. This proclamation recited the legislation directed against the Klan and stated that the order had in large measure accomplished the objects of its existence. At a time when the civil law afforded inadequate protection to life and property, when robbery and lawlessness of every description were unrebuked, when all the better elements of society were in constant dread for the safety of their property, persons, and families, the Klan had afforded protection and security to many firesides and in many ways contributed to the public welfare. But greatly to the regret of all good citizens, some members of the Klan had violated positive orders; others, under the name and disguises of the organization, had assumed to do acts of violence, for which the Klan was held responsible. The Grand Wizard had been invested with the power to determine questions of paramount importance to the interests of the order. Therefore, in the exercise of that power, the Grand Wizard declared that the organization that had been known as the Ku-Klux Klan was dissolved and disbanded.

For several years after March, 1869, the papers reported and commented on "Ku-Klux outrages" committed at various places.[1] The authors of these outrages no doubt acted in the name of the Klan and under its disguises, and it may be that in some cases they were men who had been Ku-Klux, but it cannot be charged that

---

[1] See, for example, *Nation*, March 23, 1871 (12: 192); *New York Times*, Feb. 15, 1871; *New York Times*, Aug. 26, 1873; *New York Tribune*, July 31, 1878.

they were acting by the authority of the order. The report of the joint committee of Congress appointed to investigate the "Ku-Klux conspiracy" records a great deal
of lawlessness and violence during the period 1866–71,
a part of which may be justly attributed to the Klan.
The greater part of the outrageous conduct attributed to
the Klan belongs to a date subsequent to its disband-
ment, and is chargeable merely to the influence of the
operations of the Klan. As one writer has put it, the
birth of this order was an accident, its growth a comedy,
and its death a tragedy. Its existence can be explained
only when the anomalous condition of social and political
affairs in the South during the years immediately succeeding the war is taken into account.

In this discussion of the conditions in the Southern
States which promoted recourse to lynch-law, it must
not be forgotten that at the same time the frontier type
of lynch-law was in vogue in the West. The tide of
immigration toward that part of the United States, which
had set in early in the fifties, continued with increased
vigor after the close of the Civil War. While the establishment of Territorial government, followed by admission
to the Union and State government, was remarkably
expeditious in the West, yet there was constant occasion
for recourse to lynch-law against desperadoes and persons
guilty of stealing live stock. In other sections of the
country, also, lynch-law was in operation.[1] The following statistics, obtained from an examination of the files

[1] For a list of the "Molly Maguire" outrages in the mining region of
Pennsylvania, and for an exposition of the origin, growth, and character
of that organization, see F. P. Dewees: "The Molly Maguires" (1877).

of the New York Times for the three years, 1871–73, give some idea of the distribution and character of lynchings at that time [1]:

Kentucky: 2 negroes hung for rape, 1 white hung for rape, 1 negro hung for murder, 3 negroes shot by masked men, 1 negro "murdered" by Ku-Klux.

Tennessee: 2 negroes hung for robbery and arson, 1 negro shot and hung for robbery and murder, 1 negro shot for attempted outrage, 1 negro hung and shot for murder, 1 white shot for murder of wife.

Missouri: 5 horse thieves hung, 1 negro hung for outrage, 1 white hung for murder, 3 whites hung for murder and robbery, 3 whites shot for defending and being bondsmen of county officials accused of peculation.

California: 2 whites hung for murder, 1 white hung and shot for murder, 1 Indian hung for murder, 1 Malay (steward of steamer) shot and thrown overboard near coast of California for ravishing sick girl, eleven years old.

Montana: 2 whites hung for murder.

Louisiana: 4 negroes hung for murder, 3 horse thieves hung.

Virginia: 1 desperado, horse thief and murderer hung.

Alabama: 1 white shot for murder.

South Carolina: 2 whites shot for murder, 10 negroes shot and hung by Ku-Klux.

Nevada: 1 desperado hung, 1 white hung for killing man in saloon row.

---

[1] No claim for completeness is made in regard to these statistics. Particularly in the case of lynchings in the West they are doubtless incomplete.

Wisconsin; 1 white hung for murder.

Indiana: 3 negroes hung for murder, 1 white hung for murder.

Nebraska: 1 negro and 1 white man "killed" for robbery and shooting woman.

Kansas: 2 whites hung for murder, 1 desperado and 1 horse thief "killed in jail."

Colorado: 2 whites hung for keeping gambling outfit.

Michigan: 2 whites died from beating which they received for killing a man in a German-Irish riot on the streets.

Ohio: 2 whites hung for murder.

Maryland: 1 negro hung for arson.

Total: 41 whites, 32 negroes, 1 Malay, 1 Indian.

The majority of those lynched in these three years, as given by the Times, were forcibly taken from the custody of officers of the law. In some instances, the jails were broken into, and the prisoners were taken out and hanged or were killed in the jail; in other instances, the prisoners were taken from the officers and put to death before they could be taken to the jail. Some of the lynchings were carried on by vigilance societies, others by mobs of masked persons or by "Ku-Kluxes." With two exceptions, nothing is said in the reports of these lynchings about any attempts to take legal action against the lynchers. In the two instances where attempts were made to prosecute the lynchers, it does not appear that there was any measure of success.

It thus appears that lynch-law was in operation in nearly every part of the United States during the years immediately following the close of the Civil War, and that the ordinary penalty inflicted was death. It was, however, the application of lynch-law under the anomalous conditions in the South that rendered the reconstruction period a distinctive period in the history of lynch-law. The reconstruction of the Southern States has been rightly characterized as "one of the worst periods of misgovernment and maladministration in the history of any civilized community."[1] The emancipation of the slaves and the reconstruction policy carried out by the political leaders in Congress not only brought about a changed relation between the two races, but made negro domination a real evil and an imminent danger. The Southern planters considered themselves justified in resorting to summary measures as a means of protecting their property and their families. Both the social and the political conditions in the South were such as to give a distinctively new impulse to the lynching spirit.[2]

It is true that the extreme measures taken under Ku-Klux disguises never received the approval of the mass of the Southern people, but, on the other hand, few determined efforts were made by the civil authorities in the Southern States to bring Ku-Klux offenders to justice. The outrage upon freedmen, persons of Northern origin

[1] *Outlook*, Dec. 26, 1903 (75: 984).

[2] Compare the opinion expressed in the *Nation*, Sept. 7, 1876 (23: 145) on the subject of "intimidation" at the South. In the year 1879, a "Negro exodus from the Southern States" took place, which, on account of it size and character, attracted considerable attention. Numerous reasons were assigned as the cause. See F. L. Hoffman: "Race Traits and Tendencies of the American Negro." — Publications of the American Economic Association, August, 1896 (11: 1); *Nation*, April 10, 1879 (28: 239, 242); Report and Testimony of the Select Committee of the U. S. Senate to investigate the causes of the removal of the negroes from the Southern States to the Northern States, 2d Sess., 46th Cong. (Washington, 1880).

and Southerners accused of favoring the reconstruction acts of Congress, were not stopped until after Congress had passed the so-called "force bill" in 1871. By this measure the jurisdiction of the Federal courts was extended to Ku-Klux cases, and the President was authorized to suspend the writ of *habeas corpus* when necessary to preserve order. The Federal troops were not entirely withdrawn from the South until 1877.

As a result of the doings of reconstruction times, habits of lawlessness have been perpetuated at the South, the effect of which is still to be seen. The disguises introduced by the Ku-Klux[1] have frequently given security against identification at lynchings in recent years. The modern "White Caps," so well known in the central and eastern States as well as in the South, though they are merely local and generally only temporary organizations, use the same methods that were employed by the Ku-Klux. The "White Caps" may be regarded as the successors of the Ku-Klux.

[1] It is of interest to note that the Sons of Liberty of the period 1765–1775 seem to have had a regular organization and that in their use of disguises and in their methods they were not wholly unlike the Ku-Klux.

CHAPTER VI

Lynchings

In recent years, particularly since about the year 1891, much has been said and written upon the subject of lynching. Explanations and excuses have been offered for the prevalence of the practice in the South and in other parts of the country. Remedies and means for the suppression of lynchings have been freely and widely discussed. Most of the literature, however, shows a strong sectional or partisan spirit, and is, in reality, but little more than the expression of personal opinion. Scarcely any attempt has been made to present the general facts relating to the practice of lynching for any considerable length of time. The perusal of more than seventy-five magazine articles discussing recent lynchings and dealing with different phases of the subject left upon the writer's mind no impression more distinct than this, that some facts of a statistical nature were very much needed.

The first plan that suggested itself was to make a personal investigation of the cases of lynching that have occurred in recent years, to interview personally or to correspond with individuals acquainted with the facts in such occurrences, and thus get some reliable data. Such a plan, however, has by trial been found impracticable. Mr. George C. Holt of New York had an examination made of the index and files of the New York Daily Times for the first six months of the year 1892, and a record made of all the instances of lynching reported there. His experience can best be given in his own words. He says:

"After obtaining a list of the cases reported in the Times, I drafted a circular letter of inquiry asking for information in respect to the name, age, residence, and occupation of the man lynched, the charge against him, his possible guilt, the circumstances of the lynching, and what steps, if any, were afterwards taken. In each reported case of lynching I mailed three copies of the circular letter, with a stamped envelope for reply, addressed one to the district attorney of the county, one to the postmaster, and one to any clergyman of the city or town where the lynching occurred.

"To the printed circulars sent out answers were received in relation to 16 out of the 30 cases of lynching. No answers were received in 14 of the cases, although the envelopes bore the usual direction to the postmaster to be returned if not delivered, and only one of them was returned. Of the 16 cases in respect to which answers were received, there were 3 cases in which 3 answers were returned, 5 in which 2 were returned, and 8 in which one was returned. Most of the answers were unsigned; many were very vague; a few declined to state the facts; and several requested secrecy. The general impression derived from the attempt to obtain information by the circular was that there was, in many cases, a strong disinclination, for some cause, to give any information." [1]

In an attempt to verify some reports of lynchings in

[1] "Lynching and Mobs," *American Journal of Social Science*, No. 32, p. 67 (November, 1894).

the years 1902 and 1903, the writer has met with a similar experience. A letter addressed to the mayor of a town in Arkansas was returned with the following penciled at the bottom of the sheet: "if you will give me some idea as to your reasons for wanting this information I might give you some information regarding same." A letter addressed to the mayor of a town in Georgia was returned with the following written at the bottom of the sheet: "In answer to the above I will say that I don't know anything about it." No name was signed in either case. These two replies, together with Mr. Holt's experience, are sufficient to indicate the difficulties attendant upon the collection, by any such method, of data in regard to lynchings covering any considerable period of time.

For more than twenty-two years the Chicago Tribune has published at the close of each year an itemized summary of the disasters and crimes in the United States for the year. An editorial in the Tribune for January 1, 1883, reads as follows: "Elsewhere in this issue will be found a series of reviews of the happenings during 1882. A necrological table is furnished, also a list of the more important crimes, casualties, suicides, lynchings, and judicial executions for the last year. The tables have been prepared with great care from the columns of *The Tribune*, and furnish as complete a review of the unpleasant features of the dead year as could possibly be obtained."

This annual review published by the Tribune supplies the most available and practically the only source for statistics of lynchings. The following facts are given: the date of the lynching, the name of the victim, his color and his nationality, the alleged crime for which he was lynched, and the town and State where the lynching took place. Only the names of those who have suffered death at the hands of mobs are included. No account is taken of attempted lynchings or of persons to whom mob violence was done but who recovered from their injuries.

In using this record as the basis of this investigation such means as were available have been employed for purposes of correction and verification. In every case where an error was apparent, or there was any reason for doubt, the original report of the lynching has been examined in some newspaper of the proper date, either the Chicago Tribune, or the New York Times, or the New York Tribune. Only a very few points have been left unsettled because of insufficient information. The Cyclopedic Review of Current History gives confirmatory evidence for a period covering the last twelve years. It, however, mentions only the "notable crimes" and this evidence, therefore, applies to a comparatively small number of cases.

For the last six months of the year 1902 a subscription to a newspaper clipping agency was maintained as a further means of determining the reliability and completeness of the Tribune record. The agency selected was an old and well established one. Instructions were given the readers to send full accounts of every lynching, together with a few editorial comments from various parts of the country. Clippings on lynchings were received from newspapers in every section of the United States. Out of the fifty-three victims of lynching given in the summary published by the Chicago Tribune for the six months, July—December, 1902, forty-six were reported by the newspaper clipping agency and no errors of any importance were shown. A few additional cases were mentioned in the clippings, but they were mainly on the border line between murder and lynching and could rightly be disregarded.

Undoubtedly there are errors and inaccuracies in particular cases in the Tribune record.[1] Any one who has endeavored to sift the truth from conflicting newspaper reports will readily appreciate the difficulty of obtaining an accurate account of a lynching from such a source. For the purpose of this investigation, however, only the most general facts are required, and it is believed that in regard to these the reporter or the newspaper correspondent is less likely to indulge his imaginative powers. Furthermore, by reason of the popular excitement which usually attends lynching-bees and the extraordinary methods of execution oftentimes employed, it is fair to presume that but few lynchings escape the reporter; the details of most lynchings exhibit so clearly the journalistic idea of facts of contemporaneous human interest that the publication of such news is not often intentionally omitted. There is neither the motive nor the opportunity to keep lynchings from the newspapers that there often is in the case of suicides and murders; not only indeed is every

[1] Edward Leigh Pell, writing on "Prevention of Lynch-law Epidemics," in the *Review of Reviews*, March, 1898 (17: 321), questions the accuracy of the *Tribune* figures for Alabama, Florida, and Virginia in the year 1897. It is to be noted, however, that he refers to lynchings and seems to have regarded number of lynchings as synonymous with number of persons lynched.

such motive for secrecy absent, but there is usually, more or less strongly expressed, a public sentiment approving or excusing a lynching.

What the likelihood is of every lynching in the United States having been reported to the Chicago Tribune during the last twenty-two years, and whether the probability has been uniform throughout the period, there is no means of determining. The annual review of disasters and crimes has, however, been made a special feature throughout the period, and this gives at least a presumption in favor of fullness and completeness in the record. It is at any rate safe to say that the cases of lynching actually reported probably afford a fair average basis of cases for statistical investigation.

In view of these considerations, together with the corrections and verifications that have been made, it is believed that the Tribune record has reliability sufficient for its examination to lead to the deduction of trustworthy and valuable conclusions.

On January 1, 1904, the Chicago Tribune published the following "table of lynchings" covering the last nineteen years[1]:

1885	184	1890	127
1886	138	1891	192
1887	122	1892	235
1888	142	1893	200
1889	176	1894	190

[1] In a recent article, entitled "The Facts about Lynching," written by George P. Upton, who for a number of years has been associate-editor of the *Tribune*, a similar table may be found. [See the *Independent*, Sept. 29, 1904 (57: 719)]. In this table, however, there are numerous inaccuracies, and the fact that Mr. Upton does not discriminate between number of lynchings and number of persons lynched detracts materially from the value of all of his statistical summaries on the subject.

1895..........171	1900..........115
1896..........131	1901..........135
1897..........166	1902.......... 96
1898..........127	1903..........104
1899..........107	

After carefully going over the lists of names, as published each year, of the persons lynched during the last twenty-two years, the writer obtained the following table which is based throughout on the number of persons lynched. If only the number of lynchings were taken into account the numbers given would be considerably smaller.[1]

NUMBER OF PERSONS LYNCHED

1882..........114	1893..........200
1883..........134	1894..........197
1884..........211	1895..........180
1885..........184	1896..........131
1886..........138	1897..........165
1887..........122	1898..........127
1888..........142	1899..........107
1889..........176	1900..........115
1890..........128	1901..........135
1891..........195	1902.......... 97
1892..........235	1903..........104

Total.......3337

This table agrees with the Tribune table for the nineteen years with the exception of the years 1890, 1891, 1894, 1895, 1897 and 1902. In some of these cases the difference is due merely to an error which had been made in footing up the lists. Some instances are given of a father and son being lynched, or of five horse thieves, or of two negroes, and each of these instances had been

[1] Compare p. 182.

counted as one in making up the totals. In other cases
an error was found in the instance reported. In 1902, a
report of a negro having been lynched for murder in Alabama was found later to be untrue and his name was
dropped from the list.[1] Two names have been added
to the list for 1902 from information which the writer
obtained through the newspaper clipping agency and
subsequent correspondence.

In 1903 a record of persons lynched, kept by the writer
from newspapers other than the Chicago Tribune,[2] contained sixty-three out of the one hundred and four reported by the Tribune, and corroborated the Tribune
record with reference to these sixty-three. In the writer's
record seven lynchings were reported which did not
appear in the Tribune record. Letters of inquiry in regard to these resulted in only four replies, one denying
that the reported lynching had taken place, the remaining three not stating definitely whether any lynching
whatsoever had taken place. No alteration, therefore, has
been made in the Tribune record for 1903.

Chart I has been prepared from the above table and
shows at a glance the relative prevalence of lynching
during the twenty-two years, 1882–1903.[3] The solid line,

---

[1] The negro had escaped from the mob and gone to a neighboring
county where he gave himself up to the authorities for protection. Later,
according to a letter received by the writer from the mayor of the town
where he sought protection, he was taken back by the sheriff and brought
before a justice for a preliminary hearing. The evidence was considered
insufficient to bind him over to the grand jury and he was released.

[2] Principally New York City and New Haven, Conn., papers.

[3] To be strictly accurate the number of lynchings should be taken
rather than the number of persons lynched, but for the purpose of comparison from year to year the latter may be considered sufficiently exact.
See p. 185.

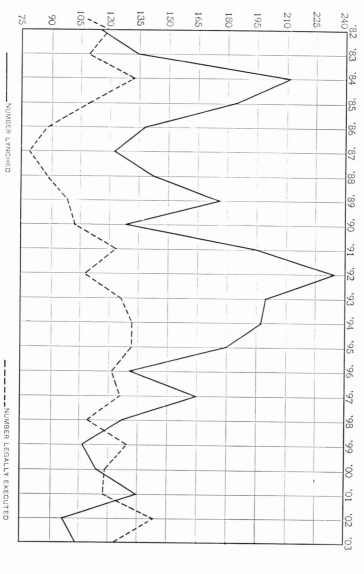

1. NUMBER LYNCHED COMPARED WITH NUMBER LEGALLY EXECUTED 1882-1903

——————— NUMBER LYNCHED

– – – – – NUMBER LEGALLY EXECUTED

II. NUMBER LYNCHED ACCORDING TO MONTHS IN DIFFERENT SECTIONS OF THE U.S. 1882-1903

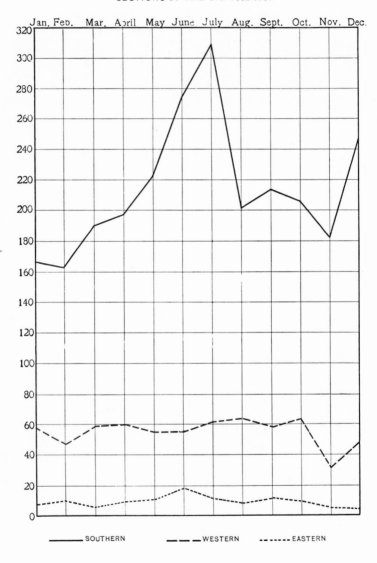

SOUTHERN ━━━━━   WESTERN ━ ━ ━   EASTERN ▪▪▪▪▪▪

representing the number of persons lynched, begins at
114 in 1882, goes up to 211 in 1884, falls to 122 in 1887,
rises again to 176 in 1889, falls again the following year
to 128, and then rises to 235 in the year 1892. From
1892 on the line shows a general downward tendency.

The large number in 1884 was due to the work of
vigilantes in Montana and Colorado. According to the
record, 40 horse thieves and cattle thieves received summary justice in Montana during the year and the lynching of seventeen cattle thieves was reported from Colorado.
The large number in 1892 was due to the lynching of
negroes in the South. These facts are shown in another
form in Chart IV.

For purposes of comparison the broken line has been
drawn on Chart I to represent the number of persons
legally executed during the twenty-two years. The
figures for legal executions have also been taken from the
Tribune record, but no further verification has been made
of them than merely to foot up the lists of names and
verify the totals. The Tribune record of legal executions
is no doubt incomplete, but it is here given for what it is
worth. In a general way the broken line follows the
solid line with the exception of the year 1892 and the last
five years. In the review of the year 1881, the Tribune
reported ninety-one legal executions but gave no record
of lynchings. To indicate the direction of the broken
line previous to 1882 a short line has been drawn at the
left of the chart.

On the whole, Chart I seems to indicate a relationship
between legal executions and lynchings. There is an
indication that the upward tendency in the broken line

since 1887 may have contributed to the downward tendency in the solid line since 1892 — the punishment of crimes by law may tend to make recourse to lynching less frequent. Another factor is needed, however, to make this reasoning conclusive; some way of measuring the amount of crime in the country during these several years is requisite. For this purpose the writer took the number of murders reported by the Tribune and plotted them on a trial chart in connection with the number lynched and the number legally executed. The result was so unsatisfactory and inconclusive, however, that any attempt to make such a comparison was abandoned.[1]

In Chart II is shown the number of persons lynched according to months throughout the twenty-two years, 1882–1903. Because of the difference in the characteristics of lynchings in different sections of the United States, and because of the differences in climate, the States have been divided into three groups as follows: (1) The Southern Group, comprising Maryland, Virginia, West Virginia, North Carolina, South Carolina, Georgia, Florida, Kentucky, Tennessee, Alabama, Mississippi, Missouri, Arkansas, Louisiana, and Texas; (2) The Western Group, comprising all the other States and Territories west of the Mississippi River; (3) The Eastern Group, comprising all the other States east of the Mississippi River.

In the Southern Group the fewest are lynched in the months of January, February, and November. The

[1] Henry M. Boies has shown from the *Tribune* record of murders that there has been, within the last twenty years, "an alarming increase of homicides, accompanied by a proportionate decrease of executions by law and lynching." — "Science of Penology" (1901), p. 120.

largest number are lynched in June, July, and December. By dividing the twenty-two years into three periods and drawing lines to show the monthly fluctuations for each of these periods, it can be shown that these same tendencies are characteristic of shorter periods of time, the tendency toward an increase in December being less marked, however, in the period 1896–1903. Several explanations suggest themselves. Perhaps the best explanation of the fall in the line from the high point in June and July to a much lower point in August is suggested by the fact that since most of the persons lynched in the Southern Group are negroes and their time is largely occupied with their camp-meetings and various religious exercises during the month of August, — a custom which originated in the time of slavery,[1] — they commit a smaller number of crimes against the whites and thus there is less occasion for lynching during that month. During the months of June and July, on the other hand, when there is work to be done in tending the growing crops, disagreements and quarrels frequently arise between the whites and the blacks, the latter often retaliating upon the former by some offense against property or person, thus giving greater occasion for lynching. The increase in December is possibly due to indulgence in excesses and to the commission of a greater number of offenses by the negroes in connection with their celebration of Christmas. Idleness on the part of the negroes probably has much to do with the whole matter. It has long been true that "the Devil finds work for idle hands to do."

[1] See W. S. Drewry: "Slave Insurrections in Virginia" (1900), pp. 22–25.

In the Western Group there is comparatively little variation in the number lynched in the different months. The drop in the line in the months of February and November is probably explained by the fact that those two months are the busy seasons of the year for the cattlemen. The "fall round-up" takes place in November and the "spring round-up" about February.

In the Eastern Group the line shows very little variation in the number lynched in the different months. A slight increase in the month of June is indicated.

Chart III shows the percentages lynched for various causes by months for the entire period of twenty-two years and for the total number of persons lynched in the United States during that time.

Before proceeding to an analysis of this chart a word of explanation is necessary concerning the classification of causes that has been adopted. The various causes assigned for the lynchings in the Tribune record have been grouped into eight classes as follows: Murder, Rape, Assault, Minor Offenses, Desperadism,[1] Theft, Arson, Unknown.

The class Murder includes murder, attempted murder, accessory to murder, suspected murder, alleged murder, conspiracy to murder, complicity in murder.

The class Rape includes rape, attempted rape, alleged rape.

The class Minor Offenses includes race prejudice, mis-

---

[1] The liberty has been taken of coining this word to designate the cause for lynching the class of individuals known as desperadoes. No other word seems to express the idea so clearly. The word "brigandage" is too narrow in meaning and too nearly obsolete; the word "outlawry" is not sufficiently inclusive and is generally used only in its technical sense.

cegenation, and various minor offenses; such as (for whites) wife beating, cruelty, kidnapping, saloon keeping, turning state's evidence, refusing to turn state's evidence, being obnoxious, swindling, political prejudice, seduction, giving information, frauds, informing, protecting a negro, giving evidence, mob indignation, illicit distilling, disorderly conduct, incest, elopement, revenue informer, disreputable character, arrest of a miner, aiding escape of murderer, suspected of killing cattle, prospective elopement; (for negroes) grave robbery, threatened political exposures, slander, self-defense, wife beating, cutting levees, kidnapping, voodooism, poisoning horses, writing insulting letters, incendiary language, swindling, jilting a girl, colonizing negroes, turning state's evidence, political troubles, gambling, quarreling, poisoning wells, throwing stones, unpopularity, making threats, circulating scandals, being troublesome, bad reputation, drunkenness, strike rioting, rioting, insults, supposed offense, insulting women, fraud, criminal abortion, alleged stock poisoning, enticing servant away, writing letter to white woman, asking white woman in marriage, conspiracy, introducing smallpox, giving information, conjuring, to prevent evidence, being disreputable, informing, concealing a criminal, slapping a child, shooting at officer, passing counterfeit money, felony, elopement with white girl, refusing to give evidence, giving evidence, disobeying ferry regulations, running quarantine, violation of contract, paying attention to white girl, resisting assault, inflammatory language, resisting arrest, testifying for one of his own race, keeping gambling-house, quarrel over profit sharing, forcing white boy to commit crime, lawlessness.

The cause "race prejudice" is given, almost without exception, only in the case of the lynching of negroes by whites and does not appear at all in the earlier years of the period 1882–1903. The probable reason for giving race prejudice as a cause for lynching is that no offense had been committed which was considered worthy of mention as a cause. This is borne out by the following instances. On February 22, 1898, a negro by the name of F. B. Baker was lynched at Lake City, South Carolina, for accepting the office of postmaster. In the Tribune record the cause is given as "race prejudice." On February 10, 1894, a negro named Collins was lynched in Georgia for "enticing servant away." One newspaper in reporting this occurrence gave "race prejudice" as the cause. The colored victims credited to "race prejudice" in 1902 by the Tribune were lynched because they were supposed to have made some insulting remarks about several white men. In December, 1903, Eli Hilson, colored, was killed by "Whitecaps" in Lincoln County, Mississippi, because he refused to leave the county in response to their warning. In the Tribune record "race prejudice" is given as the cause for the lynching of Hilson. These facts constitute the justification for placing "race prejudice" under Minor Offenses.

The class Theft includes theft, larceny, burglary, robbery, suspected robbery, safe breaking, cattle stealing, horse stealing, mule stealing.

The class Desperadism includes the action of desperado, outlaw, highway robber, train wrecker, train robber.

The class Arson includes arson, incendiarism, barn burning.

The class Assault includes assault, murderous assault.

The class Unknown includes unknown offense, no offense, without cause, mistaken identity, by accident, no cause given. There are in the lists only a few cases of mistaken identity and only one by accident. They have been put in this class merely because there was no other place to put them.

Where more than one cause was given the following principles of classification have been observed: rape and murder under Rape, robbery and murder under Murder, arson and murder under Murder, assault and robbery under Assault, robbery and arson under Arson.

Throughout this chapter, whenever any one of the above eight classes is meant the word for the class will be begun with a capital letter. This will avoid the danger of confusing the present use of the terms with their ordinary and general use.

In an analysis of Chart III, it appears that smaller percentages of persons are lynched for Murder in the summer months than in the winter months, and that larger percentages are lynched for Rape in the summer months than in the winter months, but that if Murder and Rape be taken together larger percentages are lynched for those crimes in the summer than in the winter. The percentage lynched for Assault shows little variation throughout the year. The percentage lynched for Minor Offenses is also fairly uniform throughout the year.

With regard to Desperadism a marked difference is shown between the summer months and the winter months. Only about one per cent of the lynchings in the summer are for Desperadism, there being none in the month of April, while in January 6.4 per cent, in February 10.5 per cent, in October 4.2 per cent, in November 4.5 per cent, and in December 11.2 per cent are for that cause. The percentage lynched for Theft is relatively high in May, June, and July, but especially high in October. Nearly 20 per cent of the lynchings in October are for Theft. There is a relatively small percentage for Arson in the summer. The larger percentage of lynchings for Arson are in March, September, October, and November.

As to the influence of the seasons on crime, Mayo-Smith states that it has been pretty well determined that crimes against the person are more numerous in summer than in winter, and that crimes against property are more numerous in winter than in summer.[1] Chart III shows conformity to this law of crimes.[2] A larger percentage is lynched for Murder, Rape, and Assault — crimes against the person — in summer than in winter. A larger percentage is lynched for Desperadism, Theft, and Arson, — crimes against property, — in winter than in summer.

Chart IV shows the relative number of whites, negroes, and other persons lynched each year during the last twenty-two years. The largest number of whites were lynched in the year 1884, the majority of them being in the Western Group of States. Since that year there has been a general but irregular decline in the lynching of whites. If the tops of the columns representing the whites were joined together by a line, the line would rise and

---

[1] "Statistics and Sociology" (1900), p. 271.

[2] This may be taken as an indication of the trustworthiness of the *Tribune* record of lynchings as a basis for statistical investigation.

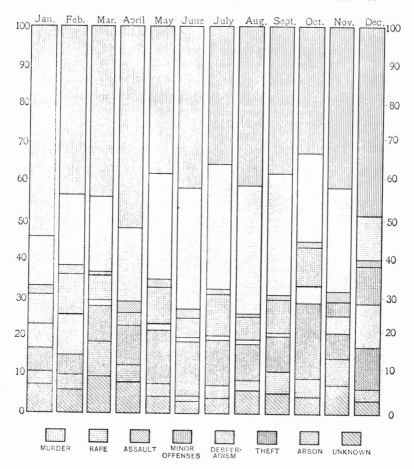

III. PERCENTAGES LYNCHED FOR VARIOUS CAUSES BY MONTHS 1882-1903

MURDER   RAPE   ASSAULT   MINOR OFFENSES   DESPER-ADISM   THEFT   ARSON   UNKNOWN

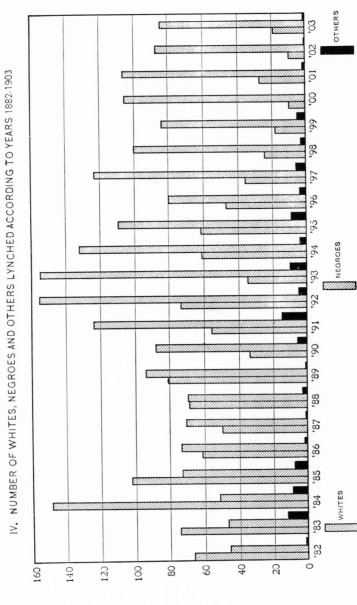

IV. NUMBER OF WHITES, NEGROES AND OTHERS LYNCHED ACCORDING TO YEARS 1882-1903

WHITES

NEGROES

OTHERS

fall with more or less regularity, suggesting the conclusion that lynchings tend to recur in groups from year to year, or, in other words, that the lynching mania spreads in successive waves over the country. If the tops of the columns representing the negroes were joined together by a line, the same tendency would be noticeable, but the waves would appear less regular and less marked. The waves for the whites and the negroes do not correspond at all from year to year, but this perhaps can be explained by the fact that the lynching of negroes is characteristic of the Southern States while the lynching of whites is characteristic of the Western States. There is no psychic connection between the lynching of a negro in the South and the lynching of a murderer or cattle thief in the West.

For the lynching of negroes, 1892 and 1893 are the years in which the largest number were lynched, the numbers being 156 and 155 respectively. The chart shows a general increase in the lynching of negroes from 1882 to 1892, and a general decline from 1893 to 1903. In 1903, however, nearly twice as many negroes were lynched as in 1882. The chart also shows an increase in the proportion of negroes lynched to whites lynched during the period 1882–1903.

The total number of negroes lynched during the twenty-two years is 2,060, an average of 93$\frac{7}{11}$ per year. The total number of whites lynched during the twenty-two years is 1,169, an average of 53$\frac{3}{22}$ per year.

Chart IV also shows, under the title of Others, the comparatively small number (108) of Indians, Mexicans, and foreigners that have been lynched during the twenty-two years. In the years when the larger numbers were lynched they were distributed as follows: in 1883, seven Mexicans, four Indians, and one Chinaman; in 1884, six Mexicans, one Indian, one Japanese, and one Swiss; in 1885, six Chinese and two Indians; in 1891, eleven Italians (at New Orleans), two Indians, and two Chinese; in 1893, five Italians, two Indians, two Mexicans, and one Bohemian; in 1895, five Italians (at Walsenburg, Colorado), two Indians, and two Mexicans. In all, forty-five Indians, twenty-eight Italians, twenty Mexicans, twelve Chinese, one Japanese, one Swiss, and one Bohemian were lynched during the period 1882–1903.

Chart V shows the number of females, both white and colored, lynched each year during the twenty-two years. With the exception of the years 1882, 1883, 1887, and 1899 one or more were lynched each year. In the year 1895, thirteen were lynched, eight colored and five white women. The majority of the colored females were lynched in the five years 1891–95. In all, forty colored and twenty-three white females, or a total of sixty-three females were lynched during the period 1882–1903.

The lower half of Chart V shows the causes for which the females were lynched. Of the whites, nine were lynched for murder or complicity in murder, one for being a disreputable character, one because of mob indignation, one for race prejudice, one for miscegenation, one for arson, two for theft, and seven for unknown reasons.

Of the colored, twenty were lynched for murder or complicity in murder, two for alleged well poisoning, eight for race prejudice, five for arson, one for theft, and four for unknown reasons.

V. NUMBER OF WOMEN (WHITES AND NEGROES) LYNCHED
ACCORDING TO YEARS 1882-1903

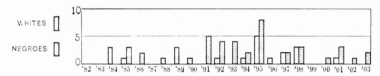

WHITES

NEGROES

PROPORTION LYNCHED FOR VARIOUS CAUSES 1882-1903
WOMEN (WHITES AND NEGROES)

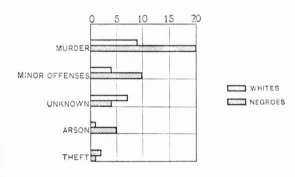

WHITES
NEGROES

VI. PERCENTAGES LYNCHED FOR VARIOUS CAUSES BY YEARS 1882-1903 WHITES AND OTHERS

MURDER RAPE ASSAULT MINOR OFFENSES DESPER-ADISM THEFT ARSON UNKNOWN

Chart V really supplements Chart IV. In Chart IV, the 3,337 persons who have been lynched during the twenty-two years are classified according to race only. In Chart V the number of females in Chart IV is shown and also the causes for which they were lynched. In the further investigation sex will be disregarded and the whites, Indians, Mexicans, and foreigners will be grouped together under the head of Whites and Others, this making a classification into negroes and those not negroes.

Chart VI shows the percentages lynched for various causes by years, 1882–1903, for Whites and Others. The percentages lynched for the various causes vary greatly from year to year. The percentage lynched for Murder varies from 24 per cent to 70 per cent. The percentage lynched for Theft varies from 3.9 per cent to 46.5 per cent. In the three years 1898–1900, and in the year 1903, none were lynched for Theft. The percentage lynched for Rape varies from 1.8 per cent to 20 per cent, none being lynched for that cause in 1902. Rape is not particularly important as a cause. The chief value of Chart VI is seen by contrasting it with Chart VII.

Chart VII shows the percentages lynched for various causes by years, 1882–1903, for Negroes. The percentage lynched for Murder does not vary greatly from year to year, the extreme variation being from 28.2 per cent in the year 1882 to 53 per cent in the year 1898. Rape appears as an important cause, the percentage varying from 22.6 per cent in the year 1901 to 56.5 per cent in the year 1882. The chart indicates in a general way a decrease in the importance of Rape as a cause for the lynching of Negroes since 1882. Minor Offenses, on the contrary, have increased in importance as a cause for the lynching of Negroes. In the later years, also, a larger percentage has been for Assault.

Comparing Charts VI and VII it appears that there is greater uniformity in the percentages lynched for the different causes from year to year in the case of the Negroes than in the case of the Whites and Others. A smaller percentage is lynched for Murder and a much larger percentage is lynched for Rape in the case of the Negroes than in the case of the Whites and Others. For the Negroes, Theft is largely larceny and burglary while for the Whites and Others it is stealing live stock. Desperadism figures to a very limited extent as a cause for lynching Negroes. Assault figures to a very limited extent as a cause for lynching Whites and Others.

Chart VIII shows the proportion lynched for various causes, 1882–1903, for Whites and Others. This chart, like Chart VI, covers the total number of Whites and Others that have been lynched during the period, without reference to particular sections of the country. Murder with 628 stands highest, and Theft, with 264, second. Rape with 109 ranks third as a cause, and Desperadism, with 93, fourth. Minor Offenses is credited with 52, Arson with 31, and Assault with 11. The number lynched which fall under the class Unknown is 89. Of the total number, 49.2 per cent were lynched for Murder, 20.6 per cent for Theft, 8.5 per cent for Rape, 7.3 per cent for Desperadism, 4 per cent for Minor Offenses, 2.4 per cent for Arson, .8 per cent for Assault, and 7 per cent is credited to Unknown. Of those lynched for Theft, nearly 90 per cent were lynched for the crime of stealing live stock.

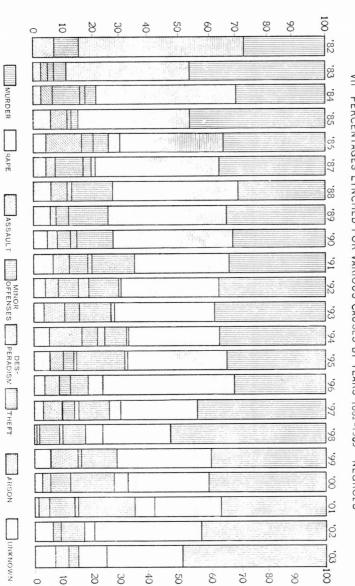

VII PERCENTAGES LYNCHED FOR VARIOUS CAUSES BY YEARS 1882-1903 NEGROES

VIII. PROPORTION LYNCHED FOR VARIOUS CAUSES 1882-1903 WHITES AND OTHERS

Chart IX shows the proportion lynched for various causes, 1882–1903, for Negroes. This chart, like the preceding chart, covers the total number of Negroes that have been lynched during the period, without reference to particular sections of the country. By far the greater number of Negroes have been lynched either for Murder or for Rape. Murder is credited with 783 and Rape with 707. Minor Offenses with 208 ranks third as a cause for the lynching of Negroes, and Arson, with 104, fourth. Theft with 101 ranks fifth. Assault is credited with 47 and Desperadism with 20. To the class Unknown 90 are credited. Of the total number, 38 per cent were lynched for Murder, 34.3 per cent for Rape, 10.1 per cent for Minor Offenses, 5 per cent for Arson, 4.9 per cent for Theft, 2.3 per cent for Assault, .9 per cent for Desperadism, and 4.3 per cent is credited to Unknown. Of the Negroes lynched for Theft only 14 per cent were lynched for stealing live stock, the remaining 86 per cent being lynched for causes that may be fairly classed under petty larceny.

By comparing Charts VIII and IX the characteristic differences in the reasons assigned for the lynching of Negroes and for the lynching of Whites and Others are readily seen. The larger number in each case is under Murder, but further than that the order of the arrangement of the causes does not agree. Rape which occupies second place in the chart for the Negroes and is nearly equal to Murder, drops to third place on the chart for the Whites and Others. Comparatively speaking, Theft, particularly the stealing of live stock, and Desperadism are much more important as causes for the lynching of

Whites and Others than for the lynching of Negroes. In the case of the Negroes, Rape, Minor Offenses, and Arson are much more important as causes than in the case of the Whites and Others. Assault is also more important as a cause for lynching Negroes than for lynching Whites and Others.

Chart X shows the proportion lynched for various causes in the Southern Group of States, 1882–1903, for Whites and Others. The majority of the Whites and Others that have been lynched in this section of the country have been lynched for Murder. The numbers lynched for the various causes are as follows: Murder 321, Rape 69, Theft 63, Minor Offenses 42, Desperadism 30, Arson 19, Assault 6, Unknown 50. The percentages lynched for the various causes are as follows: Murder 53.5 per cent, Rape 11.5 per cent, Theft 10.5 per cent, Minor Offenses 7 per cent, Desperadism 5 per cent, Arson 3.2 per cent, Assault 1 per cent, Unknown 8.3 per cent.

Chart XI shows the proportion lynched for various causes in the Southern Group of States, 1882–1903, for Negroes. As might be expected, the causes arrange themselves in the same order as in Chart IX. The numbers lynched for the various causes are as follows: Murder 753, Rape 675, Minor Offenses 206, Arson 104, Theft 96, Assault 46, Desperadism 18, Unknown 87. The percentages lynched for the various causes are as follows: Murder 38 per cent, Rape 34 per cent, Minor Offenses 10.3 per cent, Arson 5.2 per cent, Theft 4.8 per cent, Assault 2.3 per cent, Desperadism .9 per cent, Unknown 4.3 per cent.

A comparison of Charts X and XI shows how greatly

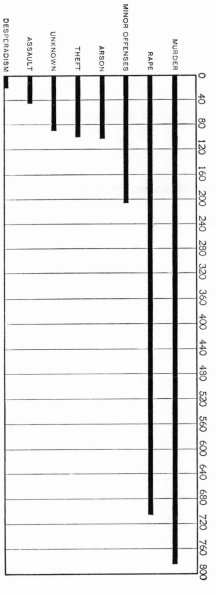

IX. PROPORTION LYNCHED FOR VARIOUS CAUSES 1882-1903 NEGROES

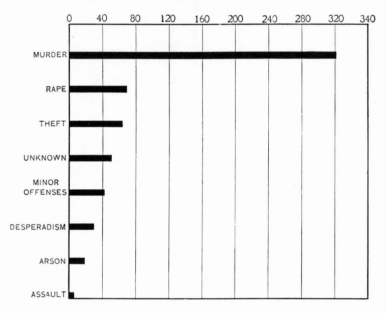

X. PROPORTION LYNCHED FOR VARIOUS CAUSES IN
SOUTHERN STATES 1882-1903 WHITES AND OTHERS

the lynching of Negroes in the South predominates over the lynching of Whites and Others. Against 600 Whites and Others lynched during the twenty-two years, 1,985 Negroes were lynched. With regard to the causes assigned for the lynchings a wide variation is observed. Only 38 per cent of the Negroes, against 53.5 per cent of the Whites and Others, were lynched for Murder. Rape stands next to Murder in order of importance in both cases, but while 34 per cent of the Negroes were lynched for Rape, only 11.5 per cent of the Whites and Others were lynched for that cause. Minor Offenses, Arson, Theft, and Assault appear as of much more importance as causes for the lynching of Negroes than for the lynching of Whites and Others.

Those who assume that the majority of the negroes lynched in the South are lynched for the crime of rape against white women, and that the lynching of negroes is therefore justifiable, will find very little satisfaction in an examination of Chart XI. In the classification of the cases the writer has put every case where both rape and murder were assigned as the cause, under Rape. It is possible that if a careful investigation were made of all the cases credited to Murder, it might be found that the motive in some cases was rape but that the actual crime committed was murder, and that it was for rape as well as for murder that the negroes in such cases were lynched. The lynchers may have considered themselves the avengers of the crime of rape as well as of the crime of murder. The statistics, however, cannot be made to show that more than thirty-four per cent of the negroes lynched in the South during the last twenty-two years have been lynched for the crime of rape, either attempted, alleged, or actually committed; and it is safe to say that if rape were connected with the offense in any case, that fact would ordinarily be stated in the report.

Chart XII shows the proportion lynched for various causes in the Western Group of States, 1882–1903. This chart covers the total number of persons lynched in that section of the country during the twenty-two years, no distinction being made either as to race or nationality. The numbers lynched for the various causes are as follows: Murder 279, Theft 199, Desperadism 64, Rape 34, Arson 12, Minor Offenses 9, Assault 4, Unknown 31. The total number lynched for all causes is 632. The percentages lynched for the various causes are as follows: Murder 44.1 per cent, Theft 31.5 per cent, Desperadism 10.1 per cent, Rape 5.4 per cent, Arson 1.9 per cent, Minor Offenses 1.4 per cent, Assault .6 per cent, Unknown 4.9 per cent. Lynchings for Theft and Desperadism are particularly characteristic of the Western States. Of the 199 lynched for Theft, 189 or 95 per cent were lynched for stealing live stock.

Chart XIII shows the proportion lynched for various causes in the Eastern Group of States, 1882–1903. The chart covers the total number of persons, without distinction as to race or nationality, who have been lynched in that section of the country during the twenty-two years. The majority have been lynched for Murder and Rape. The numbers lynched for the various causes are as follows: Murder 58, Rape 38, Theft 7, Minor Offenses 3, Assault 2, Desperadism 1, Unknown 11. None were lynched for Arson. The percentages lynched for the various causes

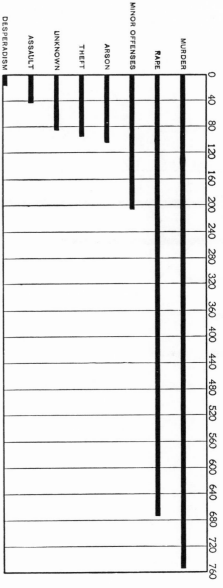

XI. PROPORTION LYNCHED FOR VARIOUS CAUSES IN SOUTHERN STATES 1882-1903 NEGROES

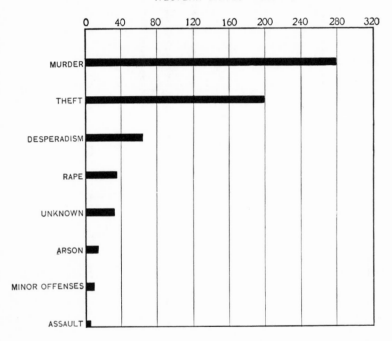

XII. PROPORTION LYNCHED FOR VARIOUS CAUSES IN
WESTERN STATES   1882-1903

are as follows: Murder 48.3 per cent, Rape 31.7 per cent, Theft 5.8 per cent, Minor Offenses 2.5 per cent, Assault 1.7 per cent, Desperadism .8 per cent, Unknown 9.1 per cent.

Thus far in this investigation the question of the distribution of lynchings has only entered to the extent of dividing the United States into three sections, the Southern Group of States, the Western Group, and the Eastern Group.[1] The following tables show the distribution of lynchings by States on the basis of the number of persons lynched, these persons being classified into Whites, Negroes and Others.

NUMBER OF PERSONS LYNCHED IN SOUTHERN STATES, 1882–1903

	WHITES	NEGROES	OTHERS	TOTAL
Mississippi	39	294	1	334
Texas	114	199	11	324
Louisiana	34	232	19	285
Georgia	28	241	..	269
Alabama	46	198	..	244
Arkansas	60	139	1	200
Tennessee	49	150	..	199
Kentucky	64	103	..	167
Florida	19	115	..	134
South Carolina	8	109	..	117
Missouri	49	42	..	91
Virginia	21	70	..	91
North Carolina	15	48	1	64
West Virginia	19	27	..	46
Maryland	2	18	..	20
Total	567	1985	33	2585

[1] See p. 164.

NUMBER OF PERSONS LYNCHED IN WESTERN STATES,
1882–1903

	WHITES	NEGROES	OTHERS	TOTAL
Indian Territory .... (Oklahoma)	73	7	15	95
Montana	80	1	4	85
Colorado	55	3	6	64
Nebraska	52	2	2	56
Kansas	34	17	..	51
California	29	..	12	41
Wyoming	37	..	..	37
Dakota .... (North and South)	28	1	6	35
New Mexico........	30	1	3	34
Arizona	25	..	3	28
Washington	20	..	6	26
Idaho	14	..	5	19
Oregon	15	1	3	19
Iowa	15	..	1	16
Alaska	4	..	4	8
Utah	4	1	2	7
Minnesota	5	..	1	6
Nevada	3	..	2	5
Total	523	34	75	632

NUMBER OF PERSONS LYNCHED IN EASTERN STATES,
1882–1903

	WHITES	NEGROES	OTHERS	TOTAL
Indiana	41	11	..	52
Ohio	10	11	..	21
Illinois	11	10	..	21
Michigan	7	1	..	8
Pennsylvania	2	5	..	7
Wisconsin	6	..	..	6
New York..........	1	1	..	2
New Jersey.........	..	1	..	1
Connecticut	1	..	..	1
Delaware	..	1	..	1
Total	79	41	..	120

XIII. PROPORTION LYNCHED FOR VARIOUS CAUSES IN EASTERN STATES 1882-1903

TOTAL NUMBER OF PERSONS LYNCHED, 1882–1903

	WHITES	NEGROES	OTHERS	TOTAL
Southern 567		1985	33	2585
Western 523		34	75	632
Eastern 79		41	..	120
Total 1169		2060	108	3337

Excluding the New England States there are no States in the Union in which lynchings have not taken place during the last twenty-two years. In forty-five of the States and Territories, as they are at present organized, one or more persons have been lynched during this period. In the Southern Group of States more than three times as many negroes as whites have been lynched. In Texas the "Others" were Mexicans, with the exception of one Indian; in Louisiana the "Others" were all Italians. In the Western Group of States only about five per cent of the persons lynched were negroes while nearly twelve per cent were "Others," the majority of whom were Indians, but there were also Chinamen, Mexicans, Italians, a Japanese, a Swiss, and a Bohemian. In the Eastern Group of States about thirty-four per cent of the persons lynched were negroes and the rest were whites, there being no "Others."

Only one lynching with one person lynched is credited to the New England States. In July, 1886, in Litchfield County, Connecticut, Charles Lockwood, a farm-hand, was found early one morning hanging from the limb of a tree, evidently having been dead for several hours. According to the New York Times,[1] public opinion was divided as to whether he had been lynched or had com-

[1] See the daily issues from July 23 to July 27, 1886.

mitted suicide. The coroner's verdict said that it was a
case of suicide. To a disinterested party, however, the
evidence appears very strong in favor of the former view.
Lockwood had brutally murdered "pretty Mattie Randell,"
of Morris, Connecticut, and escaped. Searching parties
were organized and were scouring the country, and feeling ran high in the community against him. Threats
were repeatedly made against his life. His body was
found one morning dangling from the limb of a tree. In
the writer's opinion, formed from reading various newspaper accounts of the occurrence, the Chicago Tribune
rightly included Charles Lockwood in the list of persons
lynched in the year 1886.

For the purpose of studying the distribution of lynchings with a view to determining what particular characteristics of the population, if any, promote and foster the
practice of lynching, it is the number of lynchings that
have occurred in specified districts which should be considered rather than the number of persons who have been
lynched in those districts. Not infrequently several persons have been lynched at one time and such cases would
tend to vitiate any conclusions drawn from an investigation made on the basis of the number of persons lynched.
The circumstances which surround lynchings do not vary
in any respect according to the number of victims at
particular lynchings. The following tables have therefore been prepared to show the distribution of lynchings
by States on the basis of the number of lynchings. In
making up these figures it was found necessary to establish some standard length of time for a lynching. There
were a number of cases where persons were lynched on

NUMBER OF LYNCHINGS BY YEARS IN SOUTHERN STATES, 1882-1903

	'82	'83	'84	'85	'86	'87	'88	'89	'90	'91	'92	'93	'94	'95	'96	'97	'98	'99	'00	'01	'02	'03	Total
Mississippi	3	10	10	12	12	10	10	22	11	20	11	12	14	13	6	15	12	11	15	11	9	14	263
Georgia	3	5	5	9	6	4	12	9	17	11	13	11	16	14	8	13	12	17	14	13	9	10	231
Texas	10	13	15	20	14	6	10	10	22	13	8	8	10	17	4	14	3	6	2	7	5	6	223
Louisiana	5	3	5	2	6	9	7	8	8	14	18	12	11	4	21	10	8	9	9	14	10	11	204
Alabama........	5	4	3	4	4	4	9	6	8	14	14	17	12	10	13	16	8	5	8	12	4	2	182
Tennessee	2	6	..	9	6	4	6	5	8	12	20	14	12	11	12	5	7	2	6	9	4	4	164
Arkansas	2	7	6	7	3	8	2	5	6	10	20	9	6	7	4	10	10	5	6	5	6	10	154
Kentucky	6	4	6	3	5	6	6	8	5	7	9	11	16	12	6	7	5	3	1	4	8	2	140
Florida.........	2	1	2	3	4	3	2	..	3	8	7	6	7	8	7	6	1	4	7	5	3	6	95
South Carolina ..	6	3	1	1	4	2	2	5	4	1	5	11	5	5	4	6	5	1	2	5	2	5	85
Missouri	3	2	3	6	2	1	1	7	1	1	5	4	5	4	5	3	5	3	2	4	4	3	76
Virginia	2	1	5	4	2	3	3	7	3	4	5	8	5	2	..	5	4	1	5	2	4	..	73
North Carolina ..	..	2	3	6	2	3	6	3	2	2	5	2	1	1	1	2	2	2	3	2	3	1	53
West Virginia ...	1	..	2	1	3	2	2	4	..	1	1	..	1	1	1	1	1	1	2	1	2	1	34
Maryland	..	..	2	3	1	2	..	1	..	1	1	..	..	3	1	1	2	..	1	1	..	..	20
Total......	50	61	68	90	76	66	78	100	98	120	146	125	123	111	93	113	85	70	83	93	73	75	1997

NUMBER OF LYNCHINGS BY YEARS IN WESTERN STATES, 1882–1903

	'82	'83	'84	'85	'86	'87	'88	'89	'90	'91	'92	'93	'94	'95	'96	'97	'98	'99	'00	'01	'02	'03	Total
Indian Territory (Oklahoma)	..	1	..	3	3	2	3	4	..	2	1	5	6	5	4	1	3	1	..	3	..	..	47
Kansas	2	2	2	5	5	1	3	2	..	..	3	3	3	1	..	..	1	3	1	2	1	..	40
Nebraska	..	2	6	1	3	4	4	6	2	2	..	..	2	3	..	..	..	..	..	..	..	..	35
Colorado	6	1	3	1	3	..	4	..	2	2	..	1	1	2	2	..	..	..	3	..	1	..	32
Montana	..	5	9	2	..	..	3	2	..	3	1	1	..	..	..	1	1	..	..	2	..	..	32
California	..	3	2	2	1	3	3	1	2	1	4	1	1	4	..	1	..	..	..	2	..	3	31
New Mexico	5	2	4	3	..	1	..	2	1	..	..	4	..	1	..	..	..	..	..	..	..	..	23
Dakota (North & South)	1	1	3	2	..	..	3	..	1	2	1	1	1	1	..	2	..	..	..	..	1	..	20
Washington	2	1	2	2	1	..	..	1	..	3	1	1	1	1	..	..	1	..	..	..	..	1	18
Arizona	4	1	1	1	..	2	2	..	1	..	2	..	..	..	..	2	..	..	..	..	..	1	17
Wyoming	2	..	1	..	..	..	1	3	2	1	4	..	..	..	..	..	1	..	..	..	1	2	16
Iowa	..	3	..	2	..	2	..	1	2	..	..	2	2	..	..	..	..	..	..	..	..	..	12
Oregon	..	..	4	3	..	1	..	..	2	..	..	..	..	..	..	..	..	..	..	..	..	..	11
Idaho	1	..	1	2	..	..	1	..	..	..	1	1	..	..	..	..	1	..	..	1	..	..	8
Alaska	..	..	..	..	..	..	..	..	..	..	..	..	..	..	..	3	..	..	..	..	..	..	6
Minnesota	2	2	..	..	..	..	..	..	..	..	..	2	..	..	1	..	1	..	..	..	..	..	5
Utah	..	3	2	..	..	..	..	..	..	..	..	..	..	..	..	..	..	..	..	..	..	..	5
Nevada	..	..	..	..	..	..	1	..	1	..	..	..	..	..	..	2	..	..	..	..	..	1	5
Total	25	27	40	29	16	16	28	22	12	16	18	22	17	18	7	11	8	4	4	10	5	8	363

NUMBER OF LYNCHINGS BY YEARS IN EASTERN STATES, 1882–1903

	'82	'83	'84	'85	'86	'87	'88	'89	'90	'91	'92	'93	'94	'95	'96	'97	'98	'99	'00	'01	'02	'03	Total
Indiana	4	3	3	..	5	5	..	2	4	3	..	2	2	..	1	1	1	..	2	1	1	..	40
Ohio	2	1	1	3	2	1	..	..	..	1	4	..	2	2	..	1	..	..	..	..	..	..	20
Illinois	..	1	..	2	1	..	2	..	..	1	1	2	1	1	1	1	1	..	..	..	2	3	20
Michigan	..	..	..	..	..	..	1	1	..	1	1	1	..	..	..	..	..	..	..	..	1	..	7
Pennsylvania	1	2	1	..	..	..	1	1	..	2	..	..	1	..	..	..	..	1	..	..	..	..	7
Wisconsin	..	..	1	..	..	..	1	1	..	2	..	..	1	..	..	..	..	..	..	..	..	..	6
New York	..	..	..	..	..	..	..	..	..	..	1	..	..	..	1	..	..	..	..	..	..	..	2
Connecticut	..	..	..	..	1	..	..	..	..	..	..	..	..	..	..	..	..	..	..	..	..	..	1
Delaware	..	..	..	..	..	..	..	..	..	..	..	..	..	..	..	..	..	..	..	..	..	1	1
New Jersey	..	..	..	..	1	..	..	..	..	..	..	..	..	..	..	..	..	..	..	..	..	..	1
Total	7	7	6	5	10	6	5	4	4	10	6	5	7	3	3	3	2	1	2	1	4	4	105

TOTAL NUMBER OF LYNCHINGS BY YEARS, 1882–1903

	'82	'83	'84	'85	'86	'87	'88	'89	'90	'91	'92	'93	'94	'95	'96	'97	'98	'99	'00	'01	'02	'03	Total
Southern States	50	61	68	90	76	66	78	100	98	120	146	125	123	111	93	113	85	70	83	93	73	75	1997
Western States	25	27	40	29	16	16	28	22	12	16	18	22	17	18	7	11	8	4	4	10	5	8	363
Eastern States	7	7	6	5	10	6	5	4	4	10	6	5	7	3	3	3	2	1	2	1	4	4	105
Total	82	95	114	124	102	88	101	126	114	146	170	152	147	132	103	127	95	75	89	104	82	87	2465

succeeding or subsequent days at or near the same place, and the question arose as to whether there was one lynching or more than one lynching in such cases. It would seem that ordinarily, if one whole day intervened between the lynching of one person and the lynching of another person, sufficient time had elapsed for the excitement over the lynching of the first person to abate somewhat and that the lynching of the second person in such a case could not rightfully be considered a part of the preceding act of mob violence. Using this as a criterion, all cases in which persons were lynched on two succeeding days at or near the same place have been classified as one lynching, but all cases in which at least a day intervened in the lynching of two or more persons at or near the same place have been classified as two or more lynchings.

If much that has been said and written in recent years on the subject of lynching is true; if the presence of the colored race, because of the character of the crimes which negroes commit, is largely responsible for the practice of lynching; if the immigration into this country of "the scum of Europe" is also responsible for the practice; if lynching is, in addition, a relic of barbarism and a sign of degeneracy in American civilization, — then there ought to be some correlation between the distribution of lynchings and the proportion of the white element to the colored and the foreign elements in the population, and also between the distribution of lynchings and the degree of illiteracy in the population. With this idea in mind an attempt has been made to find out whether any such correlations exist with reference to the lynchings that have occurred during the last twenty-two years in the Southern

Group of States and in the three States of the Eastern
Group in which lynchings have been most numerous.
In the following table the percentage which the total
number of lynchings bears to the total population of
these several States has been placed alongside the percentage of the negroes in the population, the percentage
of foreign born in the population, and the percentage of
illiterates in the population. In the same table also there
have been given the percentage of the persons lynched in
these several States who were whites, and the percentage
of the persons lynched who were negroes.

From this table there appears to be no distinct correlation between the distribution of lynchings and the percentage of negroes in the population. In a general way
the percentage of lynchings to the population is highest
in the States where the negro element is largest, but Virginia, North Carolina, and notably South Carolina, are
exceptions. So far as any correlation at all can be traced
between the percentage of lynchings and the percentage
of foreign born, the latter varies inversely to the former.
The percentage of illiterates varies from State to State
in about the same way that the percentage of negroes does;
and hence there is the same general conclusion to be
drawn with reference to the correlation of lynchings to
illiteracy as with reference to the correlation of lynchings
to the percentage of negroes, namely, that there is no distinct correlation. When the percentage of the persons
lynched who were negroes is compared with the percentage of negroes in the population, however, it is at once
apparent that there is a correlation between them. If
plotted graphically the lines representing the two per-

	PER CENT OF LYNCH-INGS TO POPULA-TION 1900	PER CENT OF WHITES IN POPULATION		PER CENT OF NEGROES IN POPULATION		PER CENT OF LYNCHED WHO WERE WHITES	PER CENT OF LYNCHED WHO WERE NEGROES	PER CENT OF FOREIGN BORN IN POPULATION		PER CENT OF ILLITERATES IN POPULATION	
		1890	1900	1890	1900			1890	1900	1890	1900[1]
Mississippi	.0169	42.2	41.3	57.6	58.5	11.67	88.02	0.6	0.5	40.0	32.0
Georgia	.0104	53.2	53.3	46.7	46.7	10.40	89.59	0.7	0.6	39.8	30.5
Texas	.0073	78.1	79.6	21.8	20.4	35.18	61.41	6.8	5.9	19.7	14.5
Louisiana	.0147	49.9	52.8	50.0	47.1	11.92	81.40	4.4	3.8	45.8	38.5
Alabama	.0099	55.1	54.7	44.8	45.2	18.85	81.14	1.0	0.8	41.0	34.0
Tennessee	.0081	75.6	76.2	24.4	23.8	24.62	75.37	1.1	0.9	26.6	20.7
Arkansas	.0117	72.6	72.0	27.4	28.0	30.0	69.5	1.3	1.1	26.6	20.4
Kentucky	.0065	85.6	86.7	14.4	13.3	38.32	61.67	3.2	2.3	21.6	16.5
Florida	.0179	57.5	56.3	42.5	43.7	14.17	85.82	5.9	4.5	27.8	21.9
South Carolina	.0063	40.1	41.6	59.8	58.4	6.83	93.16	0.5	0.4	45.0	35.9
Missouri	.0024	94.4	94.8	5.6	5.2	53.84	46.15	8.8	7.0	9.1	6.4
Virginia	.0039	61.6	64.3	38.4	35.6	23.07	76.92	1.1	1.0	30.2	22.9
North Carolina	.0027	65.2	66.7	34.7	33.0	23.43	75.0	0.2	0.2	35.7	28.7
West Virginia	.0035	95.7	95.5	4.3	4.5	41.30	58.69	2.5	2.3	11.4	2.5
Maryland	.0016	79.3	80.2	20.7	19.8	10.0	90.0	9.0	7.9	15.7	11.1
Indiana	.0015	97.9	97.7	2.1	2.3	78.8	21.1	6.7	5.6	6.3	4.6
Ohio	.0004	97.6	97.7	2.4	2.3	47.6	52.3	12.5	11.0	5.2	4.0
Illinois	.0004	98.5	98.2	1.5	1.8	52.3	47.6	22.0	20.1	5.2	4.2

[1] These figures are taken from the Twelfth Census, where the term "illiterates" is used to designate all persons ten years of age and over who can neither read nor write, or who can read but cannot write.

centages would rise and fall in almost perfect uniformity, only Georgia and Tennessee presenting slight exceptions to the general tendency.

For the purpose of further investigating the subject of the distribution of lynchings in relation to particular characteristics of the population, the lynchings which have occurred during the last twenty-two years in the Southern Group of States and in the three States of the Eastern Group in which lynchings have been most numerous were classified according to the counties in which they occurred in these several States. On the basis of this classification a careful study was made of the same characteristics of the population by counties as were considered above with reference to the population by States. The percentage of lynchings to the population in the several counties where lynchings have taken place was compared with the percentage of negroes, the percentage of foreign born, and the percentage of illiterates in those several counties.[1] To facilitate comparison, trial charts were drawn on which the percentages were plotted in graphic form, and the results were carefully noted.

In the comparison of the percentage of lynchings with the percentage of negroes in the population by counties no correlation can be clearly distinguished. In many counties where the negroes constitute between sixty per cent and eighty per cent of the population the percentage

[1] The figures given by the Twelfth Census were used. The figures of the Eleventh Census would be more nearly typical for the period under consideration than those of the Twelfth Census, but a difficulty was met with in an attempt to use them, owing to the fact that new counties have been formed since 1890. It was found that counties in which lynchings have occurred did not appear at all in the Eleventh Census, and that for the sake of completeness it was necessary to use the Twelfth Census.

of lynchings is high, but there are also numerous exceptions.

In the comparison of the percentage of lynchings with the percentage of foreign born in the population by counties there appears to be no distinguishable correlation. It is shown pretty conclusively, however, that there is no tendency for the percentage of lynchings to increase where the percentage of foreign born in the population is large.

In the comparison of the percentage of lynchings with the percentage of illiterates in the population by counties there appears to be not the slightest correlation.

The net result of this investigation into some characteristics of the population in relation to the distribution of lynchings is negative rather than positive. The proportion between the white and colored elements in the population does not seem to affect the prevalence of lynchings. It is only the proportion of whites lynched to negroes lynched that seems to bear any relation to the proportion between the white and colored elements in the population. The percentage of foreign born in the population does not seem to influence the prevalence of lynchings and there is not the slightest indication that the practice of lynching is anything else than a thoroughly American practice. So far as the percentage of illiterates in the population is an indication of the degree of culture and civilization possessed by a community, it does not appear that lynchings are confined to backward communities. The deductions which may be drawn as a result of this investigation afford no explanation why, for instance, a greater number of lynchings occurred in

Decatur County, Georgia, than in any other county in that State, or why there were ten lynchings in Dallas County, Alabama, but only one lynching in Lowndes, an adjoining county. It is probably true that the distribution of lynchings is largely affected by entirely local conditions, conditions which cannot be represented by statistics.[1]

In this chapter nothing has been said about the methods adopted for lynching during the twenty-two-year period. In the record of lynchings published by the Chicago Tribune no mention is made of the manner of death which the victims suffered. It is probably true that most of the lynchings were either by hanging or by shooting, or by both hanging and shooting. Additional indignities and cruelties have not infrequently been inflicted, however, and there have been a number of cases where the victims have been burned alive. The following cases of lynching by burning alive have come to the writer's notice: in 1884, one in Texas; in 1891, one in Texas, one in Louisiana; in 1892, one in Arkansas; in 1893, one in Texas; in 1894, one in Kentucky; in 1895, one in Texas; in 1897, one in North Carolina; in 1899, one in Georgia, one in Mississippi, one in Kentucky; in 1901, one in Kansas; in 1902, three in Mississippi, one in Arkansas, one in Texas, one in Colorado; in 1903, one in Illinois, one in Delaware; in 1904, one in Mississippi, one in Georgia, at each of which

[1] Alfred Holt Stone, in a paper read before the American Economic Association in December, 1901, attributed the amicable relations existing between the whites and the negroes in the Yazoo-Mississippi delta to the absence of a white laboring class, particularly of field laborers. In his opinion one of the gravest causes of trouble between the two races is contact on a common industrial plane. — "Publications of the American Economic Association," February, 1902 (3d Ser., Vol. III, No. 1, p. 235).

two persons were burned at the stake, in the former instance one of them being a woman. In all these cases the victims were negroes and they were believed to be either guilty of several crimes or of a single atrocious crime. The majority were lynched for the double crime of rape, or attempted rape, and murder.

If these cases of burning alive form a list that is at all complete, there is ground for believing that as the practice of lynching continues the punishments inflicted tend to increase in severity and the victims are tortured more and more before death comes to their relief.

While the exact figures have been given in this investigation of lynchings in recent years based on the Chicago Tribune record, it is to be remembered that these figures are probably only approximations. It is extremely doubtful whether exactly 3,337 persons have been lynched in the United States during the last twenty-two years, or whether there have been exactly 2,465 lynchings. It is probable, however, that these approximations are as nearly correct and as reliable as any that we shall ever get, and there seems to be no reason why they should not form a sound basis for the statistical study attempted in this chapter.

CHAPTER VII

Lynch-law and its Justification

For more than a century the principle laid down by the legislature of Virginia has been appealed to as a justification for recourse to lynch-law. In Revolutionary times it was held that the immediate urgency and imminent danger of the situation justified the summary and extralegal measures that were taken to suppress conspiracies against American patriots. On the frontier it was urged that the imminence of the danger warranted summary procedure against desperadoes and marauders, at first merely whipping and banishment, later hanging and summary execution. In the time of the anti-slavery agitation circumstances had arisen under which measures, though not strictly warranted by law, were held to be justifiable from the nature of the offense. In the opinion of the slave-holder summary treatment in the form of flogging, tarring and feathering, and banishing the abolitionist was wholly justifiable. The doctrine that " when the law is inefficient to take hold of a man the people should" was again and again referred to in support of the summary punishment of the abolitionists.

Hidden away in Judge Lawless's charge to the St. Louis grand jury is the same principle.[1] If the lawless violence was the work of the "many," if it was committed

[1] See p. 109.

by a representative number of the citizens while in a state of frenzy and excitement, it must be considered beyond the reach of human law. In 1839, W. E. Channing stated the principle in the following words: "Undoubtedly there may be crimes, so unnatural, so terrible to a community, that a people may be forgiven, if, deeming the usual forms of justice too slow, they assume the perilous office of inflicting speedy punishment. . . . There is, indeed, as I have intimated, one case where popular commotion does comparatively little harm, I mean that which is excited by some daring crime, which the laws sternly forbid, and which sends an electric thrill of horror through a virtuous community. In such a case, the public without law do the work of law, and enforce those natural, eternal principles of right, on which all legislation should rest."[1]

Governor Lynch, of Mississippi, in his message to the State legislature in 1836, used the following language with reference to the hanging of the Vicksburg gamblers: "However we may regret the occasion, we are constrained to admit that necessity will sometimes prompt a summary mode of trial and punishment unknown to the law."[2]

A few years later Captain Marryat wrote:

"Englishmen express their surprise that in a moral community such a monstrosity as Lynch law should exist; but although the present system, which has been derived from the original Lynch law, cannot be too severely condemned, it must, in justice to the Americans, be considered that the original custom of Lynch law was forced upon them by circumstances.

[1] *Liberator*, April 19, 1839 (9: 63).
[2] *Liberator*, April 30, 1836 (6: 72).

. . . In its origin the practice was no more blameable than were the laws established by the Pilgrim fathers on their first landing at Plymouth, or any law enacted amongst a community left to themselves, their own resources, and their own guidance and government. Lynch law, as at first constituted, was nothing more than punishment awarded to offenders by a community who had been injured, and who had no law to refer to, and could have no redress if they did not take the law into their own hands; the *present* system of Lynch law is, on the contrary, an illegal exercise of the power of the majority in opposition to and defiance of the laws of the country, and the measure of justice administered and awarded by those laws.

"It must be remembered that fifty years ago, there were but few white men to the westward of the Alleghany Mountains; that the States of Kentucky and Tennessee were at that time as scanty in population as even now are the districts of Ioway and Columbia; that by the institutions of the Union a district required a certain number of inhabitants before it could be acknowledged as even a district; and that previous to such acknowledgment, the people who had *squatted* on the land had no claim to protection or law. It must also be borne in mind, that these distant territories offered an asylum to many who fled from the vengeance of the laws, men without principle, thieves, rogues, and vagabonds, who escaping there, would often interfere with the happiness and peace of some small yet well-conducted community, which had migrated and settled on these fertile regions. These communities had no appeal against personal violence, no protection from rapacity and injustice. They were not yet within the pale of the Union. . . .

"It was, therefore, to remedy the defect of there being no established law, that Lynch law, as it is termed, was applied to; without it, all security, all social happiness would have been in a state of abeyance. By degrees, all disturbers of the public peace, all offenders against justice met with their deserts; and it is a query, whether on its first institution, any law from the bench was more honestly and impartially administered than this very Lynch law, which has now had its name prostituted by the most barbarous excesses and contemptuous violation of all law whatever. The examples I am able to bring forward of Lynch law, in its primitive state, will all be found to have been based upon necessity, and a due regard to morals and to justice."[1]

In 1843 the practice of employing lynch-law in frontier settlements was justified in the following way: "Until the law . . . is completely established the Lynch tribunals assert a concurrent jurisdiction, so to speak, with the ordinary courts; and this jurisdiction they preserve until the population loses the habit of resorting thereto, and acquires that of confiding in the protection afforded by the legal tribunals; a change of habit which takes place, we believe, as soon as those tribunals have power to protect. In a new and thinly peopled country every man feels that he may at any time be called upon to act as his own protector. A habit of self-reliance is thus generated which time alone can convert into a habit of relying upon the law."[2]

In a book descriptive of border life in Texas, which was published in 1852, the frontier type of lynch-law received the following justification:

"It is the stern primary law of self-preservation — this border custom of bringing criminals before the whole body of

[1] "Diary in America" (1839), III, 226–230.
For a description of the beginnings of legal procedure in isolated settlements on the frontier, see "Narrative of the Life of David Crockett," written by himself (1843), pp. 132–135. (M.)
[2] *British and Foreign Review*, 14: 29 (1843).

citizens for judgment — from which men sitting beside law-guarded hearths recoil in dismay, and hearing only its cruel side, stigmatize as the utterly unpardonable Lynch Law. Most true it is, that nothing but urgent and deplorable necessity will drive a just and merciful man to participate in its tribunals, but it is not less true that in frontier settlements, if the fear of its quick vengeance did not overawe the wicked, the innocent and peaceful would be in hourly danger of wrong and outrage. . . .

"The wild verdicts borderers sometimes enact, in the faith that they are just and needful, sound uncouthly to those fenced round with regular courts, and must seem dreadful to Christian men accustomed to the solemn decorum with which constituted courts deal out their legal awards of chains, lashes, and hangings; yet, seen close at hand, with a knowledge of the situation of the community, and of the life and deeds of the evil-doer, many of Judge Lynch's verdicts will appear more just and necessary than half of the sentences of the regular courts. . . .

"Statute law is but the formal expression of what the larger community deems wisest and most just for the general welfare, the small, crude, remote settlement does the same for itself; only without writing down its enactments, and in the more summary way enforced by its peculiar situation. It has no prison houses in which to detain a criminal, no courts in which to try him, no funds wherewith to support him in long duress. If a crime is committed the accused has the whole community for judges and jury, and if he is found guilty by common suffrage they proceed to execute the verdict."[1]

[1] Cora Montgomery (Jane M. Cazneau): "Eagle Pass; or Life on the Border" (1852), pp. 153, 164–167.
    Compare the justification of the frontier type of lynch-law given by Owen Wister in his recent novel, "The Virginian." After describing the lynching of some Wyoming cattle-thieves, and emphasizing the fact that "many an act that man does is right or wrong according to the time and place which form, so to speak, its context," the author puts into the

Another writer carries the vindication of the frontiers-men and pioneers still further by attributing culpability to the United States government for not providing remote settlements with legal tribunals, so that recourse to lynch-law would have been unnecessary. He writes: "The greater share of the sin and disgrace falls upon the government, which leaves to its citizens a heavy and responsible office, that ought to be guarded by all the solemnities and securities of law."[1]

Such are the arguments and the lines of reasoning by which the operation of lynch-law previous to the Civil War was generally justified.[2]   Vindication was urged on grounds of necessity or self-preservation and the nature of the offense, and it was lynch-law as applied to whites that was thus vindicated.

The anti-slavery agitation and the emancipation of the slaves brought to the support of lynch-law procedure another factor — that of race prejudice.   The number

mouth of "Judge Henry" these words: "They (the ordinary citizens) are where the law comes from, you see.   For they chose the delegates who made the Constitution that provided for the courts.   There's our machinery.   These are the hands into which ordinary citizens have put the law.   So you see, at best, when they lynch they only take back what they once gave. . . .   We are in a very bad way, and we are trying to make that way a little better until civilization can reach us.   At present we lie beyond its pale.   The courts, or rather the juries, into whose hands we have put the law, are not dealing the law.   They are withered hands, or rather they are imitation hands made for show, with no life in them, no grip.   They cannot hold a cattle-thief.   And so when your ordinary citizen sees this, and sees that he has placed justice in a dead hand, he must take justice back into his own hands where it was once at the beginning of all things.   Call this primitive, if you will, but so far from being a *defiance* of the law, it is an *assertion* of it — the fundamental assertion of self-governing men, upon whom our whole social fabric is based." — pp. 435–436.

[1] C. A. Murray: "Travels in America" (1839), II, 81.

[2] Bancroft's justification of popular tribunals and vigilance societies has been referred to above.   See Chapter IV, p. 133.

of negroes lynched in recent years as compared with the number of whites lynched has indicated so clearly the existence of race prejudice that many writers have given to it the chief place among the causes of lynchings. It is a mistake, however, to consider this race prejudice as of recent origin in the United States.

Race prejudice between the whites and the negroes in this country began with the landing of the first ship-load of slaves in Virginia. In describing the condition of the negroes in the colony of Virginia, George W. Williams says: "It was not a mitigating circumstance that the white servants of the colony who came into natural contact with the Negroes were 'disorderly persons,' or convicts sent to Virginia by an order of the King of England. It was fixed by public sentiment and law that there should be no relation between the races. The first prohibition was made September 17, 1630. Hugh Davis, a white servant, was publicly flogged 'before an assembly of Negroes and others,' for defiling himself with a Negro. It was also required that he should confess as much on the following Sabbath. . . . All intercourse was cut off between the races. Intermarrying of whites and blacks was prohibited by severe laws. And the most common civilities and amenities were frowned down when intended for a Negro. The plantation was as religious as the Church, and the Church was as secular as the plantation. The 'white christians' hated the Negro, and the Church bestowed upon him a most bountiful amount of neglect."[1]

The importation of negroes from Africa into this country brought a stream of racial heredity from the torrid

[1] "History of the Negro Race in America" (1883), I, 121, 131.

zone to mingle with a similar stream which had its origin and development in the north temperate zone. When these two streams met, the chief characteristics of the former were: civilization of a very low level; no letters or art or science, language in the agglutinative state; industries confined to a very elementary agriculture, fishing, a little hunting, and some simple handicrafts; no religion except that which explains all natural phenomena by reference to spirits, mostly ill-disposed towards man; physical and psychic characteristics substantially uniform, only trained observers being able to detect differences here and there. The stream from the north temperate zone, on the contrary, was characterized by an hereditary endowment delicately adjusted to the highest civilization recorded in history. A difference and contrast better adapted to bringing about racial antagonism can scarcely be conceived.[1]

On both physical and psychic grounds there is reason for an antagonistic feeling between the white race and the black race. Physically there is great diversity between the racial types of the two races. The color of the negro's skin, his kinky hair, and his general phsyiognomy, especially his flat nose and protruding lips with receding (actual or apparent) forehead, — all are widely diverse from the white man's standard of beauty and symmetry. Measured by the Caucasian ideal the features of the negro are coarse and animal-like. To most white per-

[1] See J. A. Tillinghast: "The Negro in Africa and America" — Publications of the American Economic Association, May, 1902 (3d Ser., Vol. III, No. 2). This monograph presents an admirable historical perspective of the native characteristics and of the acquirements of the colored race in America.

sons, also, the odor arising from an assemblage of negroes is extremely disagreeable, and some negroes say that they find the odor of white persons similarly distasteful.[1] With reference to the psychic characteristics of the two races, their intellectual and moral traits, there is even greater diversity. In their religion, and essential manners, customs, and habits of thought, the differences are so great as to constitute almost opposite extremes. There is a total lack of anything like a community of interest between the two races. Members of the white race and of the black race do not find satisfaction in intermarriage and mingling together around the hearthstone. The whites and the blacks never have associated and do not to-day associate together in public and in private as one people.[2]

[1] Fanny Kemble, writing in 1838–39, attributed the "personal offensiveness" of negroes to dirt and habits of uncleanliness, asserting that the negroes had no respect for their personal appearance, and that this lack of respect was due to slavery. In her journal, these words are found: "The stench in an Irish, Scotch, Italian, or French hovel are quite as intolerable as any I ever found in any of our negro houses." In another connection, however, when describing a certain negro named Isaac, she refers particularly to his strong physical resemblance to a monkey, and says that she is much comforted by the fact that this individual "*speaks*." See "Journal of a Residence on a Georgian Plantation" (1863), pp. 23–24, 219.

In describing "The Negro in General," Ratzel writes: "The specific, but hardly definable negro smell is certainly possessed by all, in varying degrees. Falkenstein refers it to the somewhat more oily composition of the sweat, which with uncleanly habits easily develops rancid acids." — "History of Mankind" (Trans. from 2d German ed. by A. J. Butler, 1897), II, 315; see also II, 266, 301.

A practising physician in the city of New Haven, Conn., has assured the writer that the peculiar odor is again apparent very soon after a negro patient has been given a bath and a change of clothing.

[2] Compare statements made in "An Apology for the Short Shrift" — *Saturday Review*, May 28, 1898 (85: 717).

The following passage is found in "The Selling of Joseph," by Chief-Justice Samuel Sewall, printed in Boston, June 12, 1700, the first printed protest against slaveholding in Massachusetts: "and there is such a disparity in their Conditions, Colour & Hair, that they can never embody

When two races, occupying the same territory and living side by side, differ so widely in their physical features, in their interests and in their attainments, as do the white and colored races in this country, it is most natural and indeed almost inevitable that prejudice should arise between them. The institution of slavery has no doubt created a caste feeling on the part of the master race, and yet this is but the strengthening and deepening of a natural race antipathy, the causes for which are evident. Slavery merely intensified a feeling that was due to other causes. It is an error to say that slavery has been the cause of all the prejudice against the negro.[1] It is true that the black race long wore the chain of slavery and was regarded as an inferior race, and this was true in the United States as well as elsewhere; but the reason for the antagonistic feeling lies deeper than that fact.[2]

An indication of the existence of racial prejudice during the period of slavery is found in a report adopted at the "Second Annual Convention of the People of Color" which met at Philadelphia in June, 1832. This convention, composed of free negroes, adopted a resolution in which the following passage occurs: "The recent occurrences at the South have swelled the tide of prejudice

with us, and grow up in orderly Families, to the Peopling of the Land: but still remain in our Body Politick as a kind of extravasat Blood." — See "Proceedings of the Massachusetts Historical Society" for October, 1863 (Vol. 1863–64, p. 161).

[1] William Wells Brown makes this statement in his book, "The Negro in the Rebellion," pp. 361–362.

[2] Compare the manifestation of race prejudice in South Africa, in Australia, and in the Philippines. See article "The Negro Problem in South Africa," by Arthur Hawkes, *Review of Reviews*, September, 1903 (28: 325), and the editiorial comments on pp. 264–265 of the same issue. See also, article "Race Prejudice in the Philippines," by James A. Le Roy, *Atlantic Monthly*, July, 1902 (90: 100).

until it has almost revolutionized public sentiment, which has given birth to severe legislative enactments in some of the States, and almost ruined our interests and prospects in others, in which, in the opinion of your Committee, our situation is more precarious than it has been at any other period since the Declaration of Independence. The events of the past year have been more fruitful in persecution, and have presented more inducements than any other period of the history of our country, for the men of color to fly from the graves of their fathers, and seek new homes in a land where the roaring billows of prejudice are less injurious to their rights and privileges." [1]

To this view of the matter there is an apparent objection. It would seem that if race prejudice existed during the time of slavery, it should have manifested itself in the form of summary treatment of the negroes more frequently than it did. In general, however, there was no occasion for its manifestation. So long as the blacks were valuable as slaves and accepted their inferior position without protest, no one wanted to get rid of them or put them to death. The fact that slaves were property, and in that capacity were amenable to the laws, made recourse to unlawful procedure against them both unwise and unnecessary. It was only in cases of insurrection among the slaves, or when some especially brutal and barbarous crime was committed by a negro, that summary measures were adopted prior to the Civil War. At such times negroes were killed without mercy, sometimes they were tortured and their bodies mutilated while still

[1] George W. Williams: "History of the Negro Race in America" (1883), II, 72.

alive, and occasionally they were burned to death. But these were extraordinary occasions; ordinarily the law was allowed to take its course.[1]

A careful study of the relations which existed between the two races from 1619 to 1860 will reveal the presence of more or less racial antipathy. The institution of slavery, however, acted as a check to the manifestation of this antagonistic feeling as regards the manner of procedure for the punishment of negroes accused of serious offenses. "Slavery was, in its way, a thoroughgoing school; the negro race was educated in the cotton-fields and cabins of the South. In the Old South there was very little negro crime and no negro idleness. The negro worked under direction; he was taught how to work; he cheerfully accepted his work, and he was the soul of fidelity, as the history of the war proved."[2] Restraints were placed around him; he received protection and guardianship; and, above all, he received an industrial training which gave him some degree of control over his own impulses and actions. He was looked upon and governed as a child, and he was punished as a child when he committed a breach of the peace or some serious offense against person or property. The legal procedure for the punishment of negroes, based upon the property right in slaves, was in perfect accord with the order of society that had been established during two hundred years or more of slavery.

When the institution of slavery was attacked in the

[1] Evidence for this statement has been presented above. See Chapter IV.

[2] *Outlook*, Dec. 26, 1903 (75: 984).

early thirties and during the years of controversy which followed, and still more when it was finally overthrown in the sixties, race prejudice began to manifest itself in the manner of treatment accorded negro criminals. By the emancipation of the slaves in 1863, under the existing conditions, absolutely no restriction was left upon its manifestation, for the property right in the negro had been swept away and the great mass of the negroes, finding all the old restraints suddenly removed, naturally mistook liberty for license and committed many excesses. Large numbers of negroes ceased to work. "The worst instincts of the negro came to the front; the percentage of criminals among negroes increased to an alarming extent; many were guilty of crimes of violence of the most heinous and repulsive kind." [1] The result of emanicpation had not been fully anticipated and no adequate legal provision was made for the control of the freedmen. The foundation had been removed from the old legal system and no new system was established in the place of the old one which to any degree could cope with the condition of affairs.

Further, not only did the emancipation of the slaves leave no restriction upon the manifestation of race prejudice in the form of summary procedure against negro criminals, but the sudden elevation of the negroes to political equality with the whites directly encouraged its display. "Two hundred years or more of slavery educated both the white and the black to a fixed order of society, in which the negro was the servant and the white man the master. In one generation, through as devastat-

[1] *Outlook*, Dec. 26, 1903 (75 : 984).

ing a war as any country ever experienced, slavery was abolished, the vast property interests in the slave destroyed, the structure of society reversed, the master put at the bottom and the slave at the top." [1] In the light of subsequent history a greater mistake could scarcely have been made than that of giving the elective franchise to the newly emancipated slave. He was far from being a fully developed man capable of exercising the duties of citizenship in a democratic government, but in the legal institutions which were established in the South during the period of Reconstruction it was assumed that he was entitled to an equal share in the government with his former master. A legal system was established which had no basis in the order of society then existing. The result was enmity and bitterness between whites and blacks at a time when there should have been sympathy and forbearance, and summary and illegal measures were adopted by the whites to prevent negro domination.

Any one who would deal intelligently with the questions presenting themselves in the South to-day must recognize the existence of a racial prejudice. In some respects it is an unreasoning prejudice, a prejudice in the extreme sense of the word, but there is also a real and substantial basis for such racial antipathy, and it is a feeling which is not likely to disappear for generations to come. It must be taken into account in the consideration of all remedies proposed for existing evils in the South. It is something that cannot be removed by legislative enactments; neither can it be destroyed by constant crying out

[1] *Outlook*, Dec. 26, 1903 (75 : 984).

against it. While it does not justify the lynching of negroes, it does furnish a standpoint from which justification is easy, and it is a fact which makes the prevention of such lynchings extremely difficult, particularly where brutal crimes are committed upon whites by negroes.

The commonest justification for lynching negroes in recent years, the plausibility of which rests very largely on race prejudice, is the crime of rape as directed against white women. According to Tillinghast this crime has come into existence since the Civil War, and its perpetrators are overcome in many cases by primitive passions which master the criminal's whole being, a great fear being present also which impels to murder.[1] Strictly speaking, this crime has not come into existence since the Civil War. It is not a new crime to the negro. It has merely increased and become more common along with the general increase in criminality manifest in the negro race since emancipation.[2]

In colonial times laws were in force in a number of the colonies providing for the punishment of rape committed

[1] See p. 200 of monograph "The Negro in Africa and America," referred to above. That this crime is of recent origin is either stated or assumed by almost every writer who discusses the lynching of negroes. See, for example, article by Thomas Nelson Page in *The North American Review*, January, 1904 (178: 33).

[2] From a study of the prison statistics furnished by the United States census, Professor Walter F. Willcox came to the positive conclusion that "a large and increasing amount of negro crime is manifested all over the country." — See an address on "Negro Criminality," delivered before the American Social Science Association, on Sept. 6, 1899 — " Journal of Proceedings," No. 37, p. 97.

A like opinion is expressed by many writers. See, for example, *Forum*, October, 1898 (16: 167); *Outlook*, Oct. 31, 1903 (75: 493); *Outlook*, Dec. 26, 1903 (75: 984).

by negroes on white women, and there were numerous instances of the perpetration of this crime.[1]

In the year 1705 the Assembly of the Province of Pennsylvania enacted that "WHEREAS some Difficulties have arisen within this Province, about the Manner of Trial and Punishment of *Negroes* committing Murder, Manslaughter, Buggery, Burglary, Rapes, Attempts of Rapes . . . it shall and may be lawful for two justices of the Peace of this Province, who shall be particularly commissionated by the Governor for that Service, within the respective Counties thereof, and Six of the most substantial Freeholders of the Neighbourhood to hear, examine, try and determine . . . and shall be punished by Death. And for an Attempt of Rape or Ravishment on any white Woman or Maid, and for robbing, stealing, or fraudulently taking and carrying away any Goods, living or dead, above the Value of *Five Pounds*, every *Negroe*, upon Conviction of any of said Crimes, shall be whipped Thirty-nine Lashes, and branded on the Forehead with the Letter R or T, and exported out of this Province by the Master or Owner, within Six Months after Conviction, never to return into the same, upon Pain of Death, and shall be kept in Prison till Exportation at their Masters or Owners or their own Charge."[2]

By an act passed December 10, 1712, the colony of

---

[1] For a number of references on the subject of rape and its punishment, and also on the subject of burning alive as a legal punishment for crime, during the colonial period, the writer is indebted to Mr. Albert Matthews.

[2] "Acts of Assembly of the Province of Pennsylvania" (1775), pp. 45–46.

On May 5, 1722, it became the law of Pennsylvania that importers of servants who have been convicted of rape must pay a duty and enter security for good behavior for one year. — Statutes at Large of Pennsylvania, III, 264.

New York provided that "all and every Negro Indian or
other Slave, who . . . . shall murder or otherwise kill
. . . or conspire or attempt the Death of any of Her
Majesty's liege people, not being Slaves, or shall commit
or attempt any rape on any of said Subjects, or shall
wilfully burn any dwelling-house, barn, etc. . . . or shall
wilfully mutilate, mayhem or dismember any of the said
Subjects not being Slaves as aforesaid, or shall wilfully
murder any Negro, Indian or Mallatto Slave within this
Colony, and shall thereof be convicted before three or
more of Her Majesty's Justices of the Peace . . . in Con-
junction with five of the principal ffreeholders of the
County wherein such fact shall be committed, . . . or
before any Court of Oyer and Terminer or General Gaole
Delivery . . . shall suffer the pains of Death in such
manner and with such circumstances as the aggravation
or enormity of their Crimes in the Judgment of the Justices of those Courts aforesaid, or as in the judgment of
Seven of the said Justices and ffreeholders they shall
merit and require." [1]

By an act passed March 11, 1713–14, the General
Assembly of the Province of New Jersey made the above
enactment the law of New Jersey, and added the provision that "if any Negro, Indian or Mulatto Slave shall
attempt to ravish any white Woman or Maid . . . any
two Justices of the Peace are hereby authorized to inflict

[1] Colonial Laws of New York, I, 765–766.
Compare law of Aug. 8, 1688, in the Island of Barbadoes, which provided that two justices and three freeholders were to "give sentence of
Death upon" negroes, for murder, rape, burning houses, &c. — Acts
of Assembly Passed in the Island of Barbadoes, From 1648, to 1718
(1721), pp. 140–141.

such corporal Punishment, not extending to Life or Limb, upon such Slave or Slaves so offending, as to the said Justices shall seem meet."

In 1721 Delaware passed "An Act for the Trial of Negroes" the provisions of which were similar to those of the law of Pennsylvania enacted in 1705. Two justices of the peace, "particularly commissionated by the Governor for that service within the respective counties thereof," and six of the most substantial freeholders of the neighborhood, were to hear, examine, try and determine offenses committed by negro or mulatto slaves, and it was provided that "if any Negro or Mulatto slave . . . shall attempt to commit a rape on a white woman or maid, they shall be tried in manner aforesaid, and shall be punished by standing four hours in the pillory at the Court-House on some court day, with both ears nailed to the pillory, and before he be taken down from the same shall have both his ears cut off close to his head." [1]

By an act of June 8, 1751, it became the law of Maryland "that if any slave or slaves shall at any time consult, advise, conspire or attempt to raise any insurrection within this province, or to murder or poison any person or persons whatsoever, or to commit a rape upon any white woman, or to burn any house or houses, and be thereof convict by confession or verdict . . . shall suffer death, as in cases of felony, without benefit of clergy." [2]

In North Carolina, in 1758, the Assembly resolved to

---

[1] Laws of the State of Delaware (1797), I, 102–105.

By an act passed in January, 1797, thirty-nine lashes well laid on were added to the punishment for an attempted rape on a white woman or maid. — Laws of the State of Delaware (1797), II, 1321–1324.

[2] Laws of Maryland (1799), Chapter XIV.

try "a plan which would save the lives of the slaves and still act as a deterrent from further crimes." It was enacted "that except for rape or murder no male slave who had committed a crime which was ordinarily punished by death should suffer death for the first offence; but that on due conviction such an offender should be castrated, the sheriff to be allowed for the operation twenty shillings to be paid by the public. The court must fix the value of the slave before the execution of this sentence, so that if it should be the cause of his death there might be no dispute as to the value to be paid his master. Three pounds were allowed by the public for the curing of the slave's wounds. For the second offence death might be the penalty." [1]

Foregoing further quotation and reference, the statement may be made that in the colonial period, when laws were enacted for the trial and punishment of offenses committed by negroes upon whites, rape was usually one of the offenses for which capital punishment was provided, and considerable discretion was generally allowed the judicial authorities as to the manner in which the penalty should be inflicted, the methods of hanging and burning alive both being employed.

In Massachusetts, in the year 1676, Basto, a negro slave,

---

[1] See John S. Bassett: "Slavery and Servitude in the Colony of North Carolina" — Johns Hopkins Historical Studies (1896), XIV, 199. In Virginia the punishment of castration was so frequently inflicted upon slaves by the county courts that the Assembly deemed it necessary to enact that "it shall not be lawful for any county or corporation court, to order and direct castration of any slave, except such slave shall be convicted of an attempt to ravish a white woman, in which case they may inflict such punishment." — See Hening: "Virginia Statutes at Large," VI, 3; VIII, 358; Samuel Sheperd: "Virginia Statutes at Large" (New Series, 1835), I, 125.

was sentenced to be hanged for rape on the daughter of his master.[1]

In New Jersey, in the year 1731, "a negro slave called Harry, ravished Annatye Pryers, but, apparently without exercising much force; sentenced to receive forty-one lashes and to be branded on the right shoulder with the letter 'B.'"[2]

In Maryland, in 1739, "two slaves of Anne Arundel were executed, one for burglary, the other for rape on a white woman; and the body of the second, who had been a notorious offender, was hung in chains at some distance from the gallows."[3]

In Somerset County, New Jersey, in the year 1744, a young negro was burnt alive for ravishing a white child about nine years old.[4]

The punishment of burning alive, which was sometimes applied to negroes by the courts during the colonial period, was, however, usually inflicted for other offenses than rape, such as murder or conspiracy to murder (particularly by the use of poison), insurrection, and arson.[5] But this punishment was never applied to negroes during the

---

[1] "Records of the Court of Assistants of the Colony of the Massachusetts Bay" (J. Noble, 1901), p. 74.

The following passage is taken from the *Boston Chronicle*, Sept. 26 — Oct. 3, 1768 (No. 42, I, 383): "We hear that a negro fellow was tried at the Assizes held lately at Worcester, for a rape, and found guilty, and received sentence of death. — A white man was also tried and found guilty of the same crime, and sentenced to sit on the gallows."

[2] See "Proceedings of the New Jersey Historical Society" (1874), 2d Series, III, 178.

[3] See J. R. Brackett: "The Negro in Maryland" (1889), p. 131.

[4] *Pennsylvania Gazette*, Dec. 14, 1744 (N. J. *Archives*, XII, 244).

[5] The basis for these statements is a collection of notes on legal burning alive made by Mr. Albert Matthews. Compare John Fiske: "Old Virginia and her Neighbours" (1897), II, 265.

colonial period except by judicial decree. Indeed, with the possible exception of the slave insurrection in South Carolina in 1740,[1] there are no instances recorded in colonial history where slaves were publicly executed without trial.[2] Both by law and by public sentiment slaves were recognized as chattels, and when they were executed for crimes for the commission of which the owners could in no way be held responsible, such owners were entitled to indemnification and could enter suit at law for damages. It was customary for the courts when passing sentence of death upon a slave to fix the valuation of the slave, and this sum was then paid to the owner.

[1] Section LVI of "An Act for the better Ordering and Governing Negroes and other Slaves in this Province," dated the 10th day of May, 1740, reads as follows: "And *whereas*, several negroes did lately rise in rebellion, and did commit many barbarous murders at Stono and other parts adjacent thereto; and *whereas*, in suppressing the said rebels, several of them were killed and others taken alive and executed; and as the exigence and danger the inhabitants at that time were in and exposed to, would not admit of the formality of a legal trial of such rebellious negroes, but for their own security, the said inhabitants were obliged to put such negroes to immediate death; to prevent, therefore, any person or persons being questioned for any matter or thing done in the suppression or execution of the said rebellious negroes, as also any litigious suit, action, or prosecution that may be brought, sued or prosecuted or commenced against such person or persons for or concerning the same; *Be it enacted* by the authority aforesaid, That all and every act, matter and thing, had, done, committed and executed, in and about the suppressing and putting all and every the said negro and negroes to death, is and are hereby declared lawful, to all intents and purposes whatsoever, as fully and amply as if such rebellious negroes had undergone a formal trial and condemnation, notwithstanding any want of form or omission whatever in the trial of such negroes; and any law, usage or custom to the contrary thereof in any wise notwithstanding." — "Statutes at Large of South Carolina" (edited by D. J. McCord, 1840), VII, 416–417.

[2] Instances are recorded where Indians who had committed the crime of rape on white females were legally dealt with. See "Records of the Colony of the Massachusetts Bay in New England," II, 23; "New Haven Colonial Records" (Hoadly, 1858), p. 543; "Rhode Island Colonial Records," II, 420, 427, 428; "Records of the Court of Assistants of the Colony of the Massachusetts Bay" (J. Noble, 1901), pp. 21–22; "Plymouth Colony Records," VI, 98.

There is evidence to show that this crime directed against white women continued to be perpetrated down to the time of the Civil War. The Salem (Mass.) Gazette for October 5, 1813, contained this item: "At the late term of the Supreme Judicial Court, holden at Northampton, Peter Pyner, a black man, was convicted of a Rape, committed on the body of a *white female*. The circumstances of the case were of a very distressing nature, and the evidence of his guilt clear beyond a question. Sentence of Death was pronounced by his Honor Chief Justice Parsons, in a solemn and affecting manner."

The Richmond Enquirer of December 14, 1813, gives an account of the killing of a negro slave by a white woman in defense of her virtue.[1]

The following passages are taken from Niles' Register in the years 1821 and 1822. "*A Monster.* A negro fellow, armed with a gun, seized upon a respectable married lady, near Cartersville, Va., and attempted to commit a rape on her. After a long contest, she succeeded in getting out of his clutches, when he fired at her, but missed his aim. About an hour afterwards, he in like manner attacked another married lady — not succeeding, after a desperate struggle, he attempted to kill her with a knife, but she wrested it from him, and getting released, ran away, when he fired at her and lodged many shot in the back of her neck and head — and yet, thus wounded, she escaped. The fellow declared his intention of thus serving all the white women he could meet with. A reward is offered for his apprehension."[2]

[1] *Niles' Register*, Dec. 25, 1813 (5: 279).
[2] *Niles' Register*, Aug. 25, 1821 (20: 415–416).

"*A negro*, near Winchester, in Virginia, lately assailed two young ladies, tied them to trees and compelled them to endure his loathsome caresses; but was happily frustrated as to his ultimate design." [1]

"*Trial of Ned.* A negro fellow so named, was tried and condemned at Norfolk on the 19th inst. for the crime of committing a rape on the person of a respectable white woman. He was found guilty, and the decision of the court was received with a burst of applause." [2]

"These remarks were chiefly induced by reflecting on the late conspiracy at Charleston, and certain shocking enormities committed near Norfolk and in North Carolina on the persons of white women, for which the perpetrators were put to death, the relation of which is too disgusting for our pages. Thirty-five have been hung and others remain for execution at Charleston, and many were sentenced to transportation, &c. yet it appears that the trials are not yet over. The plot seems to have been well devised, its operation was extensive, and its intent terrific. . . . When the plan was nearly ripe, the conspiracy was made known, and a large number of the supposed principals were arrested — twenty-two of whom were executed in one day! . . . The system of slavery involves in itself a state of dreadful severity, for it is sustained only by force — and about 60 years ago, thirteen blacks were burnt alive in the then colony of New York for insurrectionary movements." [3]

---

[1] *Niles' Register*, June 8, 1822 (22: 238).

[2] *Niles' Register*, July 13, 1822 (22: 320).

[3] *Niles' Register*, Sept. 14, 1822 (23: 18). It was in the year 1741 that the thirteen blacks were burned at the stake in New York by judicial decree.

The following item appeared in Niles' Register for July 16, 1831 (40:345): "A young lady, in Duplin County, North Carolina, about fourteen years old, while proceeding to pay a visit to a neighbor between eleven and twelve o'clock, noon, was violated and murdered close to the road, after an apparently severe struggle, the ground at the place being much trodden. The *Infernal*, after accomplishing his first purpose, cut her throat! No clue had been discovered by which to trace the villain."

Niles' Register for August 24, 1833 (44:423) contained the following: "A free negro calling himself James Warfield, has been committed to the jail of Harford county, Maryland, charged with the commission of a rape upon a little girl aged nine years, the daughter of Mr. William Adams, a respectable resident of that county."

Such evidence shows that the crime of rape directed against white women was not unknown prior to 1860.[1] As regards other crimes frequently committed by negroes during the period of slavery, apparently it formed a rather small proportion. It was far from being a crime that was more frequently committed than any other, and yet it was one for the perpetration of which the negroes showed a marked propensity whenever an opportunity presented itself. Under the institution of slavery, however, such opportunities were few. From the nature of slavery, the negro seldom had an opportunity to ravish a white woman. The strong, burly negro who was considered dangerous and likely to commit violence was ordinarily put at hard labor in the fields and kept under

---

[1] Additional evidence has been given above in another connection. See Chapter IV.

strict surveillance. Also, the discipline to which the negro was subjected when a slave gave him a mastery over himself which it has been extremely difficult for him to obtain by his own efforts. Habits of obedience and industry, however inculcated, go very far toward restraining criminal impulses. The good effects of the discipline of the slave régime were particularly manifest during the progress of the Civil War, when the Southern planters were obliged to leave their families with no other protectors than the slaves, and these slaves discharged their trust with uniform faithfulness and loyalty.

From the colonial period to the beginning of the antislavery agitation in the early thirties, the law was regularly allowed to take its course in dealing with negro criminals. Very little inclination was shown on the part of the people to inflict punishment otherwise than as was then provided by law. With regard to the crime of rape two instances may be cited where summary measures were employed.

Niles' Register for November 15, 1823 (25:176) contained this item: "*Negro Frank* was lately tried at Frederick, Maryland, for having defloured a young white female. That the fact had taken place, and as stated, in the most brutal manner, was admitted; but Frank was acquitted for the want of sufficient proof of his person. Some of the people, however, thought he was guilty — and, after his release, he was beaten so severely, as almost to deprive him of life."

The following item appeared in Niles' Register for March 10, 1832 (42:22): "A negro fellow lately committed a horrid outrage on the body of a girl twelve or thirteen

years old, the daughter of a respectable gentleman in
Dinwiddie county, Virginia, who was almost killed by his
brutality.   The ravisher was caught by the father, and
instantly punished with 150 lashes, of which it was believed that he would die — if not he would be brought
to trial."

That there was an increasing disposition to resort to
summary methods for the punishment of negroes during
the period 1830–1860 has been shown in the evidence
cited in Chapter IV; but so far as the infliction of summary capital punishment was concerned, that did not
become a serious evil until the time of the Reconstruction of the Southern States.   Comparatively few negroes
were lynched until after the close of the War.   It may
be said, therefore, that while race prejudice and the
crime of rape against white women both existed as
causes for the summary treatment of negroes prior to the
Civil War, both were held in check by the institution
of slavery.

It thus appears that throughout the period of slavery
there was a greater reliance on legal procedure for the
treatment of negroes accused of heinous offenses than has
been manifest since that time; and not only did the institution of slavery directly bring about this greater reliance on legal procedure, by the suppression of the strongest incentives toward adopting summary and illegal procedure, but it made possible the enactment of special laws
providing for a more expeditious trial and execution of
sentence in the case of negro offenders.

In the year 1740, South Carolina made the following
provision for the trial of slaves:

"And *whereas*, natural justice forbids that any person, of what condition soever, should be condemned unheard, and the order of civil government requires that for the due and equal administration of justice, some convenient method and form of trial should be established; *Be it therefore enacted* by the authority aforesaid, That all crimes and offences which shall be committed by slaves in this Province, and for which capital punishment shall or lawfully may be inflicted, shall be heard, examined, tried, adjudged and finally determined by any two justices assigned to keep the peace, and any number of free-holders not less than three or more than five, in the county where the offences shall be committed, and who lives in the parts adjacent, and can be most conveniently assembled; either of which justices, on complaint made or information received of any such offence committed by a slave, shall commit the offender to the safe custody of the constable of the parish where such offence shall be committed, and shall without delay, by warrant under his hand and seal, call to his assistance and request any one of the nearest justices of the peace to associate with him, and shall, by the same warrant, summon such a number of the neighboring freeholders as aforesaid, to assemble and meet together with the said justices, at a certain day and place, not exceeding three days after the apprehending of such slave or slaves[1]; and the justices and freeholders being so assembled, shall cause the slave accused or charged, to be brought before them, and shall hear the accusation which shall be brought against such slave, and his or her defence, and shall proceed to the examination of witnesses and other evidences, and finally to hear and determine the matter brought

[1] By an act passed the 11th day of May, 1754, power was given the justice to postpone the trial to such time as he thought proper, owing to the frequent difficulty of procuring the justice and the freeholders and the witnesses to attend the trial within the three days. — "Statutes at Large of S. C." (edited by D. J. McCord, 1840), VII, 426–427.

before them, in the most summary and expeditious manner; and in case the offender shall be convicted of any crime for which by law the offender ought to suffer death, the said justices shall give judgment, and award and cause execution of their sentence to be done, by inflicting such manner of death and at such time, as the said justices, by and with the consent of the freeholders, shall direct, and which they shall judge will be most effectual to deter others from offending in the like manner.

"*And be it further enacted* by the authority aforesaid, That if any crime or offence not capital, shall be committed by any slave, such slave shall be proceeded against and tried for such offence in the manner hereinbefore directed, by any one justice of the peace and any two freeholders of the country where the offence shall be committed, and can be most conveniently assembled; and the said justice and freeholders shall be assembled, summoned and called together, and shall proceed upon the trial of any slave who shall commit any offence not capital, in like manner as is hereinbefore directed for trying of causes capital. And in case any slave shall be convicted before them of any offence not capital, the said one justice, by and with the consent of the said freeholders, shall give judgment for the inflicting any corporal punishment, not extending to the taking away life or member, as he and they in their discretion shall think fit, and shall award and cause execution to be done accordingly. *Provided always*, that if the said one justice and two freeholders, upon examination of any slave charged or accused before them for an offence not capital, shall find the same to be a greater offence, and may deserve death, they shall, with all convenient speed, summons and request the assistance of another justice and one or more freeholders, not exceeding three, which said justice and freeholders newly assembled, shall join with the justice and freeholders first assembled, and shall proceed in the trial, and unto final judgment and execution, if the case shall so require, in manner as is hereinbefore directed for the trial of capital offences.

"*And be it further enacted* by the authority aforesaid, That two justices and one freeholder, or one justice and two freeholders, of the said two justices and three freeholders, shall make a quorum, and the conviction or acquittal of any slave or slaves by such a quorum of them shall be final in all capital cases; but on the trial of slaves for offences not capital, it shall and may be sufficient if before sentence or judgment shall be given for inflicting a corporal punishment, not extending to life or member, that one justice and any one of the freeholders shall agree that the slave accused is guilty of the offence with which he shall be charged. . . .

"And *whereas*, slaves may be harbored and encouraged to commit offences, and concealed and received by free negroes, and such free negroes may escape the punishment due to their crimes, for want of sufficient and legal evidence against them; *Be it therefore further enacted* by the authority aforesaid, That the evidence of any free Indian or slave, without oath, shall in like manner be allowed and admitted in all cases against any free negroes, Indians (free Indians in amity with this government, only excepted,) mulattoe or mustizoe; and all crimes and offences committed by free negroes, Indians, (except as before excepted,) mulattoes or mustizoes, shall be proceeded in, heard, tried, adjudged and determined by the justices and freeholders appointed by this Act for the trial of slaves, in like manner, order and form, as is hereby directed and appointed for the proceedings and trial of crimes and offences committed by slaves; any law, statute, usage or custom to the contrary notwithstanding."[1]

---

[1] "Statutes at Large of South Carolina" (edited by D. J. McCord, 1840), VII, 400–402. It was also provided by this act, which was passed the 10th day of May, 1740, that an oath for the faithful discharge of duty

Few of the other colonies made such careful and comprehensive provision for expediting the trial of slaves, whether accused of minor or of capital offenses. A number of the other colonies, however, made similar provision for the prompt trial of slaves and followed the same general principles in their legislation affecting the punishment of offenses committed by slaves.[1] Indeed, it was generally true throughout the period of slavery that a special form of trial was provided in the case of slaves accused of serious offenses, and that special penalties were imposed upon such offenders. It is to be noted in the South Carolina Act of 1740 that free negroes were given the same form of trial as the slaves, and that the whole purport and spirit of the statute was merely that justice might be done.

So long as the negro race was in bondage to the white race, then, not only were the inciting causes of negro lynching largely held in check, but such provisions were made for the trial and punishment of miscreant slaves that resort to lynching was wholly without justification. Even after the anti-slavery agitation had begun in the early thirties and summary measures were occasionally taken against negro offenders, justification was claimed on the ground of the incendiary publications and utterances of the abolitionists rather than the specific crimes

be taken by the freeholders when they assembled with the justices for the trial of prisoners, that the evidence of slaves, without oath, be admitted against slaves, that for certain offenses certain penalties be imposed, that compensation be allowed the owners of slaves executed, that masters and other persons be compelled to give evidence, that the constables execute or punish slaves according to the judgments rendered, &c., &c.

[1] The laws of Pennsylvania, New York, New Jersey, and Delaware have been cited above.

committed by the blacks. The fact that during the period of slavery, in the case of the raping of white women, as well as of other crimes, the law was generally allowed to take its course, goes far toward refuting the argument that lynching is necessary to repress crime among the negroes in the South to-day.

History has shown it to be a fundamental mistake to assume that illegal and summary procedure against a particular offense will deter from that offense. As one writer has very forcibly said, if an argument based on this assumption were put into plain language, it would read: "Let past crime be met with present crime in order that future crime may be prevented." [1] All revengeful dealing with crime has increased crime rather than lessened it. The only deterrent from crime that men have found is the prompt and certain and solemn punishment by law, sustained and supported by a confident, unyielding body of public opinion. [2]

The attempt to justify the lynching of negroes on the plea that lynching for rape committed upon white women is necessary to repress that crime is without support in any respect. Frederick Douglass lessened the force of this plea very considerably when he pointed out that there have been three distinct excuses offered for the persecution of negroes in the United States. First, it was because of insurrections; then, it was the fear of negro domination and supremacy; then, when neither of these was any longer defensible as an excuse, the crime of

[1] "Negro Outrage no Excuse for Lynching" — *Forum*, November, 1893 (16: 300).

[2] Walter H. Page: "The Last Hold of the Southern Bully" — *Forum*, November, 1893 (16: 303).

assault upon white women was put forward to justify. their persecution.[1] The fact that not more than thirty-four per cent of the negroes lynched in the last twenty-two years have been lynched for that crime likewise vitiates such a plea of justification. The facts as known indicate that lynching for that crime, instead of having a repressive influence, has directly stimulated its perpetration. Assaults on white women have occurred again and again immediately following a lynching for such crime, and they have so occurred in the same neighborhood where the lynching took place.[2] It has been publicly stated that in one instance a negro who had witnessed a lynching for this crime actually committed an assault on his way home.[3]

The lynching of negroes in recent years can be justified on no other ground than that the law as formulated and administered has proved inadequate to deal with the situation — that there has been governmental inefficiency. Not that guilty negroes frequently escape conviction in the Southern courts, or that they fail to receive punishment to the full extent of the law, but rather that the law and its administration seem utterly unsuited to the function of dealing with negro criminals. A judicial system

[1] "Lynching of Black People because they are Black" — *Our Day*, 13: 298 (1894).

[2] The following passage is taken from an editorial in the *Houston* (Texas) *Post* of October 23, 1902: "From the same telegraph pole from which the two negroes were hanged at Hempstead on Tuesday, a rapist was hanged less than two months ago. The circumstances of the first execution were fully known to the victims of the second mob. This teaches very plainly that lynching does not deter."

[3] See "The Epidemic of Savagery," *Outlook*, Sept. 7, 1901 (69: 9); also, "The Lynching of Negroes," by Thomas Nelson Page, *North American Review*, January, 1904 (178: 33).

adapted to a highly civilized and cultured race is not equally applicable to a race of inferior civilization, and the failure to realize this fact and act upon it, by making special provision for the control of the negro population in the Southern States since slavery was abolished, is a fundamental reason for the disrepute into which legal procedure has fallen as regards negroes accused of offenses against the whites.[1]

The mistakes of Reconstruction times are not yet blotted out in the South. Abstractions still control where racial characteristics, circumstances, and conditions should be the determining factors. Ever since the Civil War the Southern people have been blindly groping after some system other than slavery whereby two races of widely different interests and attainments can live together in peace and harmony under a republican form of government, and at the same time a vast number of Northern people have been misinterpreting their motives and watching every move with a critical and suspicious eye, ready at any moment to shout across Mason and Dixon's line that the negroes must have their rights under the Constitution of the United States and the amendments thereto.[2] Under such conditions it has been practically impossible for the South to find a satisfactory solution of its problem, and herein lies all the justification that can be found for the use of summary measures in dealing

[1] Compare the conclusion arrived at by a Georgia lawyer in an article in the *Forum*, October, 1893 (16: 176).

[2] Even such a discriminating and estimable journal as the *Nation* still makes use of every possible occasion to preach the rights of man in general and of the negro in particular, utterly ignoring the question of capability and responsibility.

with the increasing criminality which has manifested itself in the younger generations of the colored race.

In the last analysis lynch-law in this country is without any justification whatsoever. In a government founded on the idea that ultimate power and authority shall rest with the people, and in which sufficient facility has been given to the expression of the collective will of the people so that the acts of the government, the formulation of the law, and the administration of justice, ought adequately to represent this collective will, there is no tenable ground on which to vindicate the practice of punishing criminals other than by the regularly constituted courts and the officers of the law. But if circumstances and conditions be taken into consideration and the history of the practice carefully noted, it is possible to see how justification has come about through the different points of view that have been taken. From the standpoint of the frontiersmen and pioneers summary procedure in certain cases was wholly justifiable. From the standpoint of the Southerners during the period of Reconstruction summary procedure was likewise wholly justifiable. To men living in a community where a particularly brutal and barbarous crime is committed upon a white person by a negro, the prompt lynching of the negro, even with some torture and cruelty, seems entirely defensible. Thus, while we cannot justify the practice of lynching on any ground whatever, yet the fact remains that it has been repeatedly justified in one way or another.

CHAPTER VIII

REMEDIES

In the consideration of remedies for lynching it is to
the type of lynch-law procedure which prevails in well
settled communities that attention is to be directed.
The type of lynch-law procedure which is characteristic
of a frontier society naturally ceases to exist with the dis-
appearance of that unorganized form of society. The
changed social conditions incident to an increasing den-
sity of the population in a frontier region, and the establishment of a regular and adequate judiciary, remove
every cause for the existence of the frontier type of lynch-
law. The rapid colonization of the western section of
the United States has thus made that phase of the lynching question no longer a serious matter. But how to
put an end to the practice of lynching in older communities possessing well established civil regulations is a
problem for which the people of the United States have
not yet found a satisfactory solution.

As has been pointed out in the preceding chapter, there
has been a strong popular sentiment in the United States,
even down to the present day, excusing and apologizing
for lynch-law procedure. On the other hand, however,
there has not been wanting at the same time a spirit of
denunciation and disapprobation[1]; although it was not

[1] See, for example, J. H. Ingraham: "The South-West" (1835), II,
185–189.

until the early nineties, when public attention was directed
to the subject by reason of the occurrence of a number of
flagrant cases of lynching, that determined efforts were
put forth to check the practice. Previous to that time
such discussion as there was of the subject brought no
effective restraint to bear on the continuance of the practice, either because of the intensely partizan character of
the discussion as between the North and the South, or
because, while the practice in general was denounced,
particular instances of lynching were excused.[1] The
newspapers and magazines took comparatively little
notice of lynchings until after the year 1890. The newspapers printed accounts of such occurrences, but the
editorial protests were few, and the magazine literature is
almost barren on the subject.

On March 14, 1891, the eleven Italians who were
accused of complicity in the murder of the chief of police
of New Orleans were summarily put to death by a mob.
On May 30, 1891, Tump Hampton, colored, was burned
at the stake in the parish of St. Tammany, Louisiana.
On January 31, 1893, a negro by the name of Henry
Smith was publicly burned at the stake with extreme torture at Paris, Texas.[2] Excursion trains were run for
the occasion and there were many women and children
in the throng which watched the sufferings of the victim.
These and other instances of a similar character, together with the increased number of lynchings in the
years 1891, 1892, 1893 (See charts I and IV), focused

[1] See, for example, *Southern Literary Messenger*, March, 1839
(5: 219).

[2] See *Public Opinion*, Feb. 11, 1893 (14: 448).

the attention of the world upon the American practice of lynching. Italy demanded from the United States an indemnity for the lynching of the Italians at New Orleans. Foreign newspapers and periodicals united in heaping abusive censure upon the United States. Repeated and insistent demands were made, in America as well as in Europe, that lynchers be brought to justice and be punished as other murderers are punished.

An effort was also made at this time to so organize foreign public opinion that it would be directly effective in putting an end to the practice of lynching. Miss Ida B. Wells, colored, who was editor of the Free Speech published at Memphis, Tennessee, and whose paper was suppressed because she so fiercely denounced the lynching of some colored young men and arraigned the authorities for failing to punish the lynchers,[1] gave a series of lectures in England in 1893–94, and started a crusade against lynching by organizing anti-lynching societies, enrolling as members several men of international prominence.[2] These bodies proposed to send a committee to this country "to collect statistics and quietly to investigate the subject of lynchings in the United States." The South rose *en masse* against such a visit and the governors of the Southern States with one or two exceptions vehemently denounced the whole project. The statement of Governor O'Ferrall of Virginia, himself an anti-lynching man, is typical of the Southern sentiment. "Things have come to a pretty pass in this country," he said in the

---

[1] See *Our Day*, May, 1893 (11: 333).

[2] See Haydn's "Dictionary of Dates" (1898), p. 681. Also, "The Cyclopedic Review of Current History" (1894), p. 647.

New York World, "when we are to have a lot of English moralists sticking their noses into our internal affairs. It is the quintessence of brass and impudence."[1] The English committee never came to this country, and Miss Wells at length recognized the futility of further work in England and returned home. She has since organized anti-lynching societies in various parts of the North,[2] and more recently, as chairman of the Anti-lynching Bureau of the National Afro-American Council, has to all appearance been working principally among her own people, urging them to take steps to prevent lynching.[3]

Out of all this discussion, agitation, and censure there came proposals for various remedies for lynching. Various reasons were assigned for the prevalence of the practice and consequently there was little agreement in the measures which were proposed for its prevention or suppression, but most of the proposed measures were of the nature of new or additional laws directed specifically against lynching or mob violence.

Early in the year 1894 a number of the citizens of Louisiana petitioned the legislature of that State to enact stringent laws against lynching, but the legislature adjourned without fulfilling the request. A number of governors at about this time, in messages to the State legislatures, called attention to the subject and recommended immediate legislation. Governor Hogg of Texas made the matter of lynching the subject of a special mes-

[1] The *New York World* secured "interviews" with nineteen governors on the subject of the proposed visit of the committee. See *American Law Review*, November — December, 1894 (28: 904).

[2] See *Literary Digest*, July 14, 1894.

[3] See *Independent*, May 16, 1901 (53: 1133).

sage, denouncing the practice and strongly urging the enactment of laws to prevent it. Governor O'Ferrall, in a message to the legislature of Virginia, recommended that the county in which a lynching occurs should be required to pay to the State treasury a sum not exceeding ten thousand dollars for the benefit of the public school fund. Recommendations of a similar character were subsequently made by the governors of Maryland and Georgia. Governor Atkinson of Georgia made the unique recommendation that if an officer in charge of a prisoner is not required to protect his charge at the hazard of his own life, he should be required to unshackle the prisoner, arm him, and give him an opportunity to defend himself. On the assumption that the law's delay or slowness is the principal cause for lynching, the governors of a number of States offered suggestions for a more expeditious judicial procedure. Of the many measures proposed, however, and of the numerous recommendations that special legislation be enacted against lynching, comparatively few have received from the various legislatures sufficient consideration to lead to the enactment of laws on the subject.[1]

The legislature of Georgia, in the year 1893, passed an act which authorized "any officer, charged with the duty of preserving the peace and executing the lawful warrants" of the State, who should have "knowledge of any violence attempted to be perpetrated upon any citizen . . . by mob violence and without authority of law," to summon a posse of citizens, who must respond or be punished for a

[1] See article by Edward Leigh Pell on "Prevention of Lynch-law Epidemics," *Review of Reviews*, March, 1898 (17: 321).

misdemeanor, whose duty it should be to use every means in their power, even to the extent of taking human life, to prevent such violence. It was made a misdemeanor for said officer to fail to call together a posse in such an emergency, and citizens who responded were authorized to carry weapons in the performance of their duties. Any person engaged in "mobbing or lynching any citizen . . . without due process of law" should be arrested and punished by imprisonment in the penitentiary for not less than one nor longer than twenty years; and if death resulted from such mob violence the person causing said death should be subject to indictment and trial for the offense of murder.[1]

The legislature of North Carolina in the year 1893 passed an act which provided that every person who should conspire to break or enter, or who should engage in breaking or entering, any jail or place of confinement of prisoners for the purpose of killing or injuring any person confined therein would be guilty of a felony and be punishable by a fine of not less than five hundred dollars and by imprisonment for not less than two nor more than fifteen years. It was made the duty of the prosecuting officer of the judicial district in which such a crime had been committed to take immediate proceedings against the guilty parties, and jurisdiction of the offense was conferred upon the superior court of any county adjoining that in which the violence was committed. It was also made a misdemeanor punishable by fine and imprisonment, one or both, at the discretion of the court, for a witness wilfully to fail to comply with the process served on him, or,

[1] See Georgia Code, 1895, Sections 356–359.

after being sworn, to refuse to answer questions pertinent
to the matter being investigated; nor was any person to be
excused from testifying on the ground that his evidence
might tend to criminate himself, for when he should be
thus examined as a witness for the State he became altogether pardoned of any and all participation in the crime
concerning which he was required to testify. The entire
cost incurred in the prosecution was to be paid by the
county in which the crime was committed, and in case
the commissioners of the county failed to provide a
sufficient guard for a jail in response to the request of the
sheriff, and the jail should be entered and a prisoner
killed, the county became responsible in damages to be
recovered by the personal representatives of the prisoner
killed.[1]

In the year 1895 the General Assembly of Georgia
enacted additional legislation on the subject of lynching
by passing an act which made penal the offense of hinder-
ing, obstructing, or interfering with sheriffs or their
deputies or constables in the execution of any order or
sentence of court after trial in criminal cases, and requiring sheriffs and constables to present to the grand jury
any and all persons so interfering. Penalties were provided for the offense and for failure to comply with the
provisions of the act, power being given the governor to
suspend a derelict sheriff or constable and to declare his
office vacant.[2]

In the constitution which South Carolina adopted in
1895, it was provided that "in case of any prisoner law-

---

[1] Public Laws of North Carolina, 1893, ch. 461.
[2] Georgia Laws, 1895, Part I, Title 7, No. 209.

fully in the charge, custody or control of any officer, State,
County or municipal, being seized and taken from said
officer through his negligence, permission or connivance,
by a mob or other unlawful assemblage of persons, and
at their hands suffering bodily violence or death," the
said officer should be deemed guilty of a misdemeanor,
and upon true bill found should be deposed from office
pending trial, and upon conviction should forfeit his
office, and, unless pardoned by the governor, should be
ineligible to hold any office of trust or profit within the
State.   It was made the duty of the prosecuting attorney
within whose circuit or county the offense might be committed to forthwith institute a prosecution against said
officer, who should be tried in such county in the same
circuit, other than the one in which the offense was committed, as the attorney-general might elect.   The fees
and mileage of all material witnesses both for the State
and the defense were to be paid by the State treasurer.
It was also provided that "in all cases of lynching when
death ensues, the county where such lynching takes place
shall, without regard to the conduct of the officers, be
liable in exemplary damages of not less than $2,000 to
the legal representatives of the person lynched," and that
"any county against which a judgment has been obtained
for damages in any case of lynching shall have the right
to recover the amount of said judgment from the parties
engaged in said lynching in any court of competent jurisdiction." [1]

[1] Constitution of South Carolina, Section 6, Article 6.   This article
of the constitution with additional provisions necessary to make its operation effective was passed by the legislature in 1896 as "An Act to Prevent
Lynching."   See Acts of South Carolina, 1896, p. 213.

In 1896 Ohio entered the list of States that have adopted anti-lynching laws. This Ohio act gave to lynching its first legal definition. A *lynching* and a *mob* are defined as follows: "That any collection of individuals, assembled for any unlawful purpose, intending to do damage or injury to any one or pretending to exercise correctional power over other persons by violence, and without authority of law, shall for the purpose of this act be regarded as a 'mob,' and any act of violence exercised by them upon the body of any person, shall constitute a 'lynching.'" Under this act any person who is taken from the hands of the officers of justice in any county by a mob, and is assaulted by the same with whips, clubs, missiles, or in any other manner, may recover damages from the county to the amount of one thousand dollars; any person assaulted by a mob and suffering lynching at their hands may recover from the county in which the assault is made five hundred dollars, or, if the injury is serious, one thousand dollars, or, if it result in permanent disability to earn a livelihood by manual labor, five thousand dollars; and the legal representative of any person suffering death by lynching at the hands of a mob may recover from the county in which such lynching occurs the sum of five thousand dollars, provision being made for the disposition of the recovery in such instances. Any person suffering death or injury at the hands of a mob engaged in an attempt to lynch another person is to be deemed within the provisions of the act, he or his legal representatives having the same right of action thereunder as one purposely injured or killed by such mob. An order to the commissioners of a county against which such recovery may be made, to include the same with costs of action in the next succeeding tax levy of said county, forms a part of the judgment in every such case. The county, however, has a right of action to recover the amount of any judgment against it, including costs, against any of the parties composing such mob, and any person present with hostile intent at such lynching is to be deemed a member of the mob and is liable to such action. In case a mob shall carry a prisoner into another county, or shall come from another county to commit violence on a prisoner brought from such county for safe keeping, the county in which the lynching was committed may recover the amount of the judgment and costs against the county from which the mob came, unless there was contributory negligence on the part of the officials of said county in failing to protect the prisoner or disperse said mob. It is also provided that nothing in the act shall be held to relieve any person concerned in such lynching from prosecution for homicide or assault for engaging therein.[1]

By an act of April 25, 1898, it is further provided in the law of Ohio that whoever shall break into or attempt to break into a jail or any prison, or to attack an officer, with intent to seize a prisoner for the purpose of lynching, shall be deemed guilty of a felony, and shall be confined

[1] 92 Ohio Laws 136. In this the original act the amount of damages that could be recovered was fixed at a certain sum; for assault, "the sum of $1000," for suffering lynching "the sum of $500," &c. In thus fixing the amount of damages it was said that the legislature had assumed judicial power and had thus rendered the act unconstitutional. To remedy this defect, the legislature on April 21, 1898, amended the act so that the amount of damages that might be recovered should be, for assault "any sum not exceeding $1000," for suffering lynching "any sum not exceeding $500," &c. See 93 Ohio Laws 161. Being Sections 4426–4 to 4426–14 of the Revised Statutes.

in the penitentiary for not more than ten years nor less than one year.[1]

In 1897, Tennessee, Kentucky, and Texas enacted laws directed against lynching. By the Tennessee act it was made a felony punishable by from three to twenty-one years' imprisonment, and by full judgment of infamy and disqualification, for two or more persons to form or remain in any conspiracy or combination, under any name, or upon any pretext whatsoever, to take human life, or engage in any act reasonably calculated to cause the loss of life; or to inflict corporal punishment or injury; or to burn or otherwise destroy property or to feloniously take the same. It was likewise made a felony punishable in like manner for any person either directly or indirectly to procure or encourage any one to become or remain a member of any such unlawful conspiracy or combination; or for any person either directly or indirectly to aid, abet, or encourage any person to engage or remain in such conspiracies or combinations, or to aid or abet in the accomplishment of any purpose or end of such conspiracies or combinations. Any person guilty of any of these offenses was declared to be incompetent to sit or serve on any grand or traverse jury, and it was made the duty of the court to carefully exclude all such persons from the juries, both grand and petit. It was provided that indictments framed under the act were not to be held insufficient by reason of the general nature of the charges preferred, or for embracing more than one of said offenses in the same indictment, and the act was to "take effect

[1] 93 Ohio Laws 411. Being Section 6908 of Title I, Part Fourth, Revised Statutes, Crimes and Offenses.

from and after its passage, the public welfare demanding it." [1]

By the Kentucky "Act to prevent lynching, &c.," which was amended by the omission of three sections and thus re-enacted in 1902, it was provided that if any two or more persons should confederate or band themselves together for the purpose of intimidating, alarming, disturbing, or injuring any persons, or to rescue any person or persons charged with a public offense from any officer with the view of inflicting any kind of punishment on them, or with the view of preventing their lawful prosecution for any such offense or to do any felonious act, they, or either of them, should be deemed guilty of felony, and upon conviction should be confined in the penitentiary not less than one nor more than five years. If any two or more persons should confederate or band together and go forth for the purpose of molesting, injuring, or destroying any property, real or personal, of another person, persons or corporation, whether the same be injured, molested or damaged or not, they should be guilty of a felony punishable by a like penalty; and if any injury should result to the person or property of any person or persons, by reason of any such unlawful acts, any one participating in, or aiding or abetting, such unlawful acts should be guilty of a felony, and upon conviction should be confined in the State penitentiary not less than one nor more than fifteen years, unless death should result, in which case the penalty for such offense should be that prescribed by law for murder. It was made no mitigation of the offense

[1] Acts of Tennessee, 1897, Chapter 52. This act was approved March 24, 1897.

for any one upon his trial, that he may have acted through
heat or passion, or that he may have acted without malice,
and the judge trying the case should so instruct the jury
in writing. It was provided, also, that any officer or
person having the custody of a prisoner should have the
power and it should be his duty to summon to his aid as
many of the able-bodied male citizens of his county as
might be necessary to protect such prisoner, any person
who should fail or refuse to respond to such summons
being liable to a fine of not less than one hundred dollars
nor more than five hundred dollars; and when any officer
in charge of a jail had reasonable grounds to believe that
said jail would be attacked by a mob or persons con-
federated or banded together for the purpose of inflicting
violence upon any inmate of said jail, he was authorized,
in his discretion, to arm said threatened inmates, with a
view to their own protection. Authority was given the
governor to offer a reward for the apprehension and
conviction of any offender of this law in any sum not exceeding five hundred dollars, and also to employ detec-
tives, in his discretion, not exceeding two at any one time,
provided the cost thereof should not exceed three thousand
dollars in any one year. The judge of the county court
of any county in which this law should be violated was
also given power to offer a reward not exceeding two
hundred dollars, or supplement the governor's reward,
for the arrest and conviction of any person violating the
act. It was also provided that any person who should
send, circulate, exhibit or put up any threatening notice
or letter, should upon conviction thereof be fined not less
than one hundred dollars nor more than five hundred

dollars, and be imprisoned in the county jail not less than three nor more than twelve months. In any prosecution under the act it should be no exemption for a witness that his testimony might incriminate himself; but no such testimony should be used against him in any prosecution except for perjury, and he should be discharged from all liability for any violation of the act so necessarily disclosed in his testimony.[1]

By the Texas law, which was enacted at a special session of the legislature, it was provided that whenever two or more persons should combine together for the purpose of mob violence, and in pursuance of said combination should "unlawfully and wilfully take the life of any reasonable creature in being by such violence," such person should be deemed guilty of murder by mob violence, and upon conviction thereof should be punished by death or confinement in the penitentiary for life, or according to the degree of murder, to be found by the jury. It was made the duty of the district judges to give this law specially in charge to the grand jury at the beginning of each term of court, and prosecution for murder under the act might be commenced and carried on in any county of the judicial district in which the offense should be committed, except the county of the offense. It was also provided that if any sheriff, deputy sheriff, constable, chief of police, city marshal or other officer in the State should permit or suffer any person in his custody charged with crime to be killed by one or more persons, or should

[1] Laws of Kentucky, 1897, Chapter 20. For the amendment and re-enactment of this law see Laws of Kentucky, 1902, Chapter 25. In the above résumé of the law nothing has been included from the sections which were repealed in 1902.

permit or suffer any such person to be taken from his custody and killed by one or more persons, he should be deemed guilty of official misconduct, and be removed from office, proceedings for removal to be conducted by the attorney-general in accordance with the provisions of the act, such cases taking precedence in all courts of all other cases. Pending trial such officer should be temporarily suspended from his office and should judgment be rendered against him he should not thereafter be elected or appointed to that office. The final section of the act reads as follows: "The fact that there is no adequate law in this State for the suppression of mob violence, creates an emergency and an imperative public necessity that the constitutional rule requiring all bills to be read on three several days be suspended, and that this act take effect and be in force from and after its passage, and it is so enacted." [1]

In 1899 an act dealing with the subject of lynching and violence by mobs was passed by the legislature of Indiana. In this act a *mob* and a *lynching* are defined as follows: "Any collection of individuals assembled for any unlawful purpose intending to injure any person by violence and without authority of law shall, for the purpose of this act, be regarded as a 'mob,' and any act of violence exercised by such mob upon the body of any person shall constitute the crime of 'lynching,' when such act or acts of violence result in death." It is provided that any person who actively participates in or actively aids or abets such lynching, upon conviction thereof, shall suffer

[1] Laws of Texas, 1897, Chapter 13. This act was approved June 19, 1897.

death or be imprisoned during life, in the discretion of the jury, and any person who, being a member of any such mob and present at any such lynching, shall not actively participate in the lynching, shall be guilty of abetting such lynching, and upon conviction thereof shall be imprisoned not less than two nor more than twenty-one years. Every person who shall, after the commission of the crime of lynching, harbor, conceal or assist any member of such mob, with the intent that he shall escape detention, arrest, capture, or punishment, shall be deemed an accessory after the fact, and upon conviction thereof shall be imprisoned not more than twenty-one years nor less than two years. Provision is made for the manner in which prosecutions shall be instituted under the act, and in case any persons shall come together in any county for the purpose of proceeding to another county, with the view of lynching any person, or in case any person or persons shall purchase or procure any rope, weapon, or other instrument in one county for the purpose of being used in lynching any person in another county, such crime of lynching, if committed, shall constitute a continuous offense from the time of its original inception, and the courts of any county in which such overt act has been committed shall have jurisdiction over the person of any member of the mob committing such overt act. Power is given the sheriff to call bystanders and others to his assistance and arm them for the protection of a prisoner, it being a misdemeanor for such persons to refuse assistance, punishable by a fine in any sum not less than one hundred dollars nor more than one thousand dollars, and imprisonment in the county jail for a period not exceeding six months. If at any time a sheriff has reason to believe that a prisoner in his custody is in danger of being lynched, and that he, with his deputies and assistants, is not able to protect the life of such prisoner, it shall be his duty at once to notify the governor of such facts; whereupon, the governor shall be authorized to furnish such militia as shall be necessary to preserve order and defend such prisoner.[1]

In 1901 the Indiana act received the following important amendment: "If any person shall be taken from the hands of a sheriff or his deputy having such person in custody, and shall be lynched, it shall be conclusive evidence of failure on the part of such sheriff to do his duty, and his office shall thereby and thereat immediately be vacated, and the coroner shall immediately succeed to and perform the duties of sheriff until the successor of such sheriff shall have been duly appointed, pursuant to existing law providing for the filling vacancies in such office, and such sheriff shall not thereafter be eligible to either election or reappointment to the office of sheriff: *Provided, however,* That such former sheriff may, within ten days after such lynching occurs, file with the governor his petition for reinstatement to the office of sheriff, and shall give **ten** days' notice of the filing of such petition to the prosecuting attorney of the county in which such lynching occurred and also to the attorney general. If the governor, upon hearing the evidence and argument, if any, presented,

---

[1] Acts of Indiana, 1899, Chapter 218. Being Sections 2065a–2065d, 2065f of the Revised Statutes (1901).

By an act approved Feb. 24, 1899, boards of county commissioners in Indiana are authorized to pay five hundred dollars reward for the arrest and conviction of a murderer or lyncher. — Acts of 1899, Chapter 100.

shall find that such sheriff has done all in his power to protect the life of such prisoner and performed the duties required of him by existing laws respecting the protection of prisoners, then such governor may reinstate such sheriff in office . . ."[1]

In 1899 the legislature of Michigan enacted a law against lynching modelled on the Ohio act of 1896, but in 1903 this law was repealed.[2]

In the constitution which was adopted by Alabama in 1901 this provision was made in regard to the responsibility of sheriffs: "Whenever any prisoner is taken from jail or from the custody of the sheriff or his deputy, and put to death, or suffers grievous bodily harm, owing to the neglect, connivance, cowardice or other grave fault of the sheriff, such sheriff may be impeached under Section 174 of this Constitution. If the sheriff be impeached and thereupon convicted, he shall not be eligible to hold any office in this State during the time for which he had been elected to serve as sheriff."[3]

In response to a general and a special message from the governor of West Virginia calling attention to the fact that within a year several persons had been "brutally murdered at the hands of riotous and lawless mobs," the legislature of that State adopted a joint resolution on February 3, 1903, condemning "such riotous and lawless acts" and empowering the governor, by and with the aid and advice of the attorney-general, to investigate and

[1] Acts of Indiana, 1901, Chapter 140. Being Section 2065e of the Revised Statutes (1901).

[2] Public Acts of Michigan, 1899, No. 252. Repealed by Public Acts of Michigan, 1903, No. 26.

[3] Constitution of Alabama, Section 138.

place on foot such means as in his judgment were necessary to bring the guilty parties to justice.[1]

Prompted by the flagrant case of lynching which occurred at Pittsburg, Kansas, on December 25, 1902,[2] the legislature of Kansas early in 1903 authorized county commissioners to offer and pay a reward in any sum not exceeding five hundred dollars for the discovery, arrest, and conviction of the perpetrator or perpetrators of the "murder or lynching of a human being committed in their county,"[3] and also enacted a statute against lynching modelled on the Indiana act of 1899 and the amendment of 1901.[4]

From this review of the legislation that has been enacted against lynching it appears that an application of the following remedies has been sought: first, an increase of the power of sheriffs and of their responsibility for the proper discharge of the duties of their office; second, heavier penalties for sheriffs and other officers who fail to protect from mob violence any person lawfully in their custody; third, heavier penalties for citizens who break into jails, or attack officers, or hinder or obstruct legal procedure; fourth, adequate provision in the law for the discovery, prosecution, and punishment of lynchers; fifth, fixing responsibility upon a community by making

[1] Acts of West Virginia, 1903, p. 305; Joint Resolution, No. 12, adopted Feb. 3, 1903.

[2] See newspapers of the date Dec. 26, 1902, and subsequent dates.

[3] Laws of Kansas, 1903, Chapter 407. This act was approved March 10, 1903.

[4] Laws of Kansas, 1903, Chapter 221. This act was approved March 11, 1903.

the county in which a lynching occurs liable for damages,[1] and giving a right of recovery to the legal representatives of the person lynched.

Direct and definite information as to the effectiveness of these measures in particular instances is somewhat meager, but the few cases that have arisen in the courts afford a basis for argument.[2]

On January 6, 1897, Lawrence Brown, colored, was lynched in Orangeburg County, South Carolina, for suspected arson. Isaac Brown, administrator of the estate of Lawrence Brown, deceased, entered suit against Orangeburg County in the common pleas circuit court of that county for the recovery of damages under Section 6, Article 6, of the constitution, and the act to prevent lynch-

---

[1] As early as the year 1796, this measure was suggested as a means of preventing the administration of popular justice by extra-legal methods. In that year Governor St. Clair, in a report to the Secretary of State concerning "Official Proceedings in the Illinois Country," after describing an affair in which some Indians were summarily put to death, the circumstances of which he characterized as "not only not blameable but laudable," continued in these words: "I am sorry however, to add that, had the affair been ever so criminal in its nature, it would have been, I believe, impossible to have brought the actors to punishment. The difficulties that have occurred in cases of that nature in various parts of the United States, as well as in this Territory, and the stain it fixes on the national character, has often led me to consider whether justice could not be secured to the Indians by adding some sanction to the law beyond what is usual between the citizens, and it has occurred to me that, were a pretty heavy pecuniary fine to be set upon the murder of an Indian, and a proportional one for lesser injuries, to be levied upon the counties where the offense was committed if the offenders were not brought to justice, it would probably have the effect, for it is often seen that the minds of men little tinctured with justice or humanity, have a pretty strong sympathy with their pockets, and I believe it to be a subject within the province of the general legislature." — The St. Clair Papers (1882), Vol. II, p. 397.

[2] For the purpose of obtaining accurate and complete information on the subject of anti-lynching laws the writer asked the following questions of thirty-three attorneys-general in the United States, inclosing in each letter a self-addressed and stamped envelope for reply:

1. What anti-lynching laws have been enacted in your State since

ing which was passed in 1896.[1] Judgment was rendered for the defendant, the presiding judge directing the jury to find a verdict in his favor, on the ground that the provision in the constitution and the act of the legislature conferred upon the plaintiff no right to recover damages against the defendant, as the person lynched was not a prisoner. An appeal from this decision was taken to the supreme court where the judgment of the lower court was reversed and the case was remanded for trial. The supreme court, construing the constitutional provision broadly and in connection with the act of the legislature, ruled that the judge had been in error in his directions to the jury, that the correct construction of the constitutional provision made a county liable for damages when the person lynched was not in the custody of the law as a prisoner. While the court declared a consideration of the question of the power of the legislature to pass such an act, independently of the constitutional provision, to be unnecessary in the case in hand, an opinion in regard to the matter was expressed in the following words: "It has been held that statutes making a community liable

1890? (Please give citation to statutes.) If there are no anti-lynching laws in your State, mention any attempts that have been made to enact such laws.

2. Have any cases been tried under any of such laws or any attempts been made to that effect, and what has been the record and the outcome in each case?

3. Are such laws effective in any respect?

Twenty-four replies were received to the thirty-three letters sent, and upon examination a fact became evident which is probably rather more than a coincidence — the nine unanswered letters were the ones which were sent to the attorneys-general of the States, with one exception, in which the greater number of lynchings have occurred. The exception is scarcely worth noting, however, because it was a reply which was very tardy and very non-committal.

[1] See p. 234.

for damages in cases of lynchings, and giving a right of recovery to the legal representatives of the person lynched, are valid, on the ground that the main purpose is to impose a penalty on the community, which is given to the legal representatives, not because they have been damaged, but because the legislature sees fit thus to dispose of the penalty. Such statutes are salutary, as their effect is to render protection to human life, and make communities law-abiding." [1]

At the January term of the supreme court of Ohio in the year 1900 a decision was rendered on the constitutionality of the "Act for the Suppression of Mob Violence" which was passed April 10, 1896.[2] Two cases were before the court. Benjamin F. Church, as the administrator of Charles W. Mitchell, deceased, filed a petition against the board of commissioners of Champaign County to recover five thousand dollars for the lynching of said Mitchell, at Urbana, in said county.[3] Defendant demurred to the petition and the demurrer was sustained by the court of common pleas and the petition dismissed. The circuit court reversed the judgment of the court of common pleas and the case then came before the supreme court. In the other case, J. W. Caldwell brought action, under the same statute, against the board of commissioners of Cuyahoga County, to recover the sum of one thousand dollars for an injury which he alleged that he had received at the hands of a mob in that county. A demurrer to the

---

[1] Brown v. Orangeburg Co., 55 S. C. 45; 32 S. E. 764. The decision of the Supreme Court was rendered on April 20, 1899.

[2] See p. 235.

[3] Mitchell was a negro and was lynched on June 4, 1897, for the crime of rape.

petition, on the ground that the petition did not state facts sufficient to constitute a cause for action and that said act was unconstitutional, was sustained by the court of common pleas, and the judgment of the court of common pleas was affirmed by the circuit court. Both cases came up to the supreme court on petitions in error to reverse the respective judgments of the circuit court.

In the opinion delivered on April 10, 1900, the supreme court fully discussed and upheld the principle involved in the act, affirming the judgment of the circuit court in Commissioners *v.* Church, administrator of Mitchell, and reversing the judgment of the circuit court and the judgment of the court of common pleas in Caldwell *v.* Commissioners. Church recovered from Champaign County five thousand dollars with interest and costs for the lynching of Mitchell, and Caldwell's action was sustained for the recovery of one thousand dollars for injuries received at the hands of a mob in Cuyahoga County.[1] The court in its opinion stated specifically that the act was constitutional; that the recovery authorized by said act was penal in its nature, and it was within the legislative power to provide therefor; that such legislation was not an exercise of judicial power, nor was it a violation of the right of trial by jury[2]; that such recovery, and the tax levy authorized and required by said act, were within the general powers of the legislature.[3]

One case has arisen under the Indiana act as amended

[1] Caldwell lost again in the common pleas and circuit courts, and went no further. — Deputy Clerk of Cuyahoga County in letter to the writer.

[2] See note, p. 236. The supreme court by this decision upheld the act in its original form.

[3] 62 O. S. 318.

in 1901. On November 20, 1902, James Dillard, a negro who had committed the crime of rape, was taken from the custody of John S. Dudley, the sheriff of Sullivan County, Indiana, and "lynched by hanging until dead." Dudley had been elected sheriff at the general election held in November, 1900, and William P. Maxwell had been elected coroner of Sullivan County. At the general election held in November, 1902, each had been elected as his own successor. On the day following the lynching of Dillard, Governor Durbin notified Maxwell that the office of sheriff of Sullivan County was vacant, and that he, as coroner, under the law succeeded to the duties of the office. Maxwell thereupon demanded of Dudley the possession of the office. This Dudley refused to give, and within ten days after the lynching occurred, as provided for in the statute, filed with the governor a petition for reinstatement in the office. After hearing the petition and the evidence in support of it, Governor Durbin denied the petition and refused to reinstate him. Governor Durbin then notified the board of commissioners of Sullivan County of the vacancy in the office of sheriff and suggested that the board appoint a successor to Dudley. The board of commissioners took no action, however, and Maxwell brought suit under a *quo warranto* statute, to oust Dudley from the office. In the circuit court of Sullivan County a judgment for the defendant was rendered, and on an appeal to the supreme court of Indiana the judgment of the circuit court was affirmed. The issues in the case were purely questions of law, it being held that Maxwell did not have ground for action under the *quo warranto* statute, and the supreme court expressed no opinion on the constitutionality of the amendatory act of 1901.[1]

Thus, the outcome of this case was, in effect, to nullify the operation of the statute which removes a sheriff from office when he allows a prisoner to be taken from his custody and lynched. The fact that Dudley continued to exercise the duties of his office after the lynching occurred, and successfully refused to vacate the office in response to the demands of the coroner, indicates that public sentiment in the community did not support the execution of the provisions of the law. Newspaper reports of the case intimate, however, that politics entered into the question to some extent.

Perhaps the present situation with reference to remedial legislation on the subject of lynching can be summed up in these few words: Comparatively few States have enacted laws defining and punishing lynching, or have enacted any statutes the specific purpose of which is to prevent lynching. Where such statutes exist very few attempts have been made to enforce them, and the validity of some is still in doubt. From the supreme court decisions in South Carolina and Ohio it would seem that the courts are likely to uphold statutes giving recovery of damages from counties in cases of lynching. The constitutionality of statutes fixing upon sheriffs the penalty of removal from office for failure to protect prisoners is open to considerable doubt, however, and no such measure has yet been enforced. In both South Carolina and Alabama provision has been made in the body of the constitution for the removal of a sheriff from office under such

[1] 68 N. E. 899.

circumstances, but neglect, connivance, or other grave fault must be proved against the sheriff.

As to the effect that this remedial legislation has had on the practice of lynching, opinions may differ, but it is difficult to point out in what way these laws have brought about a decrease in the number of lynchings.[1] It is true that not nearly so many lynchings occurred in the years 1901, 1902, 1903, as occurred in the years 1891, 1892, 1893, but it is also true that a marked decline in the number of lynchings per year began several years before the greater number of the anti-lynching laws were enacted. It is likewise true that the number of lynchings per year, in States other than those possessing anti-lynching statutes has declined in recent years. The truth would seem to be, therefore, if it be assumed that the number of crimes or offenses which occasion lynchings has been fairly uniform from year to year, that the same causes which led to the enactment of the laws also brought about the decline in the number of lynchings, namely, public discussion and condemnation of the practice of lynching, a stronger public sentiment against it, a deeper realization of the seriousness of the lynching problem in the United States.

That the measures adopted in South Carolina for the prevention of lynching, even though upheld and strongly indorsed by the supreme court, have not been altogether effective becomes apparent from a special message sent to the General Assembly of South Carolina, on January 20, 1904. Governor Heyward wrote as follows: "In my annual message to your honorable body reference was

See p. 185. Compare Chart I.

made to lawlessness in our State, the frequent occurrence
of lynchings being dealt with particularly. You, the
lawmakers, had not been assembled here a week when
another evidence of this lawless spirit is given in the
lynching at Reevesville. The Governor is popularly
credited with the power to prevent or punish these outrages against the State. In reality he is practically
powerless. When the crime has been committed his
hands are practically tied. The meager rewards he has
been empowered to offer out of his contingent fund have
proved ineffectual, and this is as far as he is permitted to
go. In the meantime the spirit of lawlessness is un-
checked.

"Any band of men may feel secure in taking the life
of a fellow-being on almost any pretext. This deplorable
condition ought to be remedied. To compel the proper
respect for the majesty of the law I recommend the enactment of special legislation in reference to lynching, that
the great responsibility of officials directly charged with
enforcing the law be brought home to them, and that more
effectual measures be taken for the apprehension of persons who take the law in their own hands. In lieu of
some such legislation, I suggest that the Governor be
provided with an adequate fund for the purpose of suppressing lynching." [1]

On March 7, 1904, Richard Dixon, a negro, was taken
from the jail and lynched at Springfield, Ohio. This
occurred in Clark County which adjoins Champaign

[1] *New York Times*, Jan. 21, 1904. Governor Sayers of Texas made
similar statements in his annual message to the legislature of Texas on
Jan. 16, 1903.

County on the south. In at least two other instances lynchings would have taken place in Ohio, since the decision of the supreme court which established the validity of the law holding counties liable in damages, had it not been for the vigilance and prompt action of the sheriffs. The possibility of an increase in the rate of taxation does not seem as yet to have had any restraining influence on the actions of people in Ohio when occasion has arisen for a lynching.

It is only within the last three or four years that determined efforts have been put forth to arrest and punish persons who have participated in lynchings, but these efforts have not been confined to the States which have special laws against lynching. Lynchers may be punished through statutory provisions defining homicide, manslaughter, murder, conspiracy, riot, malicious mischief, assault, and the like.

In November, 1903, eleven persons were indicted in St. Clair County, Illinois, for participating in the lynching of a negro school teacher the preceding June.[1]

More than twenty persons were indicted in Vermilion County, Illinois, for participation in the lynching of a negro at Danville on July 25, 1903, and verdicts of guilty of engaging in an attack on the county jail were found against eleven men and one woman, the penalty being an indeterminate sentence in the penitentiary.[2]

In January, 1903, twenty-eight white citizens of Attala County, Mississippi, were indicted for the lynching of two negroes.[3]

---

[1] *New York Times*, Nov. 3, 1903.   [2] *New York Times*, Sept. 7, 1903.
[3] *Richmond* (Va.) *Planet*, Feb. 14, 1903.

In Alabama, in 1902, some men were given a term in the penitentiary for lynching a negro, they being "the first like offenders," according to Governor Jelks, "to serve the state since the great war. No man had heretofore gone to the penitentiary for lynching a negro." [1]

On June 4, 1903, Samuel Mitchell, white, who led the mob that lynched Thomas Gilyard, a negro, at Joplin, Missouri, on April 15, preceding, was sentenced to ten years' imprisonment in the penitentiary, and two other men were still to be tried for their part in the burning of negro houses following the lynching. [2]

In California nineteen indictments were returned against persons who engaged in the lynching of four men and a boy on May 31, 1901, at Lookout, in Modoc County, and it was said that the State's attorney worked up the case against great opposition. [3]

There were several persons under indictment in Wyoming in February, 1904, for connection with a lynching which occurred in Big Horn County on July 19, 1903. [4]

No convictions of persons participating in lynchings in either Tennessee, Kentucky, or Texas have been brought about under the anti-lynching laws which were enacted by those States in 1897. [5] The case of the State vs. Hughes, charged with participating in a lynching, came

---

[1] Governor's message to the legislature, Jan. 14, 1903.

[2] *New York Evening Sun*, June 5, 1903.

[3] After a trial which lasted three months, the first man tried was acquitted. — *Denver* (Colo.) *Republican*, Feb. 28, 1902.

[4] Attorney-general of Wyoming in letter to the writer.

[5] A woman whose husband was hanged by a mob has recently filed suit against twenty-six "prominent citizens" of Fleming County, Kentucky, for $50,000 damages, claiming that they were members of the mob which lynched her husband. — *New York Times*, July 14, 1904.

up in DeKalb County, Tennessee, in July, 1902, but it was found impossible to get a jury to try the case. The court exhausted a venire of three hundred and fifty, and "found every man in the lot disqualified — probably having themselves aided in the affair."[1] On November 13, 1902, John Davis, colored, was lynched in Marshall County, Tennessee. Two men, W. P. Hopwood and W. H. L. Johnson, were later arrested on the charge of participating in the lynching. On January 7, 1903, thirty masked men appeared at the jail where the prisoners were confined, obtained the keys to the jail, and released the prisoners.[2]

The measures adopted by Georgia and North Carolina for the suppression of lynchings have likewise remained inoperative. Numerous lynchings have taken place in both of these States since 1893, but no lyncher has yet suffered any of the penalties prescribed by law. A resident of North Carolina recently made this statement with reference to the punishment of lynchers in his State: "Judges have charged juries against the crime, and Governor Aycock — risking his political fortunes for his convictions — recently offered a reward of $400 each for the conviction of a party of seventy-five who lynched a

[1] *Chattanooga* (Tenn.) *Times*, July 27, 1902. It will be remembered that by the Tennessee act any person guilty of direct or indirect participation in a lynching was declared to be incompetent to serve on a jury, and that the court was to carefully exclude all such persons from both grand and petit juries. See p. 237.

[2] Despatch from Lewisburg, Tennessee, in *New York Commercial Advertiser*, Jan. 8, 1903.

In October, 1903, a grand jury in Moore County, Tennessee, indicted twenty-two members of a lynching mob. — See *Outlook*, Oct. 24, 1903 (75: 427).

negro near Salisbury.   But never yet has the law punished
a North Carolina lyncher." [1]

In general it may be said that the laws proposed far
outnumber the laws enacted against lynching, and that
wherever such laws have been enacted their enforcement
has not as yet been such as to warrant any great reliance
on their effectiveness to prevent lynching.   It can scarcely
be said that the remedy for lynching lies at present in the
direction of additional State legislation specifically directed
against it.

By many it is thought that a federal law on the subject would be most effective in the suppression of lynchings, and several bills have been introduced in Congress
with this end in view.[2]   On January 13, 1902, Mr. Crum-
packer of Indiana introduced a bill in the House of Representatives for the punishment of persons taking part in
the lynching of aliens.   The bill was designed to cover
cases similar to the lynching of the Italians at New Orleans,
and jurisdiction over such offenses was given to the federal
courts, persons who had taken part in lynchings being
disqualified from serving as jurors.[3]

Others would have Congress enact a law making all
who lynch, whether the victims be citizens or aliens, and
all who instigate, aid, abet, or shield lynchers, guilty of a
crime against the United States.   In support of such a
law it is urged that a lyncher could be as easily discovered
and punished as a moonshiner, or a counterfeiter, or a

[1] *Atlantic Monthly*, February, 1904 (93: 155).

[2] See bills introduced during 57th Congress, 1st Session: Senate Bill
1117; House bills 21, 4572.

[3] *Congressional Record*, 57th Congress, 1st Session, p. 636.

mail robber; that if the object of our constitution is to insure domestic tranquility, promote the general welfare and secure the blessings of liberty to ourselves and our posterity, it ought to include the power to punish those who defy the government established by the constitution and take life without due process of law; and that if it was worth while to amend the constitution to prevent the denial of the electoral franchise, it is also worth while to amend the constitution to prevent and punish the denial of justice.[1]

A further ground for bringing lynching within the jurisdiction of federal courts and federal law is the fact that the lynching of an alien may involve the United States in international complications, although the federal government can take no action in the premises. Diplomatic intercourse was actually broken off between Italy and the United States during the controversy over the matter of an indemnity for the lynching of Italian citizens at New Orleans in 1891.[2] In a number of other instances foreign countries have successfully demanded indemnities from the United States through the Department of State for injuries done their citizens by mob violence. The following table gives the sums of money that have been paid to foreign countries since 1880 in the settlement of such claims.

[1] See *Green Bag*, September, 1900 (12: 466).
[2] *New York Tribune*, April 15, 1892.

INDEMNITIES PAID FOR INJURIES TO ALIENS.[1]

YEAR WHEN PAID	COUNTRY TO WHICH PAID	LOCALITY WHERE INJURIES WERE INFLICTED	AMOUNT OF INDEMNITY
1887	China	Wyoming	$147,748.74
1888	China	Pacific Coast	276,619.75
1892	Italy	Louisiana	24,330.90
1896	Italy	Colorado	10,000.00
1896	Great Britain	Louisiana	1,000.00
1896	Great Britain	Nebraska	1,800.00
1897	Italy	Louisiana	6,000.00
1898	Mexico	California	2,000.00
1901	Mexico	Texas	2,000.00
1901	Italy	Louisiana	4,000.00
1903	Italy	Mississippi	5,000.00

Total..............................$480,499.39 [2]

With the exception of the payment to China in 1887, "in consideration of the losses unhappily sustained by certain Chinese subjects by mob violence at Rock Springs, in the Territory of Wyoming, September 2, 1885," these indemnities have been paid "out of humane consideration, without reference to the question of liability therefor." While they have thus not been paid in discharge of an express obligation recognized by the United States, there has been a moral obligation recognized and the federal government has felt it to be incumbent upon itself to redress grievances of this nature.[3]

It is a peculiar situation when the United States can

[1] Some of these indemnities cover loss of property and bodily injuries as well as loss of life.

[2] See, in addition to *New York Tribune*, April 15, 1892, United States Statutes at Large, 49th Cong., 2nd Sess., Ch. 253; 50th Cong., 1st Sess., Ch. 1210; 54th Cong., 1st Sess., Ch. 373; 55th Cong., 1st Sess., Ch. 9; 55th Cong., 2d Sess., Ch. 571; 56th Cong., 2d Sess., Ch. 831; 57th Cong., 2d Sess., Ch. 1006.

[3] *American Law Review*, September — October, 1900 (34: 709).

thus be called upon to pay indemnities for lynchings and yet cannot take steps in the several States to prevent their occurrence and cannot in any way hold the State governments responsible. That this defect in the federal constitution should be remedied seems, from this standpoint, wholly desirable. It is very doubtful, however, whether such an object could be accomplished at the present time, and still more doubtful whether a federal law could be enacted and enforced against lynching at the present time, without reviving the sectionalism and many of the evils of the Reconstruction Period. When Senator Gallinger of New Hampshire offered a resolution in the 57th Congress that the Committee on the Judiciary be directed to make an inquiry into the subject of lynchings and to report whether there be any remedy for the evil, his reference to a recent lynching in a Southern State was instantly resented by the senators from that State, and the course which the debate took upon the resolution made it apparent at once that an attempt to make such an investigation would be an unwise step. The matter was dropped by Senator Gallinger's making the request that the resolution lie on the table subject to his call.[1]

Of the numerous proposals that have been made for reform in the system of legal procedure in the United States, as a remedy for lynching, none is more noteworthy or fundamental than that put forward by Justice Brewer of the United States Supreme Court. He argues that men are afraid of the law's delays and the uncertainty of its results; that if all were sure that the guilty

[1] See *Congressional Record*, 57th Congress, 1st Session, pp. 5902–5905, 5956, 6214.

ones would be promptly tried and punished, the induce-
ment to lynch would be largely taken away. He suggests, therefore, the taking away of the right of appeal in
criminal cases as one means of checking lynching.[1]

While the law's delays in criminal cases are probably
not so great as they are popularly believed to be, the
popular impression being due to over-emphasis of flagrant cases,[2] still the fact that such an impression is a
prevalent one makes it extremely easy for a community to
countenance the summary and illegal punishment of the
perpetrator of a crime which has been particularly shocking to the community, a crime for which many persons
in the community really feel that no punishment can be
quite adequate. A case in point is that of the lynching
of George White, colored, at Wilmington, Delaware, on
June 22, 1903. A refusal by the judges to grant an immediate trial on the ground that the accused could not
then have a fair and impartial trial because of the excited
state of public feeling, was publicly urged as a reason for
the people taking the law into their own hands and "up-
holding the majesty of the law." The outcome was that
White was burned at the stake and those who participated
in the lynching were allowed to go free, the coroner's jury
returning a verdict that the deceased came to his death
at the hands of persons unknown.

It is in this way that the popular idea that the law's
delays are so great as frequently to defeat the ends of
justice, whether it have much or little basis in fact,[3]

---

[1] *Leslie's Weekly*, Aug. 20, 1903; *Independent*, Oct. 29, 1903 (55: 2547).

[2] See *Harvard Law Review*, March, 1904 (17: 317).

[3] On the work of the courts in the State of New York, see "Report of
the Commission on Law's Delays," January, 1904.

contributes to the continuance of the practice of lynching. If to abolish the right of appeal in criminal cases, or to limit it to a considerable extent, will further the ends of justice, as there seems to be good reason for believing that it will, such a step will have a tendency to check lynching by making void one of the excuses most frequently urged in extenuation of the practice. Lynching is a phenomenon in American society too deeply rooted to be destroyed by merely taking away the right of appeal in criminal cases, but that a measure will render less plausible a prominent excuse for its existence and continuance makes such a measure worthy of serious consideration.

The governors of several States have recently asked that they be given more power, and that more resources be placed at their command, in order that they may take the initiative both in preventing lynchings and in punishing lynchers. Something may be accomplished by granting their requests. During the fourteen years immediately preceding Governor O'Ferrall's inauguration there were sixty-two lynchings within the bounds of the State of Virginia, but during the four years of his administration there were but three, and in neither case was the chief executive in a position either to prevent the crime or punish the offenders.[1] The most hopeful sign at the present time is the stand which the governors and minor officers in a number of States, in the South as well as in the North, have taken against lynching.[2] Governor

---

[1] *Review of Reviews*, March, 1898 (17: 321).

[2] Governor Newton C. Blanchard, at his inauguration on May 16, 1904, at Baton Rouge, Louisiana, stated his position with reference to lynchings in unmistakable language. "Lynchings," he said, "will not be permitted under any circumstances, if it be possible for the military at

Vardaman, of Mississippi, in his recent rather sensational rescue of a negro murderer from a mob,[1] has at least demonstrated the possibility of preventing lynchings and enforcing the law. Governor Jelks, of Alabama, and Governor Durbin, of Indiana, have not only been outspoken in their denunciation of lynchings but have taken active measures to prevent them. A number of sheriffs in various States have within the last two years prevented lynchings by courageously facing mobs and making it clear that they would defend their prisoners at the hazard of their own lives.[2]

So long, however, as coroner's juries empanelled to inquire into the death of victims of lynching continue to render the verdict that "the deceased came to his death at the hands of persons unknown to the jury," and so long as it is true that the coroner's verdict commonly marks the end of all legal procedure with reference to the occurrence, it is not to be expected that sheriffs and jailers will hazard their lives in the protection of prisoners.[3]

the command of the Governor to get there in time to prevent them. And if they occur before the intervention of the Executive can be made effective, inquiry and investigation will be made and prosecution instigated. Sheriffs will be held to the strictest accountability possible under the law for the safety from mob violence of persons in their custody. . . . The courts are adequate to the prompt vindication of the law and the punishment of crime." — *Outlook*, May 28, 1904 (77: 197).

[1] Governor Vardaman ordered out two companies of militia and went himself to the scene of the trouble in a special train, bringing the negro away in his private car, at a cost to the State, it was said, of $250,000. See *New York Times*, Feb. 29, 1904.

[2] Vigilance and prompt action on the part of the officers of the law, together with the presence of the militia, probably prevented the lynching of the three negroes who assaulted Mrs. Biddle at Burlington, New Jersey, on July 5, 1904. — See *New York Times*, July 16, 1904.

[3] Governor Jelks, of Alabama, in his message of Jan. 14, 1903, said in reference to the lynching in Pike County of a negro who was taken away from a constable: "His offense was probably swearing contrary to one of

Prisoners are taken from officers of the law and lynched, not because the officers are cowards, but because they are in sympathy with the sentiment in the community which demands immediate punishment. The public sentiment revealed in the following citations is not found in isolated instances, but is typical, although equal frankness of statement cannot always be secured.

A verdict rendered by a coroner's jury in Wayne County, North Carolina, in August, 1902, over the body of a negro rapist, read as follows: "We the undersigned, empanelled as a jury to inquire into the cause of the death of Tom Jones, find that he came to his death by gun shot wounds, inflicted by parties unknown to jury, obviously by an outraged public acting in defense of their homes, wives, daughters and children. In view of the enormity of the crime committed by said Tom Jones, alias Frank Hill, we think they would have been recreant to their duty as good citizens had they acted otherwise." [1]

In December, 1899, Richard Coleman, a negro ravisher and murderer, was burned at the stake at Maysville, Kentucky. In response to a letter from the governor of the State, asking for particulars, a Maysville lawyer wrote as follows: "The whole thing took place in broad daylight and in the presence of thousands. The parties to it are known, Mr. Lashbrook (husband of Coleman's victim) himself being the leader, but it will be fruitless. to attempt any prosecution of them. The people of this community are as good as the people of any other com-

his white neighbors in a justice trial on a proof of character. This was a cold-blooded murder and without excuse at all. . . The murderers go about. None of them will be hanged as they should be."

[1] The *News-Observer*, Raleigh, North Carolina, Aug. 27, 1902.

munity in the State, or, for that matter, elsewhere, and they are shocked, and, I may say, well-nigh paralyzed by this gruesome happening in their midst, but I am satisfied they will not take kindly to any attempt to hold the parties to the transaction to any responsibilities therefor." [1]

The only ultimate remedy for lynching is a strong public sentiment against it. It is necessary, in the United States particularly, to depend very largely upon public sentiment for the enforcement of law, and until there is a sentiment, in every community where a lynching occurs, which will demand the punishment of those who take part in such lynching, it can scarcely be expected that sheriffs will risk their lives to protect prisoners, or that prosecuting attorneys, judges, and juries will co-operate to secure the conviction of lynchers and to make them feel the full penalty of the law. A member of the Maryland Bar writing in 1900 said that less than a dozen lynchers had ever been tried for their crime, and only one or two had been punished. The present writer has been able to obtain no information which would warrant the statement that as many as twenty-five persons have been convicted of a crime and punished for participating in the lynching of over three thousand persons in the last twenty-two years. [2]

From the greater number of indictments that have been secured against lynchers during the last two years it

---

[1] *American Law Review*, March — April, 1900 (34: 238).

[2] For a discussion of the problem of punishing lynchers and for some statistics with reference to the punishment of persons who participated in lynchings during the first six months of the year 1892, see paper by George C. Holt, on "Lynching and Mobs," *American Journal of Social Science*, No. 32, p. 67 (November, 1894).

would seem that the practice of lynching is receiving stronger public condemnation now than formerly, but it must be remembered that the creation of a public sentiment on any subject is a slow process, particularly with reference to lynching. Lynching as a crime against society is not yet distinguished from lynching as the justifiable infliction of a deserved punishment by private citizens. Furthermore, it is difficult to create a public sentiment against lynching because of the racial antipathy which aggravates the evil in certain sections of the United States. Time will be required for the effectual application of a remedy for lynching. Any anti-lynching measures that may be adopted must be considered as palliatives rather than as remedies.

No single statute can be enacted which will put an end to the practice of lynching; nor is it likely that any single measure can be adopted which will effectually suppress lynching. Every measure which will tend to invalidate the excuses offered for the adoption of lynch-law procedure, every measure which will tend to prevent the commission of crimes provoking resort to lynch-law procedure, every measure which will tend to strengthen and maintain a popular reliance on legal procedure, every measure which will in any way tend to create a strong, uncompromising public sentiment against lynching, all of these must be adopted if the practice of lynching is to be made a thing of the past in the United States.

CHAPTER IX

SOME CONCLUSIONS

THE question naturally arises, what is the peculiarity about American society which fosters and tolerates lynching? Why is lynching a peculiarly American institution? It has been suggested that the explanation lies along racial lines. Some have said that the Scotch-Irish are responsible for the introduction into this country of the practice of illegally punishing public offenders. Others say that it is race prejudice, a result of the coming together of many races in one country, and particularly that it is the racial antagonism between the white race and the negro race, which explains the matter. Looking at the history of the practice in the United States from colonial times down to the present day, one can scarcely regard such an explanation as either adequate or conclusive. The real explanation lies along a somewhat different line, and it can be pointed out best by drawing some contrasts between the administration of the law in the United States and its administration in the older countries of Europe.

The American people are not any more disposed toward lawlessness — they are not less law-abiding — than European peoples; it is rather that they maintain a wholly different attitude toward the law. Social and political conditions are different, and the law, instead of being something in itself to reverence and respect, is little more than a device for securing freedom. The value of laws as rules of conduct is not minimized but there is no sense of sanctity pertaining to them. To outwit, avoid, defy, or forget the laws is not a serious offense so long as an appeal can be made to the individual sense of justice in support of such courses of action.

In Europe, where the statutes have grown up from tradition and ancient custom, the law is regarded as a more sacred institution; in a very real sense it is the product of a superior authority. Law in its institutional sense is as much a predetermined factor in daily affairs as is one of the laws of nature. Social and political conditions are fixed. Politics do not enter into the enforcement of law. Civilization is distributed in a more nearly equal measure and the law is enforced with equal vigor over the whole country.[1] The judicial and administrative officers are persons socially and politically distinct from the masses, and their individuality is so completely subordinated to their representative capacity that the law thus comes to have a majesty and dignity which can be given it in no other way.

In the United States, on the contrary, the body of the law lacks the support of long tradition and ancient practice. The early immigrants brought with them the European conception of law, but in the midst of new conditions, with no strong government to enforce it with an impartial and an iron hand, along with the growth of the democratic spirit, a new *esprit des lois*, as Montesquieu would call it, has been developed. Where the people, either directly or through their representatives, make the

[1] Carroll D. Wright: "Outline of Practical Sociology" (1899), p. 357.

laws and then elect the officers who are to enforce them, it is inevitable that the legal machinery will prove powerless to control popular excitements. Politics also enter very largely into the whole question. In remote districts, too, the people seldom have occasion to meet any other officers of the law than their own neighbors and friends whom they have elected to minor civil offices. It is for this reason that the execution of the law varies so greatly in different parts of the United States, being either vigorous or lax, in accordance with the moral sentiment of the community.

In a monarchy or a highly centralized form of government, the law is made for the people and enforced against them by officials who are in no sense responsible to them.

In a democracy with a republican form of government, like the United States, such is not the case. The people consider themselves a law unto themselves. They make the laws; therefore they can unmake them. Since they say what a judge can do, they entertain the idea that they may do this thing themselves. To execute a criminal deserving of death is to act merely in their sovereign capacity, temporarily dispensing with their agents, the legal administrators of the law. While not always expressed in language so unmistakable in meaning, yet this is the spirit exhibited, the vague and perhaps unconscious attitude toward the law, which seems particularly to pervade the United States.

The tendency toward public disorder has existed in this country from its earliest settlement, and as the line of the frontier has slowly moved westward there has always been a region on the border where the forces of law were unorganized. There has thus been a constant opportunity for a plea of necessity in certain cases for resorting to the popular execution of justice. In recent years the customary explanations of lynchings attribute them to mob rule, emotional insanity of the crowd, race prejudice, contempt for the "niggers," intense community feeling, vivid hatred of crime, *lex talionis* and the like. It is often asserted that lynchings occur because the courts are slow, uncertain, and unduly sympathetic with the rights of the accused, because corrupt jurymen, shrewd lawyers, the technicalities of the law or the undue sympathies of the pardoning powers frequently prolong and save a guilty person's life. While it is true on psychological grounds that punishment to be effective must be prompt and certain, and while such explanations have validity in particular cases, the fundamental explanation lies deeper. It is to be found in the peculiar and distinctively American attitude toward those institutions connoted by the term "the law." [1] There is a readiness on the part of the people in the United States to take the law into their own hands which is not found in other countries, and the consequent immunity from punishment which is generally accorded to lynchers renders an American mob exceedingly open to the suggestion of lynching.

It is on such grounds that the existence of lynching as a peculiarly American institution is to be explained. Such are the conditions and such has been the conception of

[1] This view of the matter is ably set forth in the *Green Bag* for September, 1900 (12: 466), by O. F. Hershey of the Maryland Bar.

The same idea is expressed in a different way in an article on "American Quality," by N. S. Shaler. See *International Monthly*, July, 1901.

the law which has fostered a public sentiment in the United States excusing and apologizing for lynchings. The writer of a book published in London in 1837 was not far wrong when he wrote: "The Lynch law, is not, properly speaking, an opposition to the established laws of the country, or, is at least, not contemplated as such by its adherents; but rather as a supplement to them, — a species of *common* law, which is as old as the country."[1]

To the same effect is this "Scotch View of Lynch law" which was occasioned by the lynching of the Italians at New Orleans in 1891. After reviewing the facts and circumstances connected with that lynching, the following comments were made: "This is crude and it is primitive. It is to be deplored and condemned. But it is not without a foundation of reason and justice. The people have committed the administration of justice to a certain machinery; so long as that machinery works without flagrant injustice, it will be left to do the work; but when it utterly breaks down, or goes in the teeth of what is right according to the rough-and-ready ideas of the Americans, the people will resume the function of dealing out punishment direct. The ultimate sanction is brought in. That is the American method. The Briton, when he thinks the ordinary tribunals have failed, writes to the *Times*, or gets up a monster petition to the Home Secretary, or asks a question of the Houses of Parliament."[2]

In certain sections of the United States this readiness on the part of the people to take the law into their own

[1] Francis J. Grund: "The Americans in their moral, social, and political relations" (London, 1837), I, 323. (M.)

[2] Quoted from the *Journal of Jurisprudence* (Edinborough). See *American Law Review*, May — June, 1891 (25: 461).

hands receives constant support and encouragement from the racial antipathy which exists between the whites and the negroes. It cannot be said that the lynching of negroes is due to "race prejudice" alone, but it is true that the antagonistic feeling between the two races aggravates the tendency to lynch, when offenses are committed against white persons by negroes. Other racial contrasts in the population have likewise promoted the adoption of extra-legal methods of punishment. From colonial times down to the present day the contemptuous attitude of the whites toward the Indians has undoubtedly been a potent factor in the not infrequent failure to observe due process of law in the treatment of Indians. In the summary treatment of Italians, Mexicans, Chinese, and other aliens, differences in racial characteristics have also played an important part. In very many cases of lynching a racial antipathy has acted as the most prominent contributory cause, and it is this fact that has induced many writers to find in "race prejudice" the ultimate explanation of lynching as an American institution.

The lynching of negroes is now so distinctively an American practice largely because of the racial contrast in the population which is peculiar to this country. Nowhere else in the temperate zone does a colored race of tropical origin come into contact in such numbers with a highly civilized race of European stock. The "native question" of tropical regions has here been transplanted, as it were, to the temperate zone.[1] Further-

---

[1] For a comprehensive discussion of the "native question," see "A Sociological View of the 'Native Question,'" by Albert G. Keller, *Yale Review*, November, 1903.

more, the difficulties arising from ethnic contact within
the tropics have been intensified rather than lessened by
this change of environment. There are the same fundamental differences in racial characteristics and in racial
heredity, but these become accentuated and seem even
more adverse in a climate where the struggle for existence
is of necessity much more vigorous and exacting. In
addition, there has developed between the white race and
the colored race in the United States an intolerant, in-
considerate spirit directly promoted by an unwise and
short-sighted political policy. A great many years will
doubtless be required for the effacement of the unfortu-
nate results of past errors, involving as it does a very
general understanding and recognition of the ethnic and
"societal" factors which enter vitally into the "race question." Only in so far as this comes about, however, will
it be possible to establish a new order of society with an
appropriate legal system in the place of that which formerly
existed on the basis of the institution of slavery.

The assumption made by many writers that more
negroes are lynched for the crime of rape against white
women than for any other crime is without foundation in
fact. Statistics show that not more than thirty-four per
cent of the negroes summarily put to death during the
last twenty-two years have been lynched for that crime,
either alleged, attempted, or actually committed. Lynching for that crime, however, leads to lynching for other
crimes and also furnishes a ground for an appeal to public sentiment to condone the practice of lynching.

Since the negroes were made free American citizens a
large class of the younger generation has become utterly

shiftless and worthless, many of them being vicious and dangerous individuals in a community. Professor Du-Bois, than whom there is probably no man better qualified to make a careful and conservative estimate, says that at least nine per cent of the county black population in the Black Belt are thoroughly lewd and vicious.[1] Lynching has been resorted to by the whites not merely to wreak vengeance, but to terrorize and restrain this lawless element in the negro population. Among the Southern people the conviction is general that terror is the only restraining influence that can be brought to bear upon vicious negroes. The negroes fear nothing so much as force, and should they once get the notion that there is a reasonable hope of escape from punishment, the whites in many parts of the South would be at their mercy.[2] There is no evidence, however, to show that the punishment of negroes by mob violence tends to decrease lawlessness among the negroes, or even tends to restrain the vicious element from committing offenses against the whites. On the contrary, lawlessness seems to beget lawlessness and the publicity given to revolting crimes by lynching the perpetrators of them seems really to incite others to commit similar crimes, or at least suggests to others like crimes when opportunity offers.

The frightful tortures and the burnings which have taken place in the last few years in connection with the lynching of negroes is partly to be accounted for by the fact that lynchings are now carried on by a lower class of

---

[1] W. E. B. DuBois: "The Souls of Black Folk" (1903), p. 143.

[2] William Hayne Levell: "On Lynching in the South." — *Outlook* Nov. 16, 1901 (69: 731).

whites than formerly.[1] The power of suggestion as an incentive to crime is also evident in this barbarous conduct of lynching mobs. The publicity given in the newspapers, particularly the sensational ones, to the details of such tragic scenes has undoubtedly been largely responsible for the frequency of their recurrence.[2] The relations between the younger generations of the two races are, besides, much less cordial and amicable than were those which existed between the generations immediately preceding; there is less of a mutual understanding. The relation of master and slave has been destroyed and no new relation has yet been firmly established in its place. In the process of adjustment to a new order of things there has been constant friction between the two races, and when an offense has been committed upon a white person by a negro, particularly if an assault has been made upon the person of a white woman or child, the exasperation of the whites has known scarcely any bounds.

While the decrease in the number of lynchings per year since the early nineties affords some hope for the future with reference to the suppression of lynchings, still the number of burnings and the number of cases in which the victims are subjected to extreme torture indicate that too much reliance cannot be placed upon any apparent decline in the tendency to lynch. The fact also that lynchings frequently occur in communities where such summary and illegal procedure had not previously been

[1] "Lynching and the Franchise Rights of the Negro," Annals of the American Academy of Science, May, 1900 (15: 493).

[2] On the suggestibility of crowds, see Gustave LeBon: "The Crowd. A Study of the Popular Mind" (2d ed., 1897).
See also Boris Sidis: "The Psychology of Suggestion" (1898), Part III.

permitted forebodes more lynchings in the future. The seriousness of the situation with reference to the practice of lynching in the United States is not yet fully realized. There is no little ground for apprehension in the fact that it is becoming common for cries of "Lynch him," "Hang him," "Get a rope and string him up," &c., to be heard, even on the streets of New York City, whenever a crowd gathers in response to a feeling of popular excitement and indignation over the perpetration of some atrocious crime.

In the course of this investigation into the history of lynching it has become evident that there is usually more or less public approval, or supposed favorable public sentiment, behind a lynching. Indeed, it is not too much to say that popular justification is the *sine qua non* of lynching. It is this fact that distinguishes lynching, on the one hand, from assassination and murder, and, on the other hand, from insurrection and open warfare. A lynching may be defined as an illegal and summary execution at the hands of a mob, or a number of persons, who have in some degree the public opinion of the community behind them. When the term first came into use it meant the infliction of corporal punishment, particularly whipping. The term is now used exclusively to signify the infliction of the death penalty in a summary fashion, usually by hanging. But whatever the penalty imposed or the manner of its imposition, the sentiment frequently expressed in a community where a lynching has occurred is to the effect that the victim or victims got no more than was deserved.

It further appears from this investigation that no one cause or crime can be assigned for lynching. Lynchings take place for various causes. At one time there may be a lack of ordinary tribunals of justice, at another time there may be doubt as to the efficiency of the legal machinery. Lynchings may take place because the offense is outside the law but is deemed serious enough to merit severe punishment. They may occur because of the barbarity and fiendish nature of the crime committed. They may occur for one reason or for another; the only factor that is always present is a disorganized state of society or a condition of popular excitement and resentment when reliance on ordinary legal procedure is at a minimum.

Of the legal remedies for lynching which have been proposed, few have been enacted into laws, and where such measures have been placed upon the statute-books they have not as yet been so effectively administered as to inspire confidence in them as an ultimate means of suppressing the practice. The problem of finding a remedy for lynching is really a problem of increasing and maintaining a popular reliance on the formulation and the administration of the law. Every measure which will in any way promote such a reliance, either by invalidating the excuses offered in justification of the practice or by developing a strong public sentiment against it, deserves serious consideration, and every such measure, unless likely to be productive of other evils possibly greater, should be immediately adopted and put into operation.

The existence of the practice of lynching in the United States is a national disgrace and should be so considered by every citizen no matter in what part of the country his home may be. This, however, does not justify citizens of the Northern section in violently attacking citizens of the Southern section every time that a lynching occurs in that section, or *vice versa.* Each section and indeed each community must hold itself responsible for the prevention of lynchings. Neither European philanthropists nor the Northern press or pulpit can do very much toward preventing such occurrences in the South. It is a question with which the South alone can properly deal and it is a problem which the intelligent men of the South are best able to solve. The efforts of the Southern Education Board and the General Education Board to educate both the whites and the blacks and lift them to a higher plane of living will do much toward preventing lynchings. The work done by such schools as the Hampton Institute and the Tuskegee Normal and Industrial Institute, and the principles advocated by such men as Booker T. Washington, also lead in the same direction.

It has been well suggested that the Northern papers and the Southern papers should exchange texts — the Northern press should preach against negro crime, the Southern press should preach against lawlessness and race prejudice. That this has been done in a few instances gives hope for the future.

To the extent that the colored race increases its industrial efficiency and becomes economically strong in the South will there be a decrease in negro lawlessness and viciousness, and likewise will it merit respect and confidence on the part of the white race. More than anything else the colored race needs wise and able leaders at the present time. The false notions and ideals of the Reconstruction Period have now been largely eradicated. The race is in a position to make substantial and material progress, if under able leadership, and such progress will tend to eliminate the conditions which foster lynching in the South.

If the United States had a monarchical form of government the most practicable means for the suppression of lynchings would consist merely in the publication of an edict by the monarch for the better enforcement of the law. Most lynching mobs could be easily dispersed were the officers of the law resolute and determined men intent upon protecting their prisoners and letting the law take its course; if they were responsible only to their superior officers and not more or less directly responsible to the people, and if they were not in sympathy with the mob to a greater or less degree. Our system of government, however, is in form representative and popular, and all our traditions are against a highly centralized form of government. In the United States it is therefore necessary to depend very largely upon public sentiment for a strict enforcement of the law. Lynch-law will not cease to exist in this country until there is a strong and uncompromising public sentiment against it in every community, a public sentiment which, with a full recognition of the ethnic and "societal" factors involved in the "race question," and of the necessity for a legal system consistent with these factors instead of one based on abstract principles concerning the rights of all men, will invariably condemn lynchings because they are a crime against society, if for no other reason, and will under no circumstances countenance them because they may be the administration of deserved and well-merited punishments.

LIST OF PERIODICALS CITED

American Journal of Social Science.
American Law Review.
American Whig Review.
Annals of the American Academy of Science.
Annual Reports of the American Historical Association.
Atlantic Monthly.
Boston Chronicle.
Boston Daily Advertiser.
Boston Evenir g Post.
Boston Evening Transcript.
Boston Gazette.
Boston News-Letter.
British and Foreign Review.
Brooklyn Standard Union.
Chambers' Journal.
Chattanooga Times.
Chicago Tribune.
Congressional Record.
Cyclopedic Review of Current History.
Denver Republican.
Essex Gazette.
Fortnightly Review.
Forum.
Green Bag.
Harper's Magazine.
Harvard Law Review.
Houston Post.
Howitt's Journal.

Independent.
International Monthly.
Johns Hopkins Historical Studies.
Journal of Proceedings of American Social Science Association.
Leisure Hour.
Leslie's Weekly.
Liberator.
Literary Digest.
London Gazette.
London Gazetteer.
Massachusetts Spy
Modern Philology.
Nation.
New England Gazette.
New England Magazine.
New York Commercial Advertiser.
New York Evening Post.
New York Evening Sun.
New York Evening Telegraph.
New York Gazette.
New York Times.
New York Tribune.
New York World.
Niles' Register.
North American Review.
Notes and Queries.
Our Day.

Outlook.
Publications of the American
    Economic Association.
Publications of the Southern
    Historical Association.
Public Opinion.
Raleigh News-Observer.
Review of Reviews.

Richmond Planet.
Salem Gazette.
Saturday Review.
Southern Literary Messenger.
Spectator.
Washington Times.
Yale Review.

Citations are made also to statutes, historical records, colonial archives, encyclopedias, dictionaries, etc. Full references are given in the foot-notes. For authors quoted see index.

INDEX